CW01219058

The Normalization of the European Commission

The Normalization of the European Commission:

Politics and Bureaucracy in the EU Executive

Anchrit Wille

OXFORD
UNIVERSITY PRESS

OXFORD
UNIVERSITY PRESS

Great Clarendon Street, Oxford, OX2 6DP,
United Kingdom

Oxford University Press is a department of the University of Oxford.
It furthers the University's objective of excellence in research, scholarship,
and education by publishing worldwide. Oxford is a registered trade mark of
Oxford University Press in the UK and in certain other countries

© Anchrit Wille 2013

The moral rights of the author have been asserted

First Edition published in 2013

Impression: 3

All rights reserved. No part of this publication may be reproduced, stored in
a retrieval system, or transmitted, in any form or by any means, without the
prior permission in writing of Oxford University Press, or as expressly permitted
by law, by licence or under terms agreed with the appropriate reprographics
rights organization. Enquiries concerning reproduction outside the scope of the
above should be sent to the Rights Department, Oxford University Press, at the
address above

You must not circulate this work in any other form
and you must impose this same condition on any acquirer

British Library Cataloguing in Publication Data
Data available

ISBN 978-0-19-966569-3

Printed and bound in Great Britain by
CPI Group (UK) Ltd, Croydon, CR0 4YY

Links to third party websites are provided by Oxford in good faith and
for information only. Oxford disclaims any responsibility for the materials
contained in any third party website referenced in this work.

Acknowledgements

This book has been a long time in the making. Too long, no question about that! I am indebted to a number of people who helped me along the way. A book with a single author is always a collective project and, like most works, this study owes a great deal of its content to the thoughts, comments, and efforts of others.

As a project, this book started while I was working as a research fellow at the Utrecht School of Governance (USG) at Utrecht University on a project funded by NWO. At the same time I was involved as research group manager in the EU funded CONNEX network of excellence funded under the Sixth Framework programme. I was privileged to participate in the CONNEX Research Group 2 on 'Democratic Governance and Multi-Level Accountability coordinated by Deirdre Curtin; and Research Group 1 on 'Institutional Dynamics and the Transformation of EU Politics' coordinated by Morten Egeberg. I profited very much from the discussion in these groups. Deirdre Curtin and Morten Egeberg both played a crucial role in the development of this book. Morten's ideas about evolving institutions and the normalization of the Commission inspired my approach and are used extensively throughout this book. Deirdre's insights about executive power and multi-level accountability in the EU provided a useful framework.

I thank the officials in the EU Commission who were willing to be interviewed and who took the time and shared their views and experiences. The research would not have been possible without their goodwill and cooperation. I am extremely grateful to each of them for their help and I enjoyed an exciting period in Brussels doing the interviews.

I thank Holger Döring for sharing the data with biographical information of commissioners. Didier Georgakakis's biographical data of directors-general allowed me to describe changes in the Commission's senior management. Egeberg and Heskestad's data were helpful in answering questions about the composition of the cabinets.

There are two scholars and friends to whom I owe special thanks. Mark Bovens stands out for his collegiality and generous support. This discussion here has greatly benefited from his good ideas and commentary on the manuscript at different stages of writing. His input was invaluable in getting the

Acknowledgements

argument straight. Paul 't Hart has provided commentary and encouragement for my work over the years. It was at Paul's suggestion that I continued studying political–administrative relationships after we conducted our research at the Dutch executive, a suggestion that has proved to have been a fruitful one.

I also thank colleagues and friends on whom I have relied in many different ways over the years in which this book was in the making: Frank de Zwart and Joop van Holsteyn, Carolyn Ban, Didier Georgakakis, and Hussein Kassim. I have benefited from the discussions of this project at USG and I am grateful for the interest and encouragement of colleagues there: Sebastiaan Princen, Semin Suvarierol, Madalina Busuioc, Gijs Jan Brandsma, Marian van der Steeg, Margo Trappenburg, Sandra Schruijer, Peter Leijsink, Kutsal Yesilkagit, Thomas Schillemans, Albert Meijer, Femke van Esch, Martijn van der Meulen, and Arjen Boin. From the Leiden Institute of Public Administration: Patrick Overeem, Dave Lowery, Arco Timmermans, Wim van Noort, Frits van der Meer, Caspar van den Berg, Trui Steen, Maarja Beerkens, and Kees Nagtegaal. From the SaRO project: Luc Verhey, Ilse van den Driessche, Hansko Broeksteeg, Monica Claes, Jit Peters, Olaf Tans, and Carla Zoethout. Conversations with them were stimulating and are reflected in many ways in the pages of this book.

For detailed comments and feedback on papers and draft chapters leading up to the book, I would like to thank Peter Mair, James Svara, Martijn Groenleer, Jarle Trondal, Åse Gornitzka, Ulf Sverdrup, Ragnar Lie, Johan Olsen, Hans Bekke, Thomas Christiansen, Walter van Gerven, Daniel Gaxie, Jean-Michel Eymeri-Douzans, Jon Pierre, Per Lægreid, Guy Peters, Christophe Knill, Michael Bauer, Joel Aberbach, George Ross, Michele Cini, Jozef Bátora, Celesta Braun, Andreas Warntjen, Christophe Pelgrims, Brian Cook, Eckhard Schröter, and Edoardo Ongaro. Special thanks go to Karin van Boetzelaer for her help with arranging the interviews and Karen Laird, who edited the manuscript—a necessary and much appreciated job—and Ofra Klein, for her help with the references.

Institutional support was provided by a grant of the Netherlands Organization for Scientific Research, de Nederlandse Organisatie voor Wetenschappelijk Onderzoek (NWO) by the SaRO research programme (number 450–04–740) on political control and accountability in a European and comparative perspective. I am grateful that the research has been financially facilitated most generously during its excessively long development by the Utrecht School of Governance of Utrecht University.

Dominic Byatt and the production team of Oxford University Press were very supportive throughout the publishing process. Three referees for OUP provided valuable suggestions on developing the material.

Acknowledgements

In the past years I have worked my way towards the book by publishing some pieces of it in journals and edited volumes. Some parts of the manuscript are reworked and augmented versions of articles I published earlier. I draw on material contained in previous publications, but the book is not a collection of these earlier pieces. Rather, these earlier publications trace the evolution of my thinking about the Commission. They include:

- 'Senior Officials in a Reforming European Commission: Transforming the Top?', in Micheal W. Bauer and Christoph Knill (eds), *Management Reforms in International Organizations* (Baden-Baden: Nomos, 2007), 11–243.
- 'Bridging the Gap: Political and Administrative Leadership in a Reinvented European Commission', in M. Egeberg (ed.), *Institutional Dynamics and the Transformation of Executive Politics in Europe* (Mannheim: University of Mannheim, Connex), 7–41.
- 'Van Technocratie naar "Good Governance"', *Beleid en Maatschappij*, 35/1 (2008): 40–52.
- 'Political and Administrative Leadership in a Reinvented European Commission', in J. A. Raffel, P. Leisink, and A. E. Middlebrooks (eds), *Public Sector Leadership: International Challenges and Perspectives* (Cheltenham: Edward Elgar).
- 'Politicians, Bureaucrats and the Reinvention of the European Commission: From Technical to Good Governance', in L. Verhey, P. Kiiver, and S. Loeven (eds), *Political Accountability and European Integration* (Groningen: European Law), 91–108.
- 'The European Commission's Accountability Paradox', in M. Bovens, D. Curtin, and P. 't Hart (eds), *The Real World of EU Accountability: What Deficit?* (Oxford: Oxford University Press), 63–86.
- 'Modernizing the Executive: The Emergence of Political-Bureaucratic Accountability in the EU Commission', *West European Politics*, 33/5 (2010), 1093–1116.
- 'Beyond the Reforms: Changing Civil Service Leadership in the European Commission', in Jon Pierre and Jean-Michel Emery-Douzans (eds), *Administrative Reform, Democratic Governance and the Quality of Government* (London: Routledge, 2011), 94–105.
- 'Public Sector Leadership in a "Reinvented" European Commission', in J. W. Björkman *et al.* (eds), *Public Leadership and Citizen Value* (The Hague: Eleven International Publishing University, 2011).

Acknowledgements

- 'The Politicization of the EU Commission: Democratic Control and the Dynamics of Executive Selection', *International Review of Administrative Sciences*, 78 (Sept. 2012), 383–402.

Finally, I thank my family and friends who have supported me through this process with patience and understanding. Bronte, Ofra, and Kaeye deserve far more than a written acknowledgement. I dedicate this book to them with loving appreciation.

Amsterdam, October 2012

Contents

List of Figures	xi
List of Tables	xii
Introduction: Politics and Bureaucracy in an Evolving Executive	1
1. Normalized Executive Politics	10
2. The Reinvention of the European Commission	33
3. From Technocrats to Politicians: The Commissioners	57
4. From National Agents to EU Advisers: The Chefs of Cabinet	97
5. From Mandarins to Managers: The Senior Civil Service	119
6. An Emerging Political–Administrative Dichotomy	146
7. Executive Relationships in a 'Normalized' EU Commission	162
8. The Normalization of the EU Commission	186
Epilogue: Quo Vadis?	207
Appendix: Research Design	213
References	217
Index	237

List of Figures

0.1	Overview of the Book	7
1.1	Dynamics Driving Normalization	20
1.2	A Two-Level Model of Normalization in the EU Commission	29
3.1	Number of Questions of MEPs to the Commission, 1999–2010	60
3.2	Recruitment of Commissioners	67
3.3	Box Plot of Former Positions (Scores) of Commissioners	71
3.4	Activity After Leaving the European Commission, 1981–2009	77
4.1	Recruitment of Heads of Cabinet	103
4.2	Cabinet Members having the Same Nationality as the Commissioner	104
4.3	Number of Nationalities Represented in the Cabinets	105
4.4	Cabinet (Deputy) Heads and Members with the Same Nationality as the Commissioner	105
5.1	Recruitment of Senior Officials in the EU Commission	125
5.2	The Process of Appointing Senior Commission Officials	128
5.3	Senior Managers with Studies in Foreign Countries	131
5.4	Europeanization of Directors-General	132
5.5	Directors-General who have been Member of a Cabinet	134
6.1	Zones of Political and Administrative Accountability	151
6.2	Executive Recruitment in the EU Commission	153
7.1	Political–Bureaucratic Triads in the EU Commission	166
8.1	The Changing Nature of the European Commission: Meetings of Hallstein's Commission and the Barroso II Commission	187

List of Tables

1.1	The Features of a Normalized Executive	13
1.2	Politicization of Executive Relationships	21
2.1	Institutional Features of EU Commission in Early Years (1950s) and Period Before the Santer Crisis (1990s)	42
2.2	The EU Commission in Historical Perspective, 1958–2012	43
2.3	Countries and EU Accession	44
2.4	Overview of the EU Commission's Accountability Architecture	50
3.1	The European Parliament in Treaty Reforms since 1992	59
3.2	Prior Positions of Commission Presidents	62
3.3	Early Leaves, 1958–2012	75
3.4	Overview of Early Leavers in EU Commissions, 1958–2012	76
3.5	Politicization of the Commission's Political Executive	92
4.1	Modernization of the Cabinet System	116
5.1	Overview Administrative Reforms in Commission since 2000–4	123
5.2	Professionalization of the Administration	143
6.1	Politicians and Bureaucrats: Evolving Roles	147
6.2	Separate and Shared Elements in Executive Relationships at the Top of the Commission	159
7.1	Continuum of Political–Bureaucratic Relationships	163
7.2	Characteristics of the Ideal-Typical Models of Interactions between Politicians and Administrators	167
8.1	Features of the Commission's Normalization	190
8.2	Shifts in the Core Executive Relationship in the EU Commission	196

Introduction

Politics and Bureaucracy in an Evolving Executive

> We know more about abstract agents dealing with abstract principals than we do about *real bureaucrats* dealing with *real politicians*.
>
> (March 1997: 693)

1. A View from the Top

'Commission bureaucrats are getting too powerful' stated European Commission vice-president Gunter Verheugen in an unusual open interview with the daily *Süddeutsche Zeitung* in 2006.[1] That the German commissioner should thus criticize the hunger for power of the high-ranking Commission officials in the EU executive was unprecedented. Verheugen complained about the permanent power struggle between commissioners and their high-ranking bureaucrats, which mainly takes place 'under the surface'. Verheugen continued: 'Some of the officials think: the commissioner is gone after five years and so he is just a temporary squatter (*Hausbesetzer*). But I'm sticking around.... The most important political task of the 25 commissioners is controlling this apparatus.'

Verheugen's interview dropped a bombshell, judging from the range of reactions during the following days in the European press. The Commission staff union FFPE commented critically in the *Financial Times* that the commissioner should either apologize for his remarks or resign. The Commission's top civil servant and secretary-general, Catherine Day, riposted that 'the civil service understands that we are not the bosses. It is the commissioners that are the bosses.' And the president of the Commission José Manuel Barroso indicated some support for Verheugen by simply stating that the commissioner's remarks should be seen as part of the 'creative tension' which the Commission's modernization drive inevitably evoked.

While Verheugen's stinging criticism of the bureaucracy may have caused shock waves to reverberate around the Brussels beltway, his comments were also very symbolic.[2] Not because he warned against the potential power of EU civil servants; or because he signalled an uneasy alliance between politics

Introduction

and bureaucracy in the EU Commission. His criticism is startling because it can be read as an obvious and deliberate attempt to (re)assert control over the EU bureaucracy.

Politicians in Western democracies have, in past decades, recurrently (and with a good deal of help from the media), scapegoated bureaucracies in their frustration over bureaucratic inability to respond to quickly changing policy agendas and multiple political pressures. Public complaints of political elites about the bureaucracy's inertia and rigidity, or other forms of bashing, have become a common part of symbolic politics (Edelman 1964). Framing sniping messages to fuel the public's belief that there is something wrong with bureaucracy (too large, too lazy, too incompetent, or out of control) has had compelling impact on both the general public and the alleged targets—the bureaucracy. The German commissioner's dim view of his own officials is, in this respect, no exception.

More significant is that the commissioner's message can be read as a critical indication of changing political–bureaucratic relationships at the top of this EU institution. Verheugen's desire to strengthen the hierarchical political direction of the services points to a significant redefinition of the role of commissioners and of their senior officials. The idea of the Commission as a technocratic international organization is gradually being replaced by that of an executive that is subject to the control of political officials and responsive to the EU citizenry. Verheugen's insightful remarks illuminate an important point about the EU Commission: it is slowly coming to be perceived as a 'normal' executive.

The normalization of the Commission

The central thesis of this book is that the Commission is evolving into a *normal* core executive.[3] Broadly, *normalization* is any process by which something becomes more normal, i.e. by conforming to some regularity or rule, or returning from some state of abnormality. The argument, of course, hinges upon a more explicit and meaningful definition of what a 'normal' executive is and looks like. I will examine this concept in greater detail in the next chapter. For now, it is sufficient to state that the Commission has become increasingly 'normalized', in the sense that in the 1950s it started out as a technocratic international organization, yet today embodies many of the organizational and behavioural patterns that are highly typical of the executives we are familiar with in national settings (Egeberg 2006*d*: 15). Changes arising from the processes of treaty reforms and internal administrative reform have contributed to this transformation.

Europe is not the same place it was fifty years ago, nor is the EU Commission the same kind of institution it used to be. The issues facing the current

Commission vary from daunting economic and environmental challenges, globalization, demographic shifts, and climate change, to new security threats and the need for sustainable energy sources. The EU political order has evolved almost to the point where there is virtually no area of political or social life that is potentially not within its remit. The proliferation of activities of the EU into a political union—whose policies go far beyond the original aims of eliminating barriers to cross-border economic activities—has strengthened the call for democratic decision-making and democratic accountability of European policy-makers (Curtin and Wille 2008; Curtin 2009; Bovens *et al.* 2010).

Treaty reforms designed to make the EU Commission more democratic and accountable have been implemented in tandem with the modernization of the Commission's administration. Concurrent political and administrative reforms have put new accountability regimes in place in the EU; and this has placed new demands on the working of the Commission's political executive and its bureaucracy. Political control, accountability, and legitimacy have become more central to the Commission's work. This means that its governance is expected to be democratic, and its executive democratically legitimated. 'Normalization' was unavoidable and transformed the Commission into a different type of organization. It was unavoidable as, in the long run, there was no escaping the political nature of the Commission's work.

The concept of 'normalization' will be used as an analytical device with which to explore a number of processes at work in and around the Commission at both a micro and macro level. At the micro level, the study is about the executive relationships between politicians and bureaucrats at the top of the Commission, and the changing nature of the Commission's work in the face of political and administrative reform efforts. Yet this cannot be understood without also considering the new emerging political order in the EU and its changing institutional context (Curtin and Egeberg 2008). New political constraints and altered expectations for the Commission have produced new demands on this institution's function. It is, therefore, essential to place the analysis of executive relationships at the top of the Commission in the macro context of the accountability demands that have arisen around this institution, transforming the EU Commission into a more 'political' executive.

2. Politicians and Bureaucrats: The Heart of the Executive

The Commission is the EU's executive power. Whereas the Council and the European Parliament are the focus of the legislative process, the Commission has the responsibility for the formulation and execution of EU policy. The core functions of the EU Commission are to pull together and integrate these policies. The Commission proposes legislation for adoption by the European Parliament and the Council of Ministers and is also responsible for putting the EU's common policies into practice and managing the EU's budget and programmes.

The working of the EU Commission rests on two pillars: politics and bureaucracy. A smooth operation of this system depends on the harmonious relationship between the two (cf. Heclo 1977). Previous studies have examined either the political or the administrative actors and dimensions within the EU Commission, but not both simultaneously.[4] Little has been done so far to explore the *interface* of the political and bureaucratic levels in the EU.[5] This study aims to deal with this dearth and to provide a detailed account of the political–bureaucratic relationships at the heart of the EU Commission.

At its heart we find the 'core executive' (cf. Rhodes and Dunleavy 1995; Rhodes *et al.* 2009: 24). The term refers to the web of institutions, networks, and relations which embed the commissioners, the heads of cabinet, and senior officials in the innermost part of the EU Commission. In a way, the core executive of the Commission resembles the studio of famous painters, like Rubens or Rembrandt. The finished product bore the master's name, but much of the painting, especially the routine work, was executed by students and lesser painters.[6] Here, the final result is generally not the work of the commissioners but the product of cooperation with cabinets and the top of the civil service.

The collaboration between the political and the administrative levels consists of a *ménage à trois*, a delicate triangle of commissioners, heads of cabinet, and directors-general. The *commissioners*, who are appointed and are generally politicians by background, form the College of Commissioners. The *heads of cabinet*—officials personally appointed by the commissioner—offer policy advice to the commissioner, are the gatekeepers to the commissioner's desk, and act as linchpins between the commissioners and 'their' bureaucrats. The *directors-general*—heading the services and Directorates-General (DGs), consisting of a staff of several thousand full-time European career officials—are responsible for the administration by the Commission's bureaucracy. By virtue of the office they hold and the formal powers and responsibilities they have, they are amongst the key figures in the executive policy process.

In the study of core executives, there are four key questions that generally need to be addressed to open up the black box of political–bureaucratic relationships. (1) Who is responsible for what? (2) How are they (s)elected? (3) What are they expected to do? (4) And how do actors in the core executive cooperate? Posing these questions leads to a focus on four interrelated components that lie at the 'core of the EU's core executive'.

1. *Rules and responsibilities: who is responsible for what?* What are the responsibilities of the EU commissioners, their heads of cabinet, and their senior officials? The formal-legal arrangements of political institutions are the backbone of most core executives. Rules, laws, and constitutions define the executive's responsibilities and shape the obligations of politicians and bureaucrats. Formal and legal arrangements establish the governmental processes; they guide the work of bureaucrats; and they regulate the dealings between executive and legislative, between ministers (and commissioners), civil servants and between parliament and bureaucracy.

2. *Recruitment and selection: how are they (s)elected?* How are the commissioners, heads of cabinet, and senior officials selected? In most executives, considerable attention is paid to selecting, electing, and dismissing or otherwise removing its political executive and its senior services. Executive recruitment has important implications for the composition and characteristics of the political and bureaucratic leaders who are in the position to wield executive power. Knowing how political and bureaucratic officials are recruited, which candidates are selected with what type of skills, backgrounds, and experiences, is important for understanding *who* exactly shapes executive power.

3. *Role conceptions of executives: what are they expected to do and how?* What are the role expectations of commissioners, heads of cabinet, and the senior officials? Politicians and bureaucrats have an interpretation of their own roles as well as of those of their counterparts in the core executives. What officials do, and how they do it, is not only determined by the rules and the definition of their responsibilities, but also by these role conceptions. The set of values and predispositions that executive officials bring to their job will affect their performances and the decisions they make (Putnam 1973; Heady 1974; Aberbach *et al.* 1981; Peters 1988; Mouritzen and Svara 2002; Svara 2006). The role that political executives and senior officials have adopted for themselves and see for each other, can have important consequences for the manner in which core executives are managed.

4. *Relationships between political and bureaucratic executives: how do they cooperate?* What sort of relationships do commissioners have with their heads of cabinet and their senior officials? The relationship between political and bureaucratic executives may be a function of 'what each side believes it should be doing' (Peters 1988: 177). In many ways, executives depend on a *successful interaction* between political executives and senior officials (Heclo 1977). Ministers and commissioners cannot translate their priorities and goals into policy proposals without

Introduction

the support of the services. Equally, senior officials lack the authority and clout to achieve objectives without the full support of the political level in the executive. The smooth operation of government is shaped by the capacity of cooperation between political executives and senior bureaucrats.

A further examination of these four central elements will enable a better understanding of the operations of the EU executive. These four questions will, therefore, structure the book. By exploring these aspects, it is possible to examine patterns of executive leadership; how political elites and senior civil servants work together in the EU executive; and how these core relationships have evolved into a 'normalized' executive.

3. Plan of the Book

The book is written with three different audiences in mind: those who have a fascination with political–bureaucratic relationships at the top of governmental institutions; those who care about institutional change; and those who are interested in EU governance. It describes how a series of political and administrative changes have 'normalized' the European Commission from an international organization to a regular core executive. I concentrate on the developments at the core of this EU executive since the fall of the Santer Commission in 1999. Drawing on documentary evidence during the Prodi (1999–2004) and the Barroso I (2004–9) and Barroso II (2009–14) years and on interviews held with top officials in the Commission during the Barroso presidencies, I aim to provide a deeper understanding of the normalization of the EU Commission.

Figure 0.1 presents a schematic overview of the book's chapters. The book is organized around the executive relations of the key actors at the core of the EU Commission; and it examines the changes in the four interrelated components that lie at the heart of these relationships. The first component, the *rules and responsibilities—and the question who is responsible for what*—will recur in all chapters. The second and third components, the *recruitment patterns and the role expectations* of the three main actors at the core of the EU Commission, will be dealt with in the chapters that are organized around these players. Chapter 3 describes these components for the commissioners, Chapter 4 for the cabinet chefs; and Chapter 5 deals with the senior officials in the Commission. And Chapter 6 assesses, with the help of these components, the division of labour at the top of the Commission. The final and fourth component of executive relationships will be dealt with in Chapter 7.

Plan of the Book

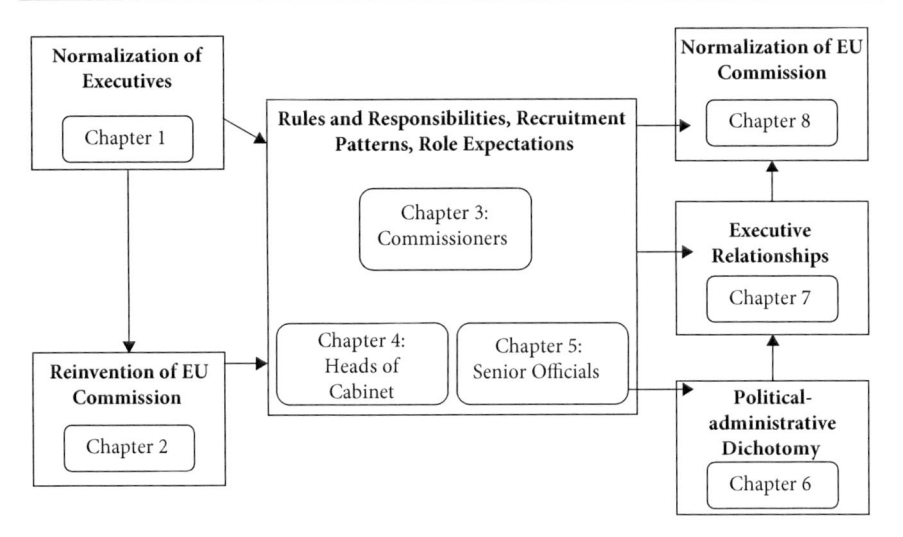

Figure 0.1. Overview of the Book

Specifically, Chapter 1 starts with an exploration of the concept of normalization. It defines the elements of a normal executive, and it describes why and through what mechanisms these normalization processes occur. It wraps up with a framework to analyse and assess normalized executive politics.

Chapter 2 describes the reinvention of the EU Commission. It explains how, in the 1990s, the Commission's values and practices grew increasingly out of step with internal and external challenges and how this crystallized in a crisis. The chapter shows how the crisis provided a 'character-defining' moment and how political and administrative reforms have changed the basic accountability system of the European Commission over the last decade.

Chapter 3 explains how political leadership in the Commission has changed due to the rise of new accountability mechanisms. The European Parliament has become a far more vociferous and demanding interlocutor and has contributed to the growth of a more politically accountable Commission. The changes in the legal and political framework governing the appointment and tasks of the commissioners are linked to the Commission's internal and external political leadership.

Chapter 4 explains how modernization of the Commission and the cabinet system has 'professionalized' the role of the heads of cabinet in the EU Commission. In response to accusations of favouritism and nepotism prompted by the cabinet structures in the EU Commission, a new listing of the roles of cabinets was designed to draw sharper lines of responsibility between cabinets and services.

Introduction

Chapter 5 shows how senior officials play a pivotal role in the Commission, linking the political to the administrative system. In past years, the Commission and its staff have been engaged in the task of overhauling administrative systems and procedures to equip the institution with a modern and effective European administration. This chapter discusses the repercussions of the reforms for the position and job of senior officials in the Commission.

Chapter 6 explains how the reforms have contributed to a differentiation between commissioners, heads of cabinet, and the top civil servants at the helm of the EU Commission. The desire to improve the accountability of the EU Commission has resulted in a clearer demarcation of the political and the administrative parts in the Commission.

Chapter 7 explains how the political–bureaucratic relationship, as part of the larger development of the institution, has evolved in the direction of the normal model. The rise of new accountability structures in and around the European Commission have turned political control and administrative responsiveness into critical rudiments of the relationship between commissioners and their senior officials. Their view of the day-to-day relationship remains, however, one of a pragmatic professional transaction.

Chapter 8 concludes that the EU Commission has become increasingly 'normalized' and summarizes the features of this normalization. The new relations were needed to comply with the new accountability demands posed by the changing political environment within which the EU Commission finds itself entrenched. At the same time, they pose a set of new complex dilemmas, as is argued in the Epilogue.

Notes

1. *Süddeutsche Zeitung*, Oct. 2006. Quotations are my translation.
2. In a follow-up interview with the *Financial Times* on 10 Oct. 2006, Verheugen explained that because of bureaucrats' obstructionism, the Commission would fail to simplify existing EU laws as part of its offensive against red tape. Some claimed that the real story behind Verheugen's attack on the Commission's services was not to be interpreted as a complaint about the undue influence of senior officials, but as a ploy to distract attention from the cause célèbre that emerged when he was photographed on an apparently romantic holiday with a long-time associate whom he had promoted to chef of his cabinet.
3. Egeberg (2006a, 2006c, 2006d) has argued repeatedly that the Commission has become increasingly 'normalized'.
4. Coombes (1970), Ross (1995), Cini (1996, 2000, 2007), Donnelly and Ritchie (1997), Egeberg (1997, 2006a, 2006b, 2006c), Nugent (1997, 2001), Page (1997), Peterson (1999, 2004), Shore (2000), Hooghe (2001), Joana and Smith (2002), Dimitrakopoulos (2004), Kassim (2004a, 2004b, 2008), Smith (2005), Spence (2006b),

Bauer (2007*b*, 2008, 2012), Suvarierol (2008), Trondal (2008, 2010, 2012), Seidel (2010), Schön-Quinlivan (2011), Ellinas and Suleiman (2012).
5. One important exception is Page's analysis of the Commission which was published in 1997.
6. I've borrowed this comparison from Kavenagh and Seldon (2003).

1

Normalized Executive Politics

> Change is an ordinary part of political life that is rule-bound and takes place through standard comprehensible processes.
>
> (Olsen 2010: 15)

1. The Normal Model

This book is about the political–administrative divide in the EU Commission, and how it is gradually acquiring the features of a 'normalized' executive. In this study, *normalization* refers to a shift of executive relations towards the political and administrative qualities of the 'normal' model, resulting from a change in existing accountability arrangements. Key in the definition of normalization are three distinct elements that will be further explored in this chapter: (1) the normal model, (2) accountability arrangements, and (3) change.

The chapter starts by giving a broad outline of the features of the 'normal' model of executive relationships. The idea of a political–administrative divide is a key central organizing principle behind this model, which is not only used to describe things as they are, but also as they ought to be. This chapter goes on to discuss how instituting political-bureaucratic accountability arrangements have changed the character of many executives. It is argued that political and administrative reforms, grounded in the principles of the 'normal' model, have contributed to the normalization of many contemporary executives, and that the classical dichotomy between politics and administration has been woven into the fabric of many executives in Western democracies, and has created a new environment for executive relationships. Then, the chapter discusses the concept of change, related as it is to normalization, and argues how valuable the normalization concept is to explain the evolution of contemporary executives. The chapter finishes with an overview of the questions that are central to the book and the research conducted into the European Commission's normalization.

The political–administrative divide

Government is often thought as being divided into two spheres: politics and administration, with separate roles assigned to politicians and administrators, each with different turfs and distinct norms of behaviour, and between which a clear, hierarchical relationship exists (Overeem 2012). The view that the *two spheres* are separate prevailed throughout much of the 20th century.[1] The politics-administration dichotomy can be traced back to the origins of theories on modern state-organizations. In the early days of the US civil service, Woodrow Wilson set out the division in his 1887 seminal essay on modern public administration, when he argued that politics should not interfere in administration. Thirty years later in Europe, Max Weber (1978) drew attention to the dichotomy in his work on the distinctiveness of vocations to political leadership and bureaucratic service.

This split between politics and administration was broadly accepted until the mid-20th century. However, from the 1950s to the 1970s, the idea of a classical dichotomy was gradually rejected until, ultimately, it became received wisdom that no such dichotomy existed (Frederickson and Smith 2003: 16). Several authors argued that a clear division is impossible, and a number of empirical studies showed varying intermeshings of the two spheres (Aberbach *et al.* 1981; Mouritzen and Svara 2002). These studies suggested that, in reality, the respective role conceptions and interaction patterns between politicians and administrators are complex and differentiated (Putnam 1975; Aberbach *et al.* 1981; Peters 1987).

However, in the 1990s the idea of a neat dichotomy between politics and administration re-emerged (Frederickson and Smith 2003). Democratization, in combination with public-sector reform, had a profound effect on the relationship between politicians and administrators in many democracies (Peters and Pierre 2001). New management techniques and the changing recruitment and career patterns of officials tended to undermine the old cooperative relationships in which jointly socialized politicians and top officials mixed smoothly. The New Public Management (NPM)-driven emphasis on performance and measurable outcomes created more tensions between the sphere of politics and administration, and contributed to a stronger distinction, both in theory and in practice (Peters and Pierre 2001).

The normal model

The political–bureaucratic divide has become the base for a particular kind of 'gold' standard institutional solution that has dominated the governing agenda in many executives. This 'gold standard' shares a design philosophy that I will call 'the normal model'. This model is a way of thinking about the organization of political–administrative functions. Much of what we see as 'normal' in executives is based on doctrines of democratic and effective government, key concerns of political analysts since Weber and Wilson. In this view, a 'good' executive would ideally be characterized by an administration outside the sphere of politics; a hierarchical order of professionally trained public servants; democratically elected politicians who exert political control over the bureaucracy; a bureaucracy governed by specific principles, all of which are designed to produce efficient administration and to serve their political masters.

Although an exact or precise definition of a 'normal' executive is difficult to give, a broad ideal-typical outline of the 'normal' model can be derived from the following four elements that describe core executives:

1. RULES AND RESPONSIBILITIES: A CLEAR DIVISION BETWEEN POLITICS AND BUREAUCRACY

In the 'normal' model, there is a functionally specific system of governmental organization that differentiates along the political–bureaucratic division. Rules allocate discrete responsibilities to politicians and bureaucrats and each group has a distinct set of behavioural norms. A clear division of responsibilities is professed as being essential for organizing a system of checks and balances and a clear line of accountability. Civil servants have a great deal of functional responsibility, while political responsibility is in the hands of political executives (Peters 1988: 150).

There is considerable variation in the formal and legal design of core executives in democracies. Parliamentary and presidential systems differ, for example, in the way executive powers and responsibilities (regarding parliament, president, or prime minister, etc.) are defined and distributed. But, for the most part, in both systems politicians and civil servants occupy two relatively distinct spaces—one political and the other administrative.

2. RECRUITMENT PATTERNS: POLITICIZED VERSUS PROFESSIONALIZED

In the 'normal' model, politicians and civil servants require distinct skills, as politicians decide on policies, while officials administer them. Despite differences in competencies, the selection procedures for political and bureaucratic roles are both based on achievement rather than on ascriptive criteria such as class or caste. Merit selection ensures that bureaucratic positions are filled with expert and highly qualified personnel (Peters 2010: 83), whose use of skills and expertise is not affected by political considerations (Ingraham 1995). Bureaucrats are educationally qualified, specialized, professionalized, and have fulltime appointments. Politicians have an appointment that is related to their political affiliation. In democratic systems, they are elected (or selected on base of elections) to represent the public interests and to manage the affairs of state. Elections serve as a natural selection struggle for political office to bring talented and competent leaders to political top positions (Weber 1978; Schumpeter 2010); and they can cause the political control over the executive to shift from one political party to another.

3. ROLE EXPECTATIONS: DISTINCT ROLES FOR POLITICIANS AND BUREAUCRATS

In a normal model of political–bureaucratic organization, there are distinct roles for political executives and their bureaucrats. Politicians act as (partisan) political leaders or as sovereign representatives to determine the political purposes and policy directions when exercising the power of their office; and it is their role to control and oversee bureaucrats and their behaviour in office. Bureaucrats contribute their expertise and technical skills to provide policy advice; they are expected to act efficiently and be unbiased by personal or partisan orientations; and to be politically responsive, following the directives and instructions from their political superiors.

4. POLITICAL–BUREAUCRATIC RELATIONSHIPS: HIERARCHICALLY ORGANIZED

In the normal understanding of the political–bureaucratic relationship, there is also a clear *hierarchical distinction* between the sphere of politics and the sphere of administration. In the normal model, politicians are expected to occupy superior positions to administrators. They are in charge, and exercise control and oversight over the performance of the bureaucracy. Civil servants are expected to be loyal towards their political bosses. In the standards of this model administrators are not only separated from politics, but also subordinated to it (cf. Svara 2006).

In brief, the four elements summarized in Table 1.1 collectively describe the core features of a 'normal' executive.[2]

The normal model as a normative theory

The normal model, which is a legacy from the writings of Wilson and Weber, functions as an empirical-analytical tool. As an ideal-typical model it helps

Table 1.1 The Features of a Normalized Executive

Rules and responsibilities	Distinct responsibilities of politicians and bureaucrats
Recruitment	*Politicized versus professionalized selection*
Role expectations	Distinct roles politicians and bureaucrats
Relationships	Hierarchical relationship between politicians and bureaucrats

in understanding and analysing executive relationships. Yet the model has also functions as a set of normative standards against which to compare and evaluate real patterns of policy-making and political–bureaucratic interactions. Verheugen's media statements described at the start of this book, about the alleged but inappropriate powers of EU senior bureaucrats and the related loss of political control, illustrate that the normal model has a widely held place in the mind of politicians.

Both Weber and Wilson argued that administration could be—and should be—separated from politics. The purpose of establishing distinct responsibilities was, in Weber's approach, to keep civil servants out of politics; and, for Wilson, to keep politics out of the civil service, i.e. to give bureaucrats more room to use their skills without political biases. Not having a clear distinction between politics and administration can have, following the normative logic of the normal model, profound implications for the realization of key governmental values such as political control, accountability, and performance.

A blurring between politics and administration makes it difficult to answer such basic questions as 'who is setting the direction?' and 'who can be held accountable for what is happening in public institutions?' Likewise, political patronage and political favouritism can undermine the technical effectiveness of administrations. On the other hand, substantive bureaucratic power flows from an administration's stability and longevity, and from its inevitable involvement in all levels of policy development and implementation (Meier and Bohte 1993). The danger of bureaucrats developing an independent power base is, therefore, great.

Political control by politicians over 'their' bureaucrats must ensure, in the prescriptions of the normal model, that the expertise and authority available in the bureaucracy is placed at the disposal of politicians. Democratically elected political representatives must be in control of these bureaucracies, because bureaucrats must not only be prevented from doing what is not wanted, but must also serve competently as an administrative organization to deliver what is 'democratically' decided (Heclo 1977: 5). A design with a clear distinction between politics and bureaucracy will remedy blurred political–bureaucratic role conceptions. Care must be taken to ensure that the powers available in public institutions are accountable to a broader public and to a broader conception of the public interest (Behn 2001: 54).

Weber and Wilson's concepts have become part of the modern ideas about governing, and of a governance paradigm, an accepted standard model for organizing the decision-making and action within governments. As a doctrine, the 'normal' model has served over the years, in several variations, to constitute the ethos of national core executives in many democracies (Savoie 2008: 5). Many attempts to reform the executive branch of government have been oriented towards improving the workings of government according to 'the standards' of this model.

Varieties of normality

The different democratic and bureaucratic traditions themselves are, inevitably, imprecise about the democratic and administrative details or procedures. This has resulted in different shades of democracy and bureaucracy, and varieties in how 'the' normal model is interpreted, organized, and institutionalized in government practices.

Democracies are commonly defined as government *by* and *for* the governed, in which the people are thought to be 'the only legitimate fountain of power'.[3] Democratic institutions should therefore reflect the will of the people (Dahl 1998; Schmidt 2006). But democracies have not inherited a *coherent* set of principles and institutions that define good government; rather, they have inherited elements from different traditions (Olsen 2010: 139). Consequently, there is no stable consensus concerning ideas about appropriate ways of organizing government, and a huge variation is found in so-called 'democracies' with regard to how the will of the people is established and implemented in practice (Huntington 1991; Keane 2009; Olson 2010: 139). There are many ways in which, in principle, a democracy can be organized and run (Lijphart 1999). Normative political theory and practice provide multiple answers and there is an ongoing 'belief battle' over democratic ideas and the desirability of particular political institutions (Sartori 1969a: 87).

The same holds for organizing public administration in democratic societies (Olsen 2010: 175–204). The task of public administration is to make democracy work through the preparation, implementation, and enforcement of laws and policies. Democratic theory, however, does not prescribe what precise administrative arrangements will support a sustainable democratic development. There are competing understandings of the proper organization of public administration within a democratic framework; and the normative ideal of the precise organization of administrative processes (rules versus results) remains largely contested.

In short, a normal executive in a presidential system looks different from a normal executive in a parliamentary system; and within these executive structures and processes there is considerable variance between the classic Westminster system and the West European consensual ones. However, the four features of the normal model that are defined here are sufficiently generic to stand as the critical dimensions of normality across the diverse institutional settings. They are part of a democratic governance paradigm that, despite differences in context and environment, has remained extremely attractive when it comes to the expansion of political or administrative reforms (Behn 2001: 60).

2. Instituting Political–Bureaucratic Accountability

In a democracy, the accountability of the executive and its officials is a vital concern. Who is accountable, to whom, and about what? The first question—who—requires the identification of responsibilities for certain parts of the executive work; the second—to whom—requires the identification of a legitimate source of authority; the third—about what—requires expectations about operations and performance. The answers to these questions lie at the heart of democratic governance and the organization of executive relationships. A range of arrangements that often have been institutionalized are in place to organize and secure accountability in these executive relationships. And it is via the set-up of these interconnected mechanisms, or accountability regimes (Bovens *et al.* 2010), that normative expectations about roles and relationships have been woven into the executives of modern governments.

Broadly conceived, accountability in public organizations is a set of mechanisms by which organizations (and their executive officials) manage the diverse expectations generated within and outside the organization (Romzek and Dubnick 1987: 228; Romzek 2000; Behn 2001: 63; Mulgan 2003; Bovens 2006, 2007, 2010; Bovens *et al.* 2010: 31–62). The presence of accountability arrangements obliges executive officials to disclose information, to explain their conduct, and to justify their behaviour. It forces officials to consider the consequences when they exercise their powers and discretion. Accountability arrangements are not designed solely to catch, reverse, and punish wrongdoings of executives. They are also designed to manage and affect prospective behaviour (Bovens 1998: 39). The mere anticipation of being called to account may provide a strong incentive to act responsibly (Mulgan 2003: 24). The fundamentals that define the mix of expectations in executive relationships are anchored in the set-up of an accountability regime.

Beyond the normal model: political–bureaucratic accountability

Accountability can have its origin in the political process, in administrative arrangements, but also in constitutional law and regulations, or professional and contractual relationships. Yet, in the basic concept of the normal model, executives find themselves confronting an accountability regime in which two main types of accountability are important: political and administrative. In *political accountability* expectations are managed through arrangements, such as elections, parliamentary instruments, ministerial responsibility, where the emphasis is on responsiveness to the agenda of the 'other', the key stakeholders, such as elected officials, the electorate. *Administrative accountability* is used for managing efficiency, fairness, and financial expectations. Accountability arrangements of this type are based on hierarchical supervision, rules, regulations, supervisory directives and are widely used for managing civil service expectations. In modern public institutions, these traditional, vertical straight-line arrangements are increasingly complemented with methods of result-based reporting and performance evaluations to manage administrative expectations.

At the same time, executives in modern democratic systems also have to deal with other accountability regimes such as *legal accountability*, in which expectations are managed through the application of common rules and laws; *professional accountability*, which relies on deference to expertise; and *public accountability*, a key part of which is ensuring that relevant information about executives activities and policies is made accessible to internal and external stakeholders (Romzek and Dubnick 1987; Bovens 2007; Bovens et al. 2010).

In theory, all types of accountability offer potentially legitimate means for managing institutional-level expectations. Each of these accountability types can be present within an organization. In reality, one or two types of accountability relationships are primary, and the others are in place, but secondary (Romzek and Dubnick 1987; Romzek 2000). The precise balance of accountability regime in an organization, at any time, depends on the nature of existing environmental, management, and governance orientations.

Organizations that transfer the authority of policy choices to technocrats, so that the choices are taken relatively isolated from politics, are more strongly linked with legal and professional accountability systems (cf. Romzek and Dubnick 1987). Such governance models are usually based on scepticism about the merits of the methods of democratic accountability, which are thought to produce policies that are short-sighted and unstable (Roberts 2011: 4). Professional expertise within the limits of legal constraints establishes the authority of these forms of technocratic governance. In contrast, democratic governance models are dominated by political and bureaucratic accountability mechanisms. Elected officials are expected to control the decisions of appointed or non-elected executive officials; and elections establish the authority of elected officials. It is via the set-up of these political–bureaucratic accountability regimes that the normal model of democratic governance has been gradually woven into the executive relationships of modern governments.

Political and administrative changes: adjusting accountability arrangements

The 20th century has been deemed the 'democratic century'; democracy in the past 100 years has taken root, has blossomed, and has now finally become consolidated, writes Peter Mair (2008).[4] Looking back at this century, political in tandem with administrative reforms have been crucial for instituting the principles of democratic government. Political reforms in the past century resulted in the worldwide establishment and expansion of democratic accountability (Huntington 1991; Dahl 2006; Keane 2009; Fukuyama 2011).[5]

Institutionalization of accountability arrangements that are anchored in the 'normal' model has augmented popular democratic control and imposed political constraints on bureaucracies and the policy-making sphere. One could argue that a considerable amount of governmental reform over the previous era was actually occupied with the task of giving effect to the proposition that 'the will of the people' should guide government behaviour (Roberts 2011: 7). First, elections have expanded the ability of citizens to choose, or influence indirectly, who holds (executive) power; and if citizens dislike their government or their policies they have a direct and effective means to correct the situation: they can vote their elected officials out of office. Second, the establishment of political assemblies, legislatures, or parliaments as central arenas of accountability created forums for the public accounting of its executive officials, and has been accompanied by an increased control over executives by legislatures (Lijphart 1984; Judge and Earnshaw 2008: 203). A variety of mechanisms (ex ante and ex post) has evolved, additionally, for effective legislative control over the executive (Strøm et al. 2010).

This democratization of government implied an increasingly active role of legislative institutions in governing political executive behaviour. It also implied an increased political professionalization. Politics became so important that it became virtually impossible to combine a political function with any other occupation. More and more, ministers and parliamentarians in Europe have become paid politicians, receiving a salary comparable to the senior civil service (Cotta and Best 2007). They have become what Weber (1978) a century ago called 'Berufspolitiker'.

This growth of professional politicians, and mass democracy, developed together with bureaucratic organization (Weber 1978: 991–2). Weber noted the increasing importance of both entities, which have grown in size, function, and power. The growing prominence and power of bureaucracy posed important problems in a democracy, because it meant that bureaucrats had greater opportunities to influence policy. This in turn made the task of elected officials especially important 'since they must oversee the bureaucracy infuse it with democratic preferences, and make it accountable to democratic processes' (Dunn 1997: 18).

The evolution of a democratic order, 'taming' the unrestrained power of executives, has been connected to a trend of rationalizing and increasing the accountability of the administrative parts of the executive (Weber 1978; Aberbach et al. 1981: 1–4; Olson 2008, 2010). Organizational and procedural rearrangements were an understandable response to democratized procedures and came with the introduction of new accountability mechanisms in the quest for more economic, efficient, and effective public organizations. Weber's ideas about bureaucratic accountability, based on three arrangements—formal hierarchical position, legal rules, and expert knowledge—fed into development of public administration in the early 20th century to stimulate the principles of fairness and efficiency. Looking back a century later, Weber's insights were remarkably prescient, as Aberbach et al. (1981: 1–2) point out: 'these twin trends have unfolded at different rates and in somewhat different phases in the several countries of Europe and North-America', but in broad outline the patterns were visible everywhere.

Since the early 1980s, a 'pandemic of public management reforms' has swept most Western countries (Pollitt and Bouckaert 2004: 1). As a result, civil services in many Western countries have changed significantly, mirroring the era of public-sector reform and reflecting ideas from a 'reinvented' normal model about how executives should operate. These reforms introduced a set of new administrative accountability mechanisms that were badged as New Public Sector Management (NPM) reforms. NPM represented a shift away from the Weberian ideas of bureaucratic organization and heavy emphasis on general rules of procedure, towards a stronger focus on getting results, while continuing to strive for professionalization and efficiency. A key theme of these NPM reforms was that of 'incentivization', the idea being to make incentives for public officials more like those for private personnel (Hood 1994: 129). These new mechanisms for 'managerial' accountability in Western public administrations emerged with the objective of prodding these administrations 'to perform better' (Pollitt and Bouckaert 2004: 16). They have compelled public institutions in a variety of settings to become more sensitive to inefficiencies, costs, and to become more responsive and accountable.

The cumulative result of decades of political and administrative reforms is an extensive accountability apparatus in most modern governments that covers the behaviours, decisions, and action of both politicians and civil servants in their use of public authority and public resources. The expansion of these political–administrative accountability arrangements contributed to an increased normalization of executive relationships.

Politicization and depoliticization: two faces of normalization

When we study normalization of executives, we must take into account that a shift at the macro level in arrangements towards a more political and bureaucratic accountability regime engenders politicization and depoliticization processes, as displayed in Figure 1.1. Both politicization and depoliticization are mediating processes impinging on the recruitment and roles expectations of political executives and their administrators at the micro level in the organization.

Normalized Executive Politics

```
Political reforms  ←——————————————→  Administrative reforms
         ↘                                    ↙
            Political and bureaucratic
                  accountability
                  arrangements
                         ↓
              Politicization and
              depoliticization of
                 the executive
                         ↓
               Normalization of
             executive relationships
```

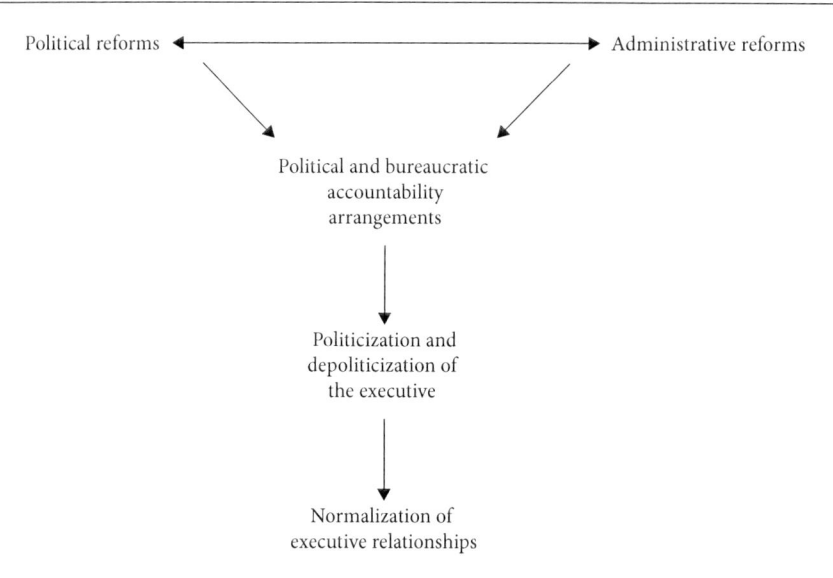

Figure 1.1. Dynamics Driving Normalization

Politicization is a complex and elusive concept (cf. Rouban 2012) and using it can easily lead to confusion. Here politicization is used in the definition of Peters and Pierre (2004: 2) as 'the substitution of political criteria for merit-based criteria in the selection, retention, promotion, rewards and disciplining' of executive officials. Depoliticization on the other hand is the polar opposite to politicization and appears when merit criteria are substituted for political-based criteria.

Given that most executives consist of a political and administrative part, we must evaluate the impact of these processes on both sides differently. Politicization contrasts with the values associated with a 'technocracy' or a 'professional bureaucracy' in which officials are expected to maintain a certain distance from political concerns (cf. Mulgan 2007: 570). But politicization goes well with officials who operate at the political level. Depoliticization, on the other hand, is a process that can underpin the neutrality of the bureaucracy, but weakens the responsiveness and legitimacy of the political executive.

A second point is that politicization can manifest itself in either of two different ways in executives: as a *bottom–up* or as a *top–down process* (cf. Peters and Pierre 2004). Table 1.2 displays the distinct features of these two politicization types. Bottom–up politicization pertains to an increased political involvement or patronage activity of public servants and includes party-political allegiance behaviour or, in international executives, activities influenced by national interests. Such 'bottom–up' politicization processes blur the political–bureaucratic divide within an executive. Top–down politicization, on the other hand, is characterized by an increased level of control exerted by political officeholders over the bureaucracy. It can be viewed as one of the more

Table 1.2 Politicization of Executive Relationships

	Bottom–Up Politicization	Top–Down Politicization
Rules	Weak political and bureaucratic accountability arrangements	Strengthened political and bureaucratic accountability arrangements
Recruitment	Political patronage	Political appointments related to elected (democratic) body; civil service appointments are merit based
Roles	Political and national loyalties	Responsiveness to directions of political 'principal'
Relationships	Fragmented, autonomous organization	Strengthened political control

important strategies adopted to achieve political influence over the arenas in which decisions are made and to ensure that the members of a civil service act in line with the political policy preferences. Political officials wield a range of tools—ex ante incentives and ex post controls—to constrain bureaucratic drift (Weingast 2005), to domesticate bottom–up political influences, and to realize more effective political (and parliamentary) control over the executive (Strøm et al. 2010). Normalization is associated with top–down politicization, in which the political executive becomes politicized and the administration depoliticized.

Historically, the institutionalization of political and administrative accountability arrangements has evoked a long-term pattern of *top–down politicization of executive relationships* in evolving representative democracies during the 19th and early 20th centuries. This has become manifest in the procedures of political executive selection. Politicization of the political executive has manifested itself in the new *demands* (and new role expectations) on eligible candidates suitable for political office at the level of the nation-states (Norris 1997; Best and Cotta 2000; Cotta and Best 2007). Developments in democratic governance and a further political professionalization have caused political qualifications (representation, partisanship, political skills) to dominate the selection for political office.

Administrative reforms aimed at depoliticization, that were an inevitable part of a historical trend towards rationalization according to Weber (1978), have been instituted in order to promote the functioning of administrative values—efficient, effective, and responsive to politicians. This was reflected in the introduction of merit-based rules, in the 19th-century bureaucracies, for the selection of civil servants as a solution to the problems that patronage or bottom–up politicization posed (Peters and Pierre 2004); and in the new role expectations introduced with NPM reforms since the end of the 1970s—stressing professional standards and supporting a detachment from politics in favour of more professional conceptions of the civil service.

In short, many of the new building blocks of accountability that have been added to Western governmental structures can be perceived as attempts to approach some of the standards of the *normal* model: the separation of administration from politics, the quest for efficiency, the need for hierarchy and the constraints (or imperative) of political control. Political and administrative reforms designed, implemented, and applied to address better governance have been persistently grounded in the normative prescriptions of the normal model. That the normal model has survived for so long speaks, in the words of Donald Savoie (2009: 6), 'both to its merits and to our inability to come up with a better one'.

3. Understanding Change

Normalization of executive politics is a form of institutional change that is transformative and that has a clear 'face'. It ensues when the professional and legal logic of accountability, around a set of executive actors, switches to a political and administrative logic of accountability. These transformative changes in institutional arrangements are rarely the result of a single dominant process, but rather a combination of sometimes interacting and co-evolving processes taking place at different levels, at different speeds, and in a different ways (Olsen 2010: 14). These processes will be addressed here briefly.

Normalization as gradual transformation

Change takes place when an entity has undergone a modification or alteration to its properties (shape, state, or quality) between time t and t1 (Capano 2009: 9). Strong punctuated equilibrium situations can lead to big changes in response to historical break points. But several authors (Pierson 2004; Thelen 2005; Streeck and Thelen 2005; Mahoney and Thelen 2010) indicate that the accumulation of small, often seemingly insignificant, adjustments may add up to historical discontinuities, too. To draw a sharp line in models of institutional change between institutional stability and institutional transformation impedes the conceptualization of a slow-moving causal process of incremental change with transformative results.

The broad view on institutional change makes it possible to think of normalization as the result of abrupt institutional breakdowns provoked by an exogenous shock that either wipes out institutions or so destabilizes them that it creates the possibility for previously unforeseen agency and innovation. But normalization may also result from an accumulation of subtle incremental changes over longer periods of time. Such a slow-moving process can take the form of a series of seemingly minor political and administrative adaptations, whereby old institutional arrangements are gradually undermined, complemented, and/or replaced by new ones, leading to an institutional reconfiguration.

Normalization as adapting and learning

If normalization does not just take place in response to exogenous shocks or shifts, then the basic types of change must be open to evolutionary modes of adapting and learning. Normalization via adaptation can be thought of as an unplanned adjustment of institutions to changing conditions in the environment. In biological terms, adaption might be comparable to biological evolution (Fukuyama 2010: 446). But normalization can also be the result of organizational learning. In the case of learning (Heclo 1974: 135; Argyris and Schön 1978; Hall 1993, 2010), institutions are deliberately reformed in order to achieve substantive purposes and ends. This form of political engineering or organizational design does not take place in a norm-free environment, but happens in a normative context, in which standards of legitimate models already exist (Rittberger 2012: 23). The 'normal model' is a loosely coupled framework that is used as a guide in processes of organizational innovation and polity- and state-building.

Modes of normalization

Thinking of normalization as the result of different modes provides a better understanding of the dynamics of this type of institutional change. Four distinct modes of change are distinguished in the literature (Streeck and Thelen 2005; Mahoney and Thelen 2010: 15–18). *Displacement*, referring to the removal of existing rules and the introduction of new ones, is often associated with abrupt and outright institutional change. The other modes of changes occur in more subtle ways. One is by means of *layering (or thickening)*, which refers to the introduction of new rules on top of or alongside existing ones. Thus the institution stays intact, but is altered by the introduction of new rules. *Conversion*, which occurs when structures and rules formally remain the same but are interpreted and enacted in new ways, and *drift*, when existing rules have a changed impact due to shifts in the environment, are evolutionary modes of change that take advantage of the ambiguities of rules themselves (Mahoney and Thelen 2010: 17). The likelihood of specific types of change depends on the character of existing rules and on the prevailing political context.

Drivers of normalization

Normalization processes can emanate from inherent ambiguities and 'gaps' that exist by design or that emerge over time between formal institutions and their actual implementation. Existing institutions that are ineffective or inappropriate in carrying out their designated tasks, or incongruities result from a perceived lack of legitimacy of the existing institution (Pierson 2004; Streeck and Thelen 2005; Olson 2010; Rittberger 2012: 22–8), can drive political and administrative reforms. But normalization can also be set in motion by what DiMaggio and Powell (1983) call 'isomorphism'—in which organizations mimic and copy popular changes because they believe that these are the structural outlines of 'good governance'. The modernization of public institutions spreads, not only because of 'functional virtues' or because this can solve government problems, but also because of the contagion effect that occurs in reforms. If something seems to work in one place (private sector, other government), chances are it will be adopted elsewhere as well.[6] Isomorphism is a constraining process that 'forces' similar organizations to adopt similar organizing approaches—through formal or informal pressures to conform, or through copying institutions which are perceived as being successful or legitimate. These types of mimetic or normative adaptations occur as a result of imitation of fashion and not because of a harsh functional necessity for increased efficiency (Pollitt 2001: 934).

Mechanisms of normalization

Several mediating mechanisms can be important for these adjustments towards 'new' democratic and administrative solutions. The pressure from accountability forums, to redirect the logic of the institution, can induce normalization. Institutional entrepreneurship may be important to make 'ideas' actionable or to contribute to the instituting of ideas or normative guides (Schmidt 2010: 15–17). And as these novel ideas and new institutional vocabularies become established in the organization, and actors gain experience in dealing with these new routines and practices (Powell and Colyvas 2008), then feedback loops (Pierson 2004) and spill-over mechanisms can lead to a further adjustment and underpinning of the normalization processes.

A normalization perspective: lessons for the present study

The normalization concept is sometimes taken as a form of 'standardization, through which ideas and actions come to be seen as regular or routine, or become taken for granted or natural in everyday practices.[7] In this study 'normalization' has a slightly different meaning and refers to a steady evolution of executive relationships in the direction of the normal model. It involves a process of adjustment of the institutional accountability architecture towards a standard solution or a generally accepted institutional design.[8]

The normalization perspective used in this study is distinctive in several respects. First, the normalization perspective allows us to focus on the *tandem* of political and administrative changes when examining the development of executive relationships. There is ample political science literature documenting democratization and political innovations and their impact on politics and political institutions. Similarly, public-sector reforms are well documented in the literature but are skewed to the separate impact these have at the various administrative levels. There is, however, little understanding of how these two types of reform *interact* in the evolution of executives. The prevailing emphasis on either political or administrative ramifications has meant that the interaction between political and administrative reforms has received little attention.

Second, the research perspective focuses both on the 'core executive' as a whole (Dunleavy and Rhodes 1990) and on the relationships between the different actors (politicians, senior officials, advisers) within the core executive. The use of the concept of 'core executive' serves to provide a neutral description of a 'working arrangement' with no normative ideals underpinning it. The concept also has the considerable advantage of being applicable to countries with radically different systems of government (Dunleavy and Rhodes 1990; Elgie 2011). The core executive arena refers to all those arrangements and structures that coordinate policy, rather than privileging an account of the power of one position-holder above that of another. It makes it possible to identify different kinds of working arrangements or 'models'.

Third, focusing on executive relationships makes it possible to examine and compare shifts in the distinct elements of executive relationships: rules, recruitment patterns, roles, and relationship patterns. It allows us to detect and explain the changes in these executive relationships by a systemic examination of these four central components.

Finally, the normalization framework makes it possible to analyse how the institutionalization of accountability arrangements in governance structures explains and affects the evolution of executive relationships—in national states, in government agencies, or international organizations.[9] Normalization is a broad process and there are clearly differences to be expected between countries and executives, closely bound up with the developments in the accountability architecture, in their administrative and democratic pathways to *normalization*.

Building on previous conceptual theories of political–administrative relationships, institutional change, and democratic and administrative reforms, it is possible to use the normalization perspective, as elaborated in this chapter, as a potentially broad agenda for further research on executive evolution across a set of cases or in individual cases. Empirically, the conceptual framework can thus be applied at different sites. The EU, as an example of a 'large scale experiment in political integration through deliberate institution building and polity formation' (Olsen 2010: 8), provides one interesting site. Analysis of the European Commission, and the institutional evolution of its accountability structures, could serve as a first exploration of the broad-ranging questions about normalization.

4. The EU Commission: A Normalized Executive?

The European Commission was officially established on 1 January 1958 when the Treaty of Rome came into force, but it was modelled on its predecessor, the 1952 High Authority of the European Coal and Steel Community (ECSC). Jean Monnet, its architect, launched the initiative to establish a new form of supranational, sector-driven interstate cooperation in 1950. He presented it as 'Europe's first government' and as the most pioneering body in the new institutional set-up of European cooperation. The plan was called a 'break with the past' (Rittberger 2005: 77–8). The catastrophe of the Second World War had opened an enormous window of opportunity for Monnet's entrepreneurial leadership to create this new, distinctive EU institution (Egeberg 2006c: 27).[10]

Over time, its institutional structure has changed, evolving into what is today's European Commission. It is clear that growth of EU accountability forums has not stood still, and that this expansion and proliferation of formal accountability mechanisms in the EU system has affected the outlook of this EU executive. The desire to foster democratic accountability and bureaucratic efficiency has ensured that the EU Commission, as a follower of international trends, has been part of the rising tide of political and administrative reform.

First, political reforms in the form of treaty revisions to foster democratic accountability mechanisms in the EU architecture have transformed the workings of the European Commission and have gradually given it the shape of a normal executive. The EU was long in a process of continuous polity-building, during which the Treaties were revised every few years by the member states. Yet the Treaty on European Union (TEU), signed in Maastricht in 1992, represented a new stage in European integration. With this treaty, the Community clearly went beyond its original economic objective to open the way to political integration. In the wake of the narrative of the 'democratic deficit', starting in the early 1990s, a strengthening of the democratic legitimacy of the EU institutions became one of the key objectives of treaty revision.[11]

The fact that the Commission was not immediately accountable to any popularly elected institution was one of the critical elements associated with the 'democratic deficit' in the EU. The remedy proposed for this was granting greater powers of scrutiny for the European Parliament (EP). The Maastricht

(1992), Amsterdam (1997), Nice (2001), and Lisbon (2007) Treaties have all given the European Parliament (EP) more power over the European executive and have led to a further 'parliamentarization' of the EU's political process (Judge and Earnshaw 2008: 273; Rittberger 2012) .

Secondly, since the early 2000s the European Commission bureaucracy has also undergone significant administrative reforms. The Commission, long perceived as the 'odd one out' when it came to public-sector reforms (Pollitt and Bouckaert 2004: 233–4; Bauer 2007*b*), has been engaged in an overhaul of administrative systems and procedures to equip the institution with a modern, efficient, and effective European civil service. The implementation of these internal reform measures has resulted in the most radical modernization since the Commission was established in 1958. What did the interaction of political treaty changes and internal administrative reforms mean for the institutional evolution of the EU Commission?

Questions of normalization

This book explores the impact of the juxtaposition of political and administrative changes on executive relationships at the top of the EU Commission. It examines how and why the Commission evolved, as a result of the reforms, into a normalized executive. The book has three general objectives.

- The first objective is to provide a *systematic documentation of the normalization of the EU Commission*. Operating at the political–bureaucratic interface, commissioners, senior officials, and heads of cabinet confront heightened demands for accountability, performance, and effective delivery. Focusing on the political–bureaucratic interface, I will examine the four elements of core executives: the rules and responsibilities, recruitment patterns, role expectations, and relationships at the top of this EU executive. What changes are there to be observed in these core elements of executive politics? And do these observations fit the normal model? These questions will be examined in Chapters 3 to 5.

- The second objective concerns the *explanation of the normalization of the EU Commission*. Discussions of the changing EU Commission tend to focus on the influence of the administrative reforms or on the political changes ensuing from the Treaties. Here I will consider the juxtaposition of their impact. In tandem, political and administrative reforms have put new accountability regimes in place in the EU. How have these reforms affected the work of commissioners, their cabinets, and their senior officials? What bearing has this juxtaposition had on executive relationships? And how has the combination of political and administrative reforms turned the Commission into a normalized executive? This issue will be explored in Chapter 2 and the following chapters.

- The third objective addresses *the consequences of normalization for executive relationships*. What did the normalization mean for politicians and bureaucrats working at the top of the Commission? What was the impact of a normalization of executive politics on political and administrative leadership and bureaucratic power in the European Commission? How have these changes affected the nature of the executive relationships between politicians and bureaucrats in the European Commission? How has the Commission's reform agenda impacted upon the political–bureaucratic divide within it? Did it produce increased cooperation or greater antagonism between the political and administrative levels? Did it lead to a strengthening of accountability, better performance, and more political control in the EU Commission? These questions will be answered in Chapters 6 and 7.

This study is both individual and institutional in its focus. The relationships between political executives and senior officials in bureaucracy are a daily and continuing feature of life in the Commission. Because of the importance of these relationships in modern governance, they are the major focus of this book, in combination with an institutional analysis to examine how political–administrative dynamics have changed the Commission's accountability architecture.

This study breaks with the idea widely held by EU specialists that EU politics should be analysed as a *sui generis* case. Although the European Commission is often regarded as a unique international organization that has no match, it also has institutional characteristics similar in very important respects to other public-sector institutions (Egeberg 2006d; Trondal 2010). Understanding these characteristics as opportunities and constraints that are part of broader classes of political phenomena (Caproso 1997; Woll 2006) implies that many of the processes within the Commission do not have to be studied as a *one of a kind* phenomenon or as an instance of $N = 1$. It also means that we need to draw more strongly on the current political science and public administration literature to analyse the European institutions.

5. Study Design

This study is predicated on the assumption that the aforementioned questions can only be answered by an empirical study. This means that I will take an essentially *empirical* approach to the study of normalization of the

Study Design

EU Commission. Two methodological considerations are of relevance in the devise of this study.

Normalization: a two-level change

The design of this study is focused on creating a 'generic' picture at two levels of analysis, namely at the level of the institution's evolution and that of its executive relationships.

It means that throughout this study, a two-level model is used to analyse the normalization of the Commission. This model distinguishes between the macro and the micro levels of institutional change, allowing the process of political and administrative reforms to be linked to the level of executive relationships. It enables us to see how these changes and newly emerging contexts have put new political pressures and demands on the working of the Commission in terms of its political executive function and its bureaucracy. Following Coleman (1990), this model can be summarized in the form of a simple graph (Figure 1.2).

In the process of normalization depicted in Figure 1.2 there are two main levels on which the transformation of EU politics is analysed. At the macro level, political and administrative reforms have created new rules, procedures, and accountability arrangements. These have defined new responsibilities (arrow B) with a range of constraints and incentives, yielding a system for more control over and accountability on the part of the actors at the top of the EU Commission (arrow C). These new constraints and incentives have influenced political and administrative leadership. The political–bureaucratic actions and interactions have accumulated at the macro level (arrow D) and have given the EU Commission a different outlook. This two-level model of institutional change explains how the Commission has normalized by adapting structures and practices to opportunities and constraints in the internal and external environments.

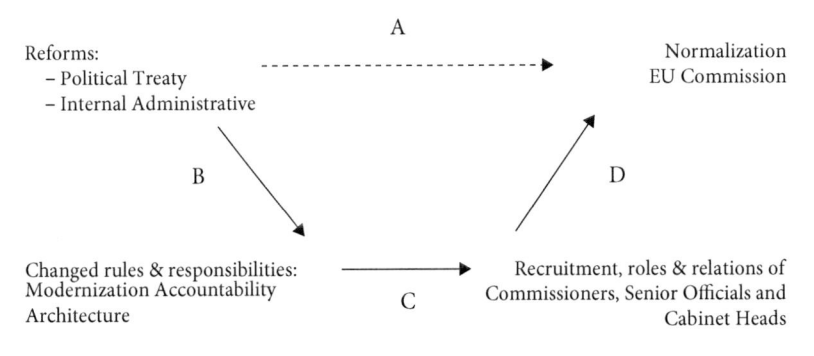

Figure 1.2. A Two-Level Model of Normalization in the EU Commission

A combination of methods

The difficulty of studying 'change' is analogous in some respects to the challenge facing a meteorologist who measures global warming, writes Putnam (1993: 26): 'We know what kind of evidence we want from the past, but time's arrows means that we can't go back to conduct those well designed studies.' Thus if we are to explore how institutions change, we must make imperfect inferences from all the evidence that we can find. The most powerful strategy in such a case is to triangulate among diverse sources of evidence.

In order to gain insight into the (changing) rules, reforms, and organizational procedures at the top of the Commission I have drawn on documentary evidence of politics during (and before) the Prodi (1999–2004), the Barroso I (2004–9), and the Barroso II (2010–15) years. I have first focused on the formal changes, which include the reorganization and rewriting of institutional forms, rules, standards, and arrangements that outline a new accountability framework and that present more or less binding behavioural claims on officials working in the Commission.

To obtain more insight into how the expansion of accountability arrangements in and around the EU Commission has affected the role interpretations of commissioners and senior officials at the helm of this organization, and the cooperation of those working at the pinnacle of the Commission, I conducted a set of qualitative in-depth interviews in the period 2006–8 with fifty high-level officials working at the apex of the Commission, i.e. commissioners, heads and members of cabinets, and directors-general.[12] Here, at the political– administrative interface, officials have to deal with the impact of the multiple initiatives and efforts to improve the accountability of the Commission. The interviews were conducted to uncover whether the new arrangements and mechanisms put in place have created new role expectations and forms of cooperation (see the Appendix for more details on the interviews). The qualitative interviews are an attempt to understand the world from the subjects' point of view, to unfold the meaning of peoples' experiences at the top of the Commission and to uncover their role expectations and interaction patterns. In order to contrast the interview data with the work of heads of cabinet in the early years of the Commission, I have drawn on the existing literature about the Commission under the previous presidencies (particularly Delors and Santer) to use this as 'proxy measures' of past behavioural patterns. Data on the biographical information of senior officials and commissioners, and secondary material on the background of Commission officials, provided insight into their career patterns, and how these have changed.

The combination of methods made it possible to widen the scope of the study and to take in contextual aspects of the executive relationships at the top of the Commission. It also was possible to generate an empirically grounded picture. In the remainder of this book, I present the results of the analysis. The quotations function as illustrations of the findings from the interviews. Having assured the respondents that they would not be identified, I have used the Commission officials' own words to describe the imperatives they face and the relationships they maintain. This offers readers a rare look at the day-to-day practices behind the EU treaty reforms and internal administrative changes that have affected the operation of the EU Commission. I have tried to portray the high-level relationships and to provide an account of what it is like to work at the top of the Commission in an era of change.

Notes

1. Although not in the public administration literature (Svara 2006).
2. The 'normal' model corresponds with the formal-legal model of Guy Peters (1988) and with image I of Aberbach *et al.* (1981). This literature about political-administrative relations will come back in Chapters 6 and 7.
3. In the words of James Madison 1788 in *The Federalist*, 49.
4. In 1900 there were no fully fledged democratic regimes at all. Around the 1950s, just 28% of independent regimes were classifiable as democratic (Mair 2009). By the year 2011 some 60% of the independent regimes in the world could be classified as electoral democracies (<www.Freedomhouse.org>).
5. After the first long wave (1828–1926) and the second wave (from 1922–62), most Western governments, starting in the 1970s, have gone through a third wave of democratization (Huntington 1991).
6. These days, the tendency of administrations and policies to grow more alike, to develop similarities in structures and processes, is international. Reforms of a similar nature have spread extensively around the globe, suggesting that the industrialized democracies are coping with similar problems (DiMaggio and Powell 1983; Dolowitz and Marsh 2000; Rose 2005; Knill 2005).
7. In sociological theory the normalization concept is found in medical sociology and science and technology studies. In these disciplines the normalization process theory provides a framework for understanding the social processes by which new ways of thinking, working, and organizing become routinely incorporated in everyday work.
8. Normalization is different from a 'normal' form of institutionalization, in which organizations acquire value and stability over time, developing their internal procedures and also becoming accepted by external actors.
9. For instance, Romzek and Dubnick (1987) show in an influential article with the use of an institutional analysis how political dynamics have changed NASA's accountability architecture.
10. The Commission was a new and distinctive executive centre at the EU level (Egeberg 2006c; Curtin 2009). Together with the Council—also assigned with

executive functions—the EU evolved into a dual executive system (Hix 1999: 21; Judge and Earnshaw 2008: 23).
11. The Treaty of Maastricht responded to five key goals: to strengthen the democratic legitimacy of the institutions; to improve the effectiveness of the institutions; to establish economic and monetary union; to develop the Community's social dimension; to establish a common foreign and security policy, see 5 Jan. 2011.
12. The interviews were conducted prior to the entry into force of the Treaty of Lisbon on 1 Dec. 2009.

2

The Reinvention of the European Commission

> Nothing is possible without men; nothing is lasting without institutions.
>
> (Jean Monnet)

1. A Defining Moment

Every organization has *defining moments*—crucial moments in which the organization faces choices and needs to take steps that shape its development and character (Selznick 1957). The European Commission experienced such a 'defining moment' when it came under increasing attack at the end of the 1990s for the handling of its executive responsibilities. Ongoing criticism of the Commission's performance in a report that was drawn up by a Commission of Independent Experts (CIE), instigated at the insistence of the European Parliament, resulted in the resignation of the Santer Commission in March 1999.

The Santer Commission stepped down on the day the Committee of Independent Experts delivered its report. A long and intense political process preceded this final unprecedented step, culminating in an open crisis during the Commission's final months in office. The recurrent accusations of mismanagement, irregularities, and fraud and, eventually, the resignation of the College of Commissioners, had generated a highly politicized atmosphere, pushed the reform of the European Commission to the forefront of the public debate, and made a fresh effort inevitable. Problems at both political and administrative levels could no longer be ignored.

The CIE painted in its report the image of an ill-managed executive power.[1] The Committee sought to explain the Commission's difficulties in functioning in terms of the relationship between the political and administrative spheres within the Commission. One of the fundamental problems observed was a lack of control at various levels and by various persons in the hierarchy, with the ultimate control and political responsibility lying with the commissioners themselves. Apparently, the collective responsibility of the College of Commissioners did not translate into an individual responsibility of commissioners for the administrative services within their respective portfolios. This failing of individual commissioners to exercise proper oversight over 'their' services contributed to a state of affairs which the Committee described as 'a growing reluctance among the members of the hierarchy to acknowledge their responsibility'. The Committee even went so far as to conclude that: 'It is becoming difficult to find anyone who has even the slightest sense of responsibility' (CIE 1999*a*: para. 9.4.25).[2]

The Commission's crisis was, in Selznick's (1957) classic terms, a 'character-defining' moment for the Commission. It acted as a catalyst for change in the Commission's inefficient administrative practices and organizational weaknesses, and bore all the hallmarks of an institutional crisis (Boin and Hart 1999: 12). Characteristically, during an institutional crisis pivotal actors and accountability forums come to realize that 'the old way of doing things' is no longer effective or appropriate; plans to refashion existing structures, or to establish new ones, emerge; and leaders make key decisions that affect the trajectory of institutional development.

At this critical moment in the Commission's history, accountability was placed squarely on its institutional agenda (Harlow 2002: 53). Fundamental reform of the Commission's accountability—along with its efficiency, effectiveness, and transparency—became one of the top priorities of the new Commission presided over by Romano Prodi, who was appointed on the basis of a mandate to reform the institution and to restore confidence in its organization. The proposals for change initiated by the new Commission favoured two objectives: modernizing the Commission's bureaucracy and instituting reforms that would guarantee that similar scandals would not occur in the future. Accordingly, the European Commission underwent the most significant internal changes since its inception. These reforms, in combination with revisions of the treaties altering the Commission's legal and political framework, challenged some deeply embedded features in its organization.

This chapter explains how political and administrative reforms have changed the basic accountability system of the European Commission: what were the driving forces behind the Commission's transformation? To understand the modernization of the Commission's accountability system, it is necessary to know something about the history of this EU institution: what were the vision and values, the organizational DNA, on which the EU Commission was built? How did those values and practices became incongruent with internal and external challenges? How did they crystallize in a crisis? Finally, the chapter shows how a strategic reorientation has affected the trajectory of institutional development: what steps were taken to reinvent the EU Commission? And what new mechanisms have become effective in the EU Commission's accountability architecture? These questions are the topic of this chapter.

2. The Commission's Organizational DNA

The European Commission of the European Union is a relatively recent creation by international public administration standards. Its central features were established in its early years by its predecessor, the High Authority, which created long-term 'path dependencies' under the presidency of Jean Monnet. The nature and architecture of the EU Commission, its foundational, normative, and organizational principles, were strongly modelled on this High Authority.

An effective understanding of the Commission begins, therefore, with a study of the organizational 'character' (Selznick 1957; Stinchcombe 1965; March and Olson 1984, 1989; Boin 1998) that emerged from its organizational DNA.[3] This means that we first have to get insight in the three core values that constitute the 'genetic make-up' of any institution: its mission; the external legitimacy and support it relies upon to authorize its actions; and the organizational capacity it relies on to deliver the desired results (Moore 1995).

Monnet's mission: the making of a unique international organization

Five years after the Second World War, the anxiety and the determination to prevent another war played a significant role in the conception of a plan to create a new international body. A number of European leaders became convinced that the only way to secure a lasting peace between their countries was to unite them economically and politically. The plan was officially announced on 9 May 1950 by the French Foreign Minister Robert Schuman, but it was his adviser, Jean Monnet, who was the actual designer of the plan. 'The fear [was] that if we did nothing we should soon face war again' writes Monnet (1978: 289) in his memoirs.[4]

'History offered no precedent' concluded Monnet (1978: 294).[5] In this plan prospective member states accepted the delegation of sovereignty in specific policy sectors to a supranational body, the High Authority, which was to have the power to make decisions that were binding for the member states. This was an innovative structure that would crack the impasse induced by unanimous decision-making and that implied a sector-by-sector, gradual delegation of national sovereignty (Rittberger 2005: 95).[6] A combination of economic and

The Reinvention of the European Commission

security motives determined the choice for the coal and steel sector. The idea of the European Coal and Steel Community (ECSC) was born.

An acceptable solution to the accountability question

The question 'to whom should it be accountable and how?' became an immediate issue of constitutional politics. The executive control and accountability of the new institution was a shared concern among the national delegations participating in the negotiations over the Schuman plan (Rittberger 2005: 78–99). The Benelux countries had great reservations about the institutional parts of the plan. The scepticism of the Dutch delegation, which criticized the High Authority as a 'dictatorship of experts', was so pronounced that they made their participation in the negotiations conditional on an 'acceptable' solution to the 'accountability question'. Two key demands of the Dutch and the Belgium delegations were: (1) a flexible and limited jurisdiction for the new institution—on an issue-by-issue basis—and (2) the High Authority should share its decision-making powers with an intergovernmental body, a council of ministers, that should be able to block decisions made by the High Authority, and to which it should be ultimately accountable (Rittberger 2005: 97).[7]

Monnet realized that the sovereignty of the High Authority would not be considered acceptable without instituting adequate control and accountability mechanisms. He became convinced that, as part of the institutional set-up, a parliamentary body was needed to which the new executive would be accountable (Rittberger 2005: 79): in 'a world where government authority is derived from representative assemblies, Europe cannot be built without such an assembly' (Monnet cited in Rittberger 2005: 98).

A strong parliamentary institution with legislative powers was, however, absolutely unacceptable to the Benelux governments because it would imply the existence of another supranational body with policy-making powers, whose decisions could be detrimental for national politics. The Benelux countries would only agree to the founding of a supranational executive as long as ex post control of the new institution would be exercised by the court and by the member states in a ministerial council (Rittberger 2005: 97). The parliamentary body would be accepted on the condition that it did not have any legislative and budgetary powers (Rittberger 2005: 102) and that it was to play only a negligible role in the Community's institutional set-up.

The Commission's organizational DNA

The ECSC treaty was signed in 1951 by the governments of Belgium, France, Germany, Italy, Luxembourg, and the Netherlands, and its institutional framework was set down in four pillars (Seidel 2010: 1): the European Court of Justice (EJC), a parliamentary body called the Common Assembly (CA), the Special Council of ministers, and the High Authority (HA).[8] This High Authority had, as an executive body, its own decision-making powers and its function was to oversee the implementation of the ECSC treaty (Seidel 2010: 1). Three core values constituted the institution's genetic make-up during its early years. Its *mission* was to pursue and protect a common European interest (Harlow 2002: 62; Egeberg 2006a: 35). Concerning its sources of *legitimacy and support*, the High Authority was meant to be able to act independently of national governments to perform its mission. In view of its *organizational capabilities*, Monnet's vision of the new institution was that of a depoliticized, supranational, functionalist technocracy.

The first steps on the path of European integration proved such a success that, within six years, the six member states decided to go further and integrate other sectors of their economies (Seidel 2010: 1). In 1957 they signed the Treaties of Rome, creating the European Atomic Energy Community (EURATOM) and the European Economic Community (EEC). The institutional framework of the EEC was modelled after that of the ECSC. This led in 1958 to the start of the first European Commission under the presidency of Walter Hallstein. The Commission was the EEC equivalent of the 'High Authority'; it was set up to perform Europe's executive functions, starting with removing trade barriers between the member states and forming a 'common market'. On 1 July 1967, the three executive bodies were combined into a single administration under the Merger Treaty.

3. Institutional Imbalances

A glance at the start of the Commission's history shows that several tensions were embedded in its organizational capabilities. Three major sources of tension between the stated ambition and actual capacity to perform stand out: the tension between professionalism and politicization; the tension between Europeanization and the role that nationality ties and loyalties traditionally played in the Commission organization; and the tension between autonomy and accountability.

The tension between professionalism and politicization

The first tension, embedded in many bureaucracies, is the dilemma between competency and political responsiveness. One of the defining features of Weber's model of bureaucracy was that hiring and promotion occurs on the basis of merit rather than political or national allegiances. This protects bureaucrats from political pressure and helps to ensure neutral competence.

But it can also make the bureaucracy less responsive to political influence 'from above', that is, to the programmes of leaders in power; or to influence 'from below', that is, to the preferences of groups in the wider society (Lewis 2008: 5; Peters 2010: 82–5).

The European Commission was designed as a technocratic body to propose solutions to policy problems, to broker deals, to operate as the 'motor of integration', and to be the guardian of the common European interest. Monnet and his peers feared that a politicized EU would produce winners and losers among its member states. This could undermine its legitimacy and stability. In the performance of their duties, the members of the High Authority were to be independent from any government.

A technocratic elite of appointed experts at the top of this body was to guide the process of European integration, mediating where necessary. Not a political elite, as this would be subject to a democratic 'majoritarian' mechanism of some kind. Politicians are bound to be short-sighted and self-seeking, as they are subject to electoral mechanisms. It would make for better governance to take the impartial, the overall, and long-term view of the technocrat. Successful integration requires consensus about practical goals and abstinence from power politics, hard political choices and conflict (Hooghe and Marks 2005). In the original design of the European Commission, politics was 'organized out'.

The Commission's role as a guardian of the European interest would depend on its expertise and its credibility as an impartial mediator between political views, conflicting national interests, and interest group pressures. The High Authority, and later the Commission, would derive its political legitimacy from its capacity to tackle problems that require collective solutions. It was interest-based rather than identity-based (Thomassen and Schmidt 2004) and would thus be legitimated on output rather than on input criteria (Majone 1994). The political elites could reasonably expect to command popular consent, as long as the beneficial results of European integration were widely accepted.

For the European Commission administration to be effective it needed a corps of competent professionals. 'Although the Commission was entitled to recruit personnel independently, concessions had to be made when it came to the nationality of staff and the special interest of a member state in a policy area' (Seidel 2010: 173). To ensure that each member state was represented in the administration, the Commission distributed posts according to informal quotas. Maintaining a national balance would enhance the legitimacy of the European administration. But use of the 'representativeness' principle was at odds with hiring and promoting on base of individual qualifications and merit and opened the European administration up to political influences.

The image of the Commission as a depoliticized, functionalist, technocratic institution started to contrast with a hidden and less palatable established reality of the Commission as *a 'politicized' bureaucracy* (Christiansen 1997; Peterson 2007). Formally, the Commission possesses many of the classic characteristics of a Weberian hierarchical organization (Page 1997; Hooghe 2001: 200). But several structural factors have contributed to a politicization of the Commission (Christiansen 1997). First, the cabinets, as the link between the political and administrative Commission, often interfered directly in the work of the DGs. This blurred the boundaries between the two. Second, a lack of integration between the political (the commissioners) and the bureaucratic level (the civil servants) created 'political control' problems. Cabinets acted as screens and fences, impeding direct communication between commissioners and departments (CIE 1999a), which resulted in a distant political-bureaucratic pecking order. Third, interdepartmental conflict and competition within and between DGs manifested itself in bureaucratic turf wars. These internal tensions, that were an expression of sector-specific interdepartmental struggles and of member state influence, politicized the Commission's political and administrative system.

The upshot of all this was that the division between politics and administration was far from clear in the Commission. It was constantly compromised by the behaviour of many officials (Fouilleux *et al.* 2005). As Hooghe (2001: 7) observed in her study: 'in the complex setting of the European Union, Commission officials often find it impossible to resolve the tension between politics and expertise and impartiality'.

The tension between Europeanization and nationality

The Commission was set up from the start to act as an autonomous supranational institution with an Europeanization vocation;[9] Monnet expected the officials working in the European administration to develop a strong 'European spirit'. They not only had to take the lead in uniting the countries of Europe, they were expected to play a pioneering role in the European integration process (Seidel 2010: 1). The Commission is 'the only body paid to think European',[10] as one Commission official explained in an interview. But thinking European was no easy task. From the very start, it became fairly clear that running the Commission was a balancing act between autonomy and dependence on the member states (Christiansen 1997; Egeberg 2006a: 35).

Being a multinational bureaucracy had a fundamental impact on its cohesion, demographic character, and form of political control (Page 1997). Studies in the 1990s showed that its staff maintained allegiance to national identities and an attachment to their cultural and linguistic routines (Abélès *et al.* 1993; Abélès and Bellier 1996; Mazey and Richardson 1996; McDonald 2000); and that national affinities in the Commission were important for network-building and sometimes became institutionalized in units, divisions, and even in whole DGs (Egeberg 1996; Christiansen 1997: 83; Hooghe 1999). Several structural conditions, such as preserving a nationality balance in the organization, forced the Commission to placate member-state interests and to induce intergovernmental elements into its functioning. Nation-states proved reluctant to take their hands completely off the instruments of governance.

As a result, promotions at the top depended on nationality and support from the national government—not on merit or loyalty to the Commission hierarchy. For instance, in the past, senior officials in the Commission were often 'parachuted' in from national administrations—and there was an informal system of 'flagging' where certain director-general posts were expected to be held by nationals of particular countries (agriculture was French, competition German). Moreover, the large share of national civil services under secondment in the services was often considered to play a national 'meddling' role in the Commission. National quotas and temporary contracts 'politicized' the Commission bureaucracy. This took on such proportions that national governments were stopping just short of claiming certain posts as being theirs by right (Cini 1996: 126).

The tension between autonomy and accountability

A third tension embedded in the Commission's DNA is the tension between autonomy and accountability. In Monnet's blueprint, Europe needed an institution that was able to act as an executive, relatively independently of national governments. But 'organizing autonomous institutions within a political setting immediately raises questions about accountability' (Egeberg 2006*a*: 31).

The structure of the Commission was not designed with direct political accountability in mind. The origins of the EU Commission lie in a period when the EEC and the process of European integration were conceived in elite terms (Harlow 2002: 57; Judge and Earnshaw 2008). Like other international organizations, the EU Commission was legitimized indirectly by the consent of the participating governments and above all by their capacity to solve the problems that led to its creation (Held and Koenig-Archibugi 2005). The consensus about European integration at that time had a significant impact on the development and management of the Commission in its early years (Christiansen 1997; Harlow 2002; Judge and Earnshaw 2008). It developed an enlightened 'community model' which commanded a degree of accountability sufficient for the limited governance it had to bear. The

Institutional Imbalances

ethos of consensual democracy legitimized decision-making by elites, with the role of the parliament being confined to that of ratifying these decisions. In a way, it looked more like a quasi-autonomous executive agency (Majone 1996; Harlow 2002: 57).

Also, bureaucratic accountability was not part of the initial design of this European administration. Monnet saw the new institution as a small, organizationally flexible and adaptive, multinational hub of individuals and experts that would develop ideas—a so-called 'administration de mission'. Bureaucracy and implementation would be left to the national administrations (Hooghe 2001: 37; Seidel 2010: 12). These circumstances would allow the new European administration to become a special kind of bureaucracy, that in the early years was characterized by a strong degree of expertise operating under a system of *professional* accountability.

The new Commission organization in 1958, under the presidency of Hallstein, adopted an administrative structure based on that of its predecessor, the High Authority. But there were also differences. Monnet supported the idea of a small and flexible organization for the High Authority, while Hallstein was in favour of creating a large administration with a clear-cut, hierarchical organizational structure (Seidel 2010: 69). He shaped an organizational structure with nine directorates-general (DGs), correspondingly roughly to the policy areas stipulated in the EEC treaty and to the number of commissioners. A hierarchy was created by subdividing the DGs into directorates, which served as the 'executive core'.

The bureaucratization in the 1960s left its imprint on the Commission and, by the 1970s, dysfunctional bureaucratic features challenged the operation of its organization: red tape, the multinational character of the organization, the prevalence of principles of proportionality and mutual veto that were present in the administration (Hooghe 2001: 177), the acceptance of alternative hierarchies based on nationality, internal fragmentation of the organization, lack of political leadership which could have overcome these internal tendencies, the meddling role of the cabinets and the influence of 'national enclaves' (Page 1997). The Commission was commonly derided for its bureaucratic approach to policy-making and criticized for its inertia and not taking sufficiently into account the preferences of Europeans.[11]

Over time, this criticism opened up a discussion on the legitimacy and democratic calibre of the EU. The pressure to develop a politically responsive organization, in which mechanisms for managing expectations of democracy, efficiency, fairness, and performance are more strongly supported, started to emerge. A changing environment and the demands of new institutional conditions created a setting for the EU Commission that called for the strengthening of its *bureaucratic and political accountability*.

Table 2.1 Institutional Features of EU Commission in Early Years (1950s) and Period Before the Santer Crisis (1990s)

Organizational capacities	1950s	1990s
Organization	Professionalized technocracy	Politicized bureaucracy
(In)dependence	Autonomy to pursue the European interest	Dependency on national interests
Accountability	Professional, legal, and indirect political accountability dominate	Rising demands for direct political accountability; and accountability for performance

Institutional tensions

From the start, there have been organizational components in the EU Commission that have buttressed the evolution to a stronger autonomy, while others have reinforced the influence of the member states (Egeberg 2006*a*: 36). Table 2.1 summarizes the core ingredients of the tensions and how these played out over the life of the commission in its early years in 1960 and at the time of its 'defining moment' in 1999.

These three internal institutional imbalances increased the institution's problem of finding a stable equilibrium and augmented its vulnerability to crisis. The internal institutional tensions created, eventually, a gap between the Commission's mission, its operational capacities, and new externally imposed demands and expectations that started to rise. The tendency of the Union to expand its powers and competences, the impact of enlargement, and the massive changes in the character of the European Union provoked a shift in societal and political conceptions of what is appropriate—as we will see in the next section. Finding a new workable 'fit' between the Commission's key institutional values and its practices became a critical question.

4. An Ever-Expanding Executive

There have been fourteen colleges since the first meeting of the European Economic Community (EEC) in 1958 and much has changed since then. The names and chronology of the colleges are shown in Table 2.2. Fifty years after Hallstein, the Barroso I Commission was the first full Commission of twenty-seven members, following the 2004 enlargements, where larger member states no longer had two commissioners.

The larger Commission reflects the increased size—by series of enlargements (see Table 2.3)—and heterogeneity of the Union. Starting as the 'Europe of Six' (France, West Germany, Italy, and the Benelux countries), taking in the UK, Denmark, and Ireland to become the 'Europe of Nine', after which

Table 2.2 The EU Commission in Historical Perspective, 1958–2012

College	Period	Size	Holders	Treaties effective
Hallstein I	1958–61	9	12	Treaty Rome 1958
Hallstein II	1962–7	9	10	Merger Treaty 1965
Rey	1967–70	14	14	
Malfatti/Mansholt	1970–2	9	10	
Ortoli	1973–6	13	17	
Jenkins	1977–80	13	13	
Thor	1981–4	14	17	
Delors I	1985–8	14+3	18	SEA 1987
Delors II	1989–92	17	17	TEU Maastricht 1993
Delors III	1993–4	17	18	
Santer	1995–9	20	20	Treaty Amsterdam 1999
Prodi	1999–2004	20+10	35	Treaty Nice 2003
Barroso I	2005–9	25+2	34	
Barroso II	2010–14	27	28	Treaty Lisbon 2009

it grew larger and became the 'Europe of Twelve' with the addition in the 1980s of Greece, Spain, and Portugal. Austria, Sweden, and Finland joining in 1990s brought its number to fifteen (Judt 2011) and by 2007 the EU had twenty-seven members.

The Commission's historic development also shows an ever-expanding executive in terms of policy competences. Usually, new areas of competences are incorporated during a new treaty negotiation. Originally, the Community's responsibility was for only economic and trade matters. Throughout the past fifty years the EU has adopted a steady stream of regulatory policies, as well as distributive and redistributive spending policies which grew particularly quickly during the Delors and Santer years of the late 1980s and early 1990s (Majone 1996; Pollack 2003). At the end of the 1960s, after completion of the customs union and with the common agriculture policy fully functional, the Commission needed to identify new goals (Seidel 2010: 177). Due to the economic crisis of the 1970s, the EU integration (Peterson and Shackleton 2006: 2) process slowed during the 1970s and 1980s. But under Delors's leadership, a great number of policies were initiated, such as the plan for finalizing the Internal Market, the Single European Act (SEA), and the launch of the Economic and Monetary Union (EMU) (Grøn 2009: 40).

The Maastricht Treaty in 1992 was to some extent a natural follow-up to the Single European Market. A new treaty (and some form of political partnership) was needed that could further advance the economic union (Franklin *et al.* 1994); the Single European Market required a single currency. A single currency required a single Central Bank. A single Central Bank required a single monetary policy. A single monetary policy required coherent policy-making in many areas (including foreign and defence policy) that were previously beyond the scope of the EU decision-making. This illustration of the logic of 'spillover' (Haas 1958) shows how the achievement of the Single European

Table 2.3 Countries and EU Accession*

Enlargement Type	Applicant	Accession Date
Founding member	Belgium France Germany, W Italy Luxembourg Netherlands	23 July 1952
First Enlargements	Denmark Ireland United Kingdom	1 January 1973
Mediterranean Enlargements	Greece Portugal Spain	1 January 1981
Post Cold War Enlargement	Austria Finland Sweden	1 January 1995
Eastern Enlargements	Cyprus Italy Czech Republic Estonia Hungary Latvia Lithuania Malta Poland Slovakia Slovenia	1 May 2004
	Bulgaria Romania	1 January 2007

* Applications to the European Coal and Steel Community, European Communities and European Union depending on date.

Market opened the need for a stronger political union that would complement this new economic union.

The EU political order has evolved almost to the point where virtually no area of political or social life falls outside its remit. It has built up a considerable body of independent policy and regulation in fields like environmental protection, consumer protection, and occupational health and safety. In addition, it has branched out to include issues such as immigration policies, justice and home affairs, and a common foreign and defence policy. The issues in which the present Commission engages cover a wide spectrum of EU policies: foreign aid, illegal immigrants, asylum seekers, climate change, terrorism, external relations, financial reforms, and crisis management in the banking sector, to name only a few.

Changing political arenas and an expanding social and economic agenda, changes in the world economy, and the EU's desire to strengthen Europe's role in the world have all combined to push the need for comprehensive institutional reforms.

Emerging demands for good governance

As integration intensified and more national competences were transferred to the European level, so too did the problems of public mistrust and the lack of obvious legitimacy for the EU's central institutions increase. After the Maastricht ratification, the benefits of integration could no longer simply be taken for granted. The institutional forms of the European Union were increasingly out of step with the popular forces behind modern democratic government.

Questions regarding the accountability and democracy of the EU, its governance, and its institutions were seriously raised in the discussions that preceded the Maastricht Treaty of 1992. The development of the EU into a political union, whose policies go far beyond the original aims of eliminating barriers to cross-border economic activities, has strengthened the call for democratic decision-making and democratic accountability of European policy-makers (Curtin and Wille 2008). The fact that an independent and technocratic elite in the Commission was allowed to play such an important agenda-setting role became one of the democratic concerns. More and more, the exercise of executive power at the EU level was expected to be democratic and its executive to be democratically legitimated. European institutions adopting binding rules and spending public money were to be answerable to citizens through elected bodies; and if a decision was to be taken at the European level, especially one involving majority voting, an elected European body capable of directly channelling citizens' concerns and exercising political control on their behalf should also be in place.

Much of the political debate surrounding the notion of the 'democratic deficit' that arose in debates at the start of the 1990s, about the future of a legitimate order in Europe, revolved around the role of parliaments in the EU political process (Magnette 2001; Rittberger 2005, 2012; Judge and Earnshaw 2009). The question of the democratic deficit of the EU seemed to have obvious solutions. In Magnette's (2001: 292) words: 'As democracy had been synonymous with parliamentary politics for two centuries the Community could only be democratic, or so it was said, if its parliaments became central in the political system.' This was not simply an issue of representation, but also one of the accountability of executive decision-makers to parliamentary representatives. Despite conflicting views over political objectives and policy outcomes, member states accepted these liberal democratic values as the fundamental standards of legitimacy (Rittberger and Schimmelfennig 2006).[12] The implementation of these ideas would, it was thought, solve the EU democratic deficit. This has been the main functional logic behind the successive increase in the powers of the European Parliament. The EU has seen the preparation, negotiation, or ratification of a treaty reform every few years in order to streamline the internal workings of the EU and to align the existing institutional structures with the democratic forces, in order to answer the call for a more democratic decision-making process and democratic accountability. Accordingly, with every treaty change in the past years—Maastricht, Amsterdam, Nice, and Lisbon—the EP has successfully managed to extend its legislative and co-decisional powers in the EU system, at the expense of the Commission.

Not only the Commission's traditionally weak democratic credentials (input legitimacy) but also its diminishing problem-solving efficiency (output legitimacy) increasingly drew public attention. The period under Jacques Delors had resulted in an extreme expansion of policy responsibilities but also in a managerial overstretch (Grøn 2009: 45). Consequently, the Commission's organization came under increasing attack in the mid-1990s for the handling of its executive responsibilities. The Commission suffered from a substantial 'management deficit', in the words of Les Metcalfe (2000: 891), which was just as challenging to its legitimacy as the much discussed 'democratic deficit'. As a response to these problems, the Santer Commission launched several reform initiatives, which were intended to improve executive performance (Nugent 2001: 177), most of which foundered during implementation (Cini 2000; Stevens and Stevens 2006). This resulted not only in a weakening of the organization, but also in a credibility loss between the European Parliament and the EU heads of state.

In this way, the Commission forfeited much of the authority it had enjoyed under Delors. Weak leadership and ineffective management eroded its standing *vis-à-vis* other EU institutions. Dissatisfaction with the way the Commission functioned, especially among the largest and more powerful EU member governments, meant that none of the big players were prepared to spend political capital defending it (Peterson 2004: 15). Lack of support in the major capitals contributed to a political marginalization of the Commission. In fact, the larger states, led alternately by France, the UK, and Germany, have often shown themselves keen to clip the Commission's wings (Spence 2006c: 26). Many national leaders were less than enthusiastic about entrusting it with new powers, preferring to cooperate among themselves on issues they considered to be at the core of national sovereignty.

From vulnerability to crisis

The series of scandals and inefficiencies that surrounded the Commission at the end of the 1990s left its mark. The sudden resignation of all twenty commissioners of the European Union's executive body in March 1999, accused by the Committee of Independent Experts of sloppy management, irresponsibility in administering public funds, of corruption, and incompetence, marked a critical moment in the history of the Commission. For the first time, democratic accountability was breaking through at the European level in a way that ordinary citizens could easily understand. At that moment in March, the Commission's defining moment came.

5. The Politics of Reform

'Defining moments' open up paths that are decisive to the future. They can be occasions for leadership, during which policy-makers and elites use their formal positions and leadership skills to resolve the problems besetting the institutions in question. It may even prepare the stage for strategic reorientations and critical decisions about the future of institutions (Boin and Hart 1999).

It was against the background of the post-1999 institutional crisis of the Commission that political leaders of the institutions of the EU and the member states were faced with the issue of how to recalibrate the Commission's power, legitimacy, and credibility. Whilst baffling to actors within the Commission, the crisis that engulfed the Santer Commission did provide a window of opportunity to address the ongoing criticism of its inefficient administrative practices and organizational weaknesses. Problems at both political and administrative levels could no longer be ignored; and the issue of the problematic accountability of this key EU executive was pushed to the forefront of the public debate. Political leaders in the EU and from the member states were adjured to put their 'House' in order (Cram 2002: 310) and to ensure that the expertise and authority available in the Commission bureaucracy were made available to a democratically elected government.

Two developments subsequently bolstered the accountability of the EU Commission. In the first place, the European Parliament was fast gaining considerable power and influence in the EU political process. Political innovations by means of treaty revisions has led to an expansion of the EP's legislative and budgetary powers and the establishment of a stronger interconnection between the legislative and executive branches of EU government. As a consequence, the Commission was being steadily sucked into the European Parliament's orbit. The European Parliament, which was 'flexing its political muscles' in the light of the upcoming European elections in June 1999, and the member states pushed for reform, even going so far as to 'dictate' the content of this reform to a certain extent on the basis of the *Second Report on Reform of the Commission* of the Committee of Independent Experts (CIE) (Schön-Quinlivan 2007: 29). This second report included numerous (ninety, to be exact) proposals for changes in the Commission.

The second development centred on the internal reform of the Commission. Romano Prodi, Santer's successor as Commission President, was appointed with a clear mandate to reform the Commission. Neil Kinnock became the vice-president and the new commissioner in charge of administrative reforms, to accommodate the criticism raised by the Committee of Independent Experts. At the same time the EU Commission had become more presidential in its design—due to the treaty revisions. Prodi and Kinnock's leadership took advantage of this moment to define new values, and to move the institution in new strategic directions. Kinnock (2002: 21–2) explained the need for reform as follows: 'while Europe and the union have altered hugely over four decades ... the organization, structures and working methods of the Commission as the executive administration to that Union have never really been sufficiently adapted to the changes that have taken place. Europe evolved: the Commission as an organization didn't keep pace.'

The Commission had to be 'reinvented'. It searched for a new base for legitimacy, which was found in the concept of 'good governance'. In March 2000, Kinnock announced a set of proposals in a *Reform Strategy White Paper* for what he called a 'root, branch, trunk and trees' reform of the institution. A year later, in July 2001, the Prodi Commission issued a *White Paper on European Governance*, which announced a range of reform proposals that would transform the functioning and administration of the Commission and its executive responsibilities. The main objective of this internal reform strategy was to ensure that 'efficiency, accountability, transparency, responsibility and service' were applied as working conventions in the Commission administration (European Commission 2000: p. iii). The reforms were part of the fight against the loss of legitimacy and were designed to help the institution regain some of its lustre as the motor of European integration.

An overwhelming proportion of the measures were implemented within a very short space of time. The imminent arrival of the EU's largest and most complex enlargements in May 2004—the European Union was to include 10 + 2 new member states—provided further impetus for reform.

Reinventing the Commission: reforms in tandem

The Commission's reinvention focused on two aspects: the reform of the political executive, focusing on the roles and accountability of commissioners, and the reform of the administration, embracing such issues as efficiency and the management of staff. New structures and rules with a range of ex ante constraints and ex post incentives were put in place to provide a system for more control and accountability in and over the Commission.

Kinnock and his cabinet acted very much as the leaders of the reform process, shaping its strategy and pace (Schön-Quinlivan 2007, 2010). They felt the reform had to create an administration that would be more accountable and responsive to the College of Commissioners. Key issues were political control and bureaucratic power. Buttressed by NPM techniques—together with Weberian principles in the organization—the Commission's bureaucracy was meant to become a more unitary actor and, in the process, come to resemble national administrations more closely (Hooghe 2001: 200).

Important for the Commission's normalization is that these internal administrative reforms have been implemented in conjunction with revisions in the EU treaties that were directed at strengthening the political control and accountability structures around the Commission. Reforms were directed to both the political and administrative level, and stricter rules applied to both the political and administrative actors in the Commission. In conjunction these tendencies have changed the EU Commission's politicization from a bottom–up to a top–down one. This top–down politicization manifested itself in the Commission in terms of a stronger 'political' control over the appointment of commissioners and the senior service. Top–down politicization is also visible in the attempts to influence the responsibilities and role expectations of commissioners and their officials by sharpening political-bureaucratic accountability. In tandem political and administrative reforms have affected the Commission's executive responsibilities; and in tandem they have modernized the accountability structures of this EU executive.

6. Modernized Executive Accountability

Over the past decade, the accountability mechanisms of the Commission have changed immensely. Political and administrative reforms have contributed to a more rigorous regime for raising accountability in the Commission. A layering and thickening of rules is apparent in the multitude of newly introduced mechanisms and instruments of control and scrutiny, and the establishment of bodies looking over the shoulders of commissioners and their senior officials. The aim of these new political and bureaucratic accountability arrangements was a more accountable EU Commission, that is, it intended to streamline executive leadership and to integrate authority and accountability within the EU executive more tightly.

In any event, there are now more mechanisms in place than ever before. It is not viable to summarize in few pages the full complexity of the evolving accountability architecture, the new forums, arrangements, and processes. Table 2.4 gives an overview of the different types and mechanisms that have been incorporated in the EU Commission accountability architecture as part of the reform process.

As the arrangements in Table 2.4 show, the 'de jure' accountability of what once was a technocratically oriented international organization has been considerably 'beefed up'. The addition of new political, administrative, and

The Reinvention of the European Commission

Table 2.4 Overview of the EU Commission's Accountability Architecture

Accountability Type	Accountability Arrangement	Main Features
Political Accountability	Elections for European Parliament (since 1979)	Electoral process that secures change positions or offices through election. Elected and appointed officials are accountable and responsive to the European public
	European Parliament exercises democratic oversight over other EU institutions, particularly the European Commission (powers increased in different treaties)	Parliamentary scrutiny. Parties demand accounts from the executive. Parliament has tools (debates, questions) to discipline or sanction those found responsible for wrongdoings or shortcomings
	Presidential powers (1999)	Increased ex ante and ex post controls of the president over his fellow commissioners
	Principle of collegiality	Internal and collective responsibility
Administrative Accountability	Hierarchical organization	Hierarchical organization of superior–subordinate relationships. Subordinates report to superiors on their use of authority in the discharge of their responsibilities; rule-based governance
	Managerial and Performance: Strategic Programming and Planning (SPP) with Annual Policy Strategy (APS), Annual Management Plan (AMP), Annual Activity Report (AAR), Synthesis Report (since 2004)	Activity Based Management with performance-oriented reviews and reports
	Performance: Career Development Review (CDR) for senior officials (2004)	Internal performance appraisal of staff by their superiors
Administrative Financial Accountability	Financial: Decentralization of controls Separation of financial control from internal auditing (2004)	Financial rules and regulation
	Financial-Performance: Internal Audit Office (2001)	
	European Court of Auditors (1975)	External audits and performance reviews of the administration of public services; independent evaluations of policies and programmes; internal audit, monitoring and control capacities
Professional Accountability	Codes of Conduct; Declarations of Interests; Code of Good Administrative Behaviour (2001)	Protocols that explicitly or implicitly address the professional obligation and standards
	Whistleblowers Charter (2002)	Protection for officials who release information as an response to a undisclosed wrongdoing
Quasi-Legal Accountability	European Ombudsman (1995) OLAF: EU's Anti-Fraud Office (1999)	Checks, controls, and fire-alarms

Accountability Type	Accountability Arrangement	Main Features
Judicial-Legal Accountability	European Courts	Judicial review of administrative decisions, to uphold the rule of law, to prevent the misuse of power
Public Accountability	European Transparency Initiative (2005)	Public access to government information, open government (access to information and active disclosure)

financial arrangements has created a more elaborate, more demanding regime. As a result, accountability has evolved along several specific dimensions.[13]

Political accountability

The Commission's political accountability environment has moved from being intergovernmental and relatively deficient, towards a more complicated, multidimensional, and supranational arrangement. A system promoting favouritism, in which responsiveness to political interests of the member states was central, was replaced by a structure of democratic political channels of accountability through the parliamentary process, supplemented with presidential forms of control.

Strengthening of the political accountability of the Commission was realized by an enhancement of the European Parliament's capacity to hold commissioners and their officials to account. Several steps have been taken to render the Commission more directly accountable to the Parliament, as illustrated by the fact that the EP committees now scrutinize commissioners, that they play a prominent role in their appointment, and are able to dismiss the entire College by taking a vote of no confidence.

Increased responsiveness of the Commission to the EP is helped and mediated by the president's increased stature within the College and the growing control of the latter over the Commission. The EP is consulted on the choice of president, and also has the right to approve his appointment. The ex ante and ex post controls of the president over his fellow commissioners was increased by allowing him to decide who does which portfolio and to reshuffle them during their five-year term of office. This revised political accountability regime strengthened the answerability of the key political actors in the Commission.

Administrative accountability

Actions were also undertaken to improve the administrative accountability of the services. These measures focused on priority setting, allocation, and efficient use of resources. The use of performance reporting, i.e. result-based reporting, reviews, and audits, was widely expanded, in order to render senior civil servants responsible and accountable for the 'implementation' of the Commission's programme. Performance-based management created new standards of behaviour and performance. The new requirement for every Directorate General to publish an Annual Activity Report (AAR) powerfully reinforced the direct internal accountability of directors-general for expenditures authorized by them and by their staff. These new standards were intended to establish a yardstick for accountability against which senior managers in the Commission could be evaluated.

Administrative-financial accountability

To reinforce financial responsibility and accountability in the services, the Kinnock reform brought about the complete modernization of the system of financial management and control. Setting up a proper internal audit service, better fraud-proofing structures, and decentralizing the financial controls to individual Directorates General were all part of the reform plans. As a start, directors-general were given direct responsibility for making sure that proper control was carried out within their own departments and that managers bore responsibility for their financial decisions. Moreover, the establishment of an *Internal Audit Office* (IAS) in the Commission in 2001 has caused audits, monitoring, and supervision to become important mechanisms to focus on the misuse and abuse of power or on poor performance.

Legal and quasi-legal accountability

Judicial review to ensure that legal principles are properly applied is part of the legal accountability framework in which the Commission operates. Further financial-administrative scrutiny and control is exercised by external bodies operating independently of the Commission. The *European Court of Auditors* is the 'financial conscience' of the Union and makes sure that the revenues and expenditures of the EU institutions are legally and financially correct. The establishment of the 'European Anti-Fraud Office' (OLAF—Office Européen de Lutte Anti-Fraude) in 1999 also strengthened the mechanisms for conducting independent administrative anti-fraud investigations.

Professional accountability

Several additional tools were used to create shared expectations about what role and degree of responsibility are proper and desirable for commissioners and senior officials. Codes of conduct and ethical protocols have become prominent means to communicate the relevance of public-service values.

Although these mechanisms are part of the Commission's 'ethical framework' (Cini 2007), they are instruments used to instil public virtue and are relevant for creating standards to hold officials to account.

Public accountability

Increased openness and accessibility are prerequisites for effective scrutiny of public institutions (Curtin and Meijer 2006; Fung *et al.* 2007; Hood and Heald 2006; Fung *et al.* 2007; Naurin 2007; Curtin 2011; Meijer 2012). Transparency may be not an end in itself, but a critical tool to evaluate organizational accountability. The Commission honed transparency into a refined instrument of governance by launching the European Transparency Initiative (ETI) in November 2005. This consisted of a package of four main components: increasing the transparency of interest representatives seeking to influence EU decision-making and upholding minimum standards of consultation; increasing transparency of the use of EU funds; the sharpening and polishing of ethical rules and standards for public officials; and enlarging public access to documents and information from the EU institutions.

The Commission's modernized accountability architecture

Efforts to broaden the possibilities to hold the EU Commission to account therefore resulted in an expanded set of accountability arrangements being built into and around the institution. In the new accountability architecture, European institutions and actors have become an increasing important factor in ensuring the Commission's accountability. A major expansion of the mandate of the European Parliament regarding the capacity to organize audits, reviews, and the institutionalization of offices (ombudsman, audit, anti-fraud) that function as forums for intense scrutiny, has resulted in the Commission's accountability becoming positioned to an increasing extent at the supranational level.

Importantly, the changes have not exclusively focused on the role of the commissioners or of the services, but have addressed both the political and the administrative levels of the institution. Political pressures and the pressure for administrative reforms have targeted and activated *political and administrative accountability*, ensuring these were no longer secondary or peripheral to the Commission and putting them on an equal footing with *legal* and *professional* accountability. The cumulative result of the political and administrative reforms is the expansion of the accountability system; an extensive accountability apparatus and set of associated expectations cover the behaviours, decisions, and actions of commissioners and their senior civil servants in the use of public authority and resources.

New rules, new roles, new relationships

The Commission's reinvention addressed several problems. In response to the Commission's democratic control and accountability problem, ex ante and ex post structures and rules to retain political responsibility were designed. Enhancing the responsiveness of the Commission to the European Parliament was needed to fix the legitimacy problem. Meanwhile the Commission also engaged in attempts to ensure adequate managerial and financial accountability mechanisms within (and outside) the institution to oversee and improve implementation capacities as an answer to its management problems. Much of these institutional reinventions have been directed to establishing and superimposing new types and levels of accountability.

When looking at the modernized accountability system, in retrospect, we see that this evolved accountability system has not taken place in a planned, coherent, and consistent manner. Moreover, key actors contributing to the reform of the Commission's accountability apparatus were better at thickening and layering than at replacing arrangements. We also see a gradual fusion of different modes. The political accountability framework, built through successive revisions of the treaties, is organized along both presidential and parliamentary lines, whereas the administrative accountability framework evolved along Weberian and NPM principles.

New operating routines, incentives, training, and experiential learning, ex ante and ex post accountability mechanisms, other schemata of appropriate behaviour, and role expectations, introduced with the political and administrative reforms, are expected to have a major influence on what executives do and how they do it. Given that new types of accountability have become dominant, what were the consequences of these shifts for the expectations of the behaviour of commissioners and their senior officials? To what extent have these new rules and accountability arrangements also led to a carving out of new political and managerial roles? The next chapters explain how these formal reforms affecting the Commission have resulted in changing *responsibilities, recruitment patterns,* and in a *redefinition of the roles* of commissioners, their cabinet chefs, and senior-officials; and how these changes affected the executive relationships at the top of the EU Commission.

Notes

1. After having submitted its report to the European Parliament on 15 Mar. 1999, the committee was commissioned by the Parliament to prepare a second report. The second report on the Reform of the Commission was submitted to the EP on 10

Sept. 1999 and contained ninety concrete recommendations and was the basis for the series of reforms undertaken by the Prodi Commission (Van Gerven 2009: 117).
2. Later Neil Kinnock said that the report was devastating. He referred specifically to this critical sentence which had been added at the last minute to the report (Schön-Quinlivan 2011: p. xix). The Santer commissioners were appalled by this sentence and the tone of the report as a whole and the only option to express their resentment was to resign *en masse*. A decade later a member of this CIE (Van Gerven 2009: 117) wrote that the statement echoed a reluctance 'among the members of the hierarchy to acknowledge their responsibilities'; the sentence was to be understood as a 'cri de cœur' rather than something documented by hard evidence.
3. The idea of organizational DNA is inspired by Stinchcombe's (1965) so-called 'organizational imprinting hypothesis', according to which organizations are shaped by the historically specific resources upon which their founders initially draw. Organizations bear these 'birth marks' from the era in which their structural form was created and they have a long-term effect on its organizational evolution. The organizational DNA is also organizational imprinting and refers to the core values that constitute the genetic make-up of the institution. Here Moore's (1995) framework of public values is used to define the organizational DNA.
4. Cited in Rittberger (2005: 76).
5. Cited in Rittberger (2005: 95).
6. Monnet was not a big admirer of the 'intergovernmental method'. As a deputy secretary general at the League of Nations he had experienced at close quarters the failure of intergovernmental organizations to prevent wars.
7. It was the Dutch government, in particular, that suggested that a council of ministers should be instituted to which the HA should ultimately be accountable (Rittberger 2006: 97).
8. The contours of the EU Commission and the three other core institutions (Court, Council, and Parliament) of the current EU were in place from the start in 1952, although still in an emerging and embryonic condition (Egeberg 2006*a*: 28). The Commission—together with the Council—was set up with executive functions, and the EU evolved into a dual executive system (Hix 1999: 21) where there is a system of joint decision-making by the EP and the Council (Judge and Earnshaw 2008: 23).
9. This is in contrast to the Council, which represents governments, and the Parliament, which represents citizens, and the Economic and Social Committee, which represents organized civil society.
10. Interview with European Commission Secretary-General Catherine Day EurActiv, 25 Sept. 2006. <http://www.euractiv.com/en/future-eu/interview-european-commission-secretary-general-catherine-day/article-158149> (accessed Dec. 2010).
11. The Spierenburg Report of 1979 stated that over the preceding decade the Commission's 'effectiveness and reputation' had declined.
12. In the early decades of the EP's existence its legitimacy was highly contested. Proponents of the EP have successfully scandalized the lack of parliamentary

democracy at the EU level and succeeded in 'shaming' recalcitrant policy-makers into compliance with the institutionalization of representative democracy at the EU level (Rittberger 2012: 33).
13 For each of these different types of accountability there are different methods and arrangements for obtaining compliance and different potential penalties for non-compliance. It goes without saying that these different accountabilities may be separated analytically, but are interrelated and overlapping in practice.

3

From Technocrats to Politicians: The Commissioners

> We have a Treaty, we have responsibility, we have duties, we have rights and I want to say that the Commission has given all the conclusions requested to this parliament and, by the way, in full transparency.
>
> (José Manuel Barroso[1])

1. Politicization of the College

In February 2010, after eighty-one hours of hearings, around 1,750 questions, and the withdrawal of one candidate after political opposition, Jose Manuel Barroso's new 'team' of twenty-six commissioners finally received a vote of approval from the EP. At long last, with 488 votes in favour, 137 opposed, and 72 abstentions, the EP gave its endorsement to the Barroso II line-up.

Commission president Barroso's proposed new team had come under fire from the EP during the job interviews held in advance of the vote. Members of the European Parliament (MEPs) demanded information about the financial affairs and the business interests of Bulgaria's embattled nominee to the European Commission, raising the spectre of a previous rumpus during the vetting of Barroso's first team of commissioners in 2004. At that time, storms of protest led the European Parliament to force the withdrawal of the controversial Italian candidate, Rocco Buttiglione, over his views on gay rights and women, and Barroso had to reshuffle his team. Speaking to a handful of journalists after this political confrontation with parliament, Barroso waved away the controversy, saying that the uncertainty surrounding the incoming Commission was a sign of a growing political maturity: 'The EU process is becoming more political ... We have to adjust psychologically to that. ... We can't say that whenever there is a debate there is a crisis,' he said. 'If this is a crisis, then I can live with this crisis.'[2]

Six years later, as Barroso began a second five-year term at the helm of the European Union's executive arm, politicization had become a pervasive trend. 'The politicizing of the process has gone up another notch', as one senior EU official observed at that time. Debates about the approval of the Commission had become 'normal' politics, with many of the MEPs' objections coming down to political point-scoring, confirming the developing partisanship underpinning the selection process (Judge and Earnshaw 2008: 206). This chapter links changes in the legal and political framework of the EU Commission to a transformation that has turned the College of Commissioners into a genuinely political rather than a technocratic body. It will first explore how new formal powers for the EP and an increase in parliamentary activism have provided a new context for the EU executive. Subsequently, the following questions are addressed. What precisely was the effect of this 'parliamentarization' on the Commission's political leadership? How did the treaty revisions transform the recruitment and selection of commissioners, and hence the character of the Commission? Did it lead to a radically different perspective on the qualities required to lead the Commission? The chapter concludes that a top–down process of politicization has increasingly shaped the executive role of the Commission.

Parliamentarization: the increased powers of the EP over the Commission

A 'politicized bureaucracy without political control': this is how the EU Commission was wont to be described (Page 1997). The process of decision-making within the Commission was, like that of the member states, a highly political one. Yet the Commission's political leadership was perceived as being very different from that of a national ministry because 'commissioners are not commissioned by anyone to do anything in particular' (Page 1997: 115). Lack and fragmentation of executive control meant that commissioners were less likely to be the focus of authority: 'The notion of "political control" over the EU bureaucracy is not directly equivalent to the notion as it applies in member states. Normally political control over the bureaucracy refers to the degree to which elected representatives, whether as parliamentarians, … or whether as ministers, can constrain the actions of permanent officials' (Page 1997: 111).

However, the idea that the EU executive needs to be democratically legitimized has translated into a long and slow process of adaptation, involving rival claims to legitimacy and stressing notions of input legitimacy, parliamentary sovereignty, and representative government (Magnette 2001; Rittberger 2005). Political innovations by means of treaty revisions have led to an expansion of the EP's legislative and budgetary powers and the establishment of a stronger interconnection between the legislative and executive

Table 3.1 The European Parliament in Treaty Reforms since 1992

Year Signed	Treaty	Outcome
1992	Treaty on European Union Maastricht (effective: 1 November 1993)	Three-pillar structure of Europe; some co-decision for EP and extending the cooperation procedure to others
1997	Treaty of Amsterdam (ToA) (effective: 1 May 1999)	More legislative powers to EP; stronger requirements for Commission appointments. Extended co-decision to most areas of legislation, and reformed the procedure to put the Parliament on an equal footing with the Council
2001	Treaty of Nice (effective: 1 February 2003)	Co-decision EP extended to seven more areas.
2007	Treaty of Lisbon (effective: 1 December 2009)	The EP's powers are considerably increased, extending its decision-making powers to encompass a number of important policy fields, notably in justice and home affairs but also in agriculture and international trade

branches of EU government. They have enhanced parliamentary control and authorization over the Commission.

The Maastricht Treaty (1992) marked the beginning of the Parliament's metamorphosis into the role of co-legislator by introducing full legislative power ('co-decision') in certain policy areas, and by extending the cooperation procedure to others. By the time the Lisbon Treaty came into force, this procedure had become, with a few exceptions, the norm for the EU, putting the Parliament, in effect, on a legislative par with the Council. Over the years, the EP has thus become a much more powerful actor, as Table 3.1 shows, accruing ever-greater decision-making capacities with each step of treaty reform.

At the same time, the EP also progressively acquired oversight powers over the Commission. The Maastricht Treaty brought the term of office of the Commission into line with the term of the European Parliament and gave parliament the power of final approval over the membership of the Commission. This way it was possible to create a link between the preferences expressed by Union citizens in EP elections and the nomination of the College of Commissioners and its programme for the parliamentary term. Consequentially, the term of office of Colleges was extended from four to five years so as to align this more closely with the term of the EP elections and to give the EP more weight in the EU appointment procedure. Steps were taken to render the College directly accountable to the EP, as illustrated by the EP committees' examination of nominated commissioners, its vote of confidence, its right to dismiss the entire College, and the right to approve the appointment of the president.

As a result of these increases in power, the EP has considerably expanded its influence in the EU decision-making process. Not surprisingly, parliamentary

The Commissioners

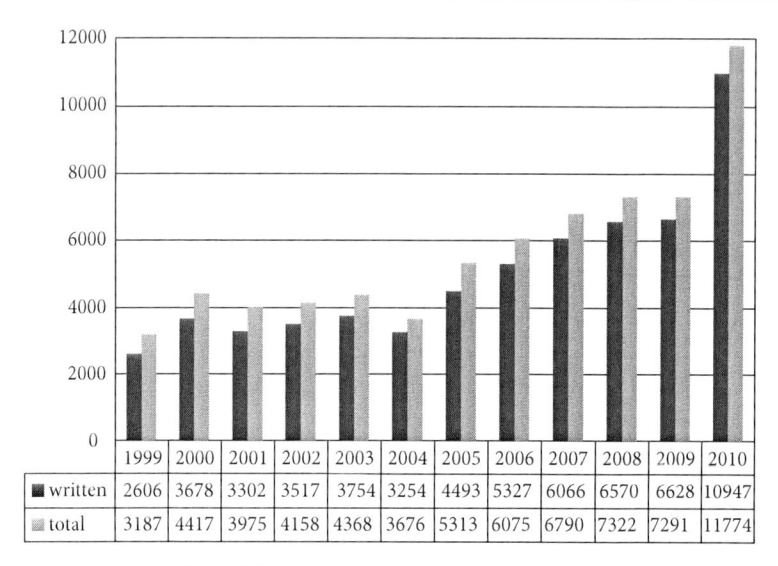

	1999	2000	2001	2002	2003	2004	2005	2006	2007	2008	2009	2010
written	2606	3678	3302	3517	3754	3254	4493	5327	6066	6570	6628	10947
total	3187	4417	3975	4158	4368	3676	5313	6075	6790	7322	7291	11774

Figure 3.1. Number of Questions of MEPs to the Commission, 1999–2010
Source: General Report of Activities of the European Union

activity has increased substantially over the past decade: more questions are being posed, more debates held, and there are more committees occupying the time of many more MEPs, receiving the written answers or oral policy statements of the Commission.

The EP's oversight function steadily continues to gain ground. One of the most popular and visible methods to perform oversight and ensure executive accountability is by posing questions (Judge and Earnshaw 2008: 217).[3] Figure 3.1 shows that the number of questions increased in the ten years between 1999 and 2009 by nearly 130 per cent. This percentage rises to a staggering 270 per cent if the enormous number of questions posed in 2010 is included. Parliamentary questions give MEPs the opportunity to obtain information, as the Commission is bound to reply to these questions orally or in writing. But questions also provide a means through which parliamentarians can inform the executive (in this case, the Commission and Council) of concerns and issues which MEPs feel should receive more attention from the executive.

Its strengthened legislative powers have provided the EP with an array of 'constraints', preventing the Commission from taking unilateral policy decisions. On some policy proposals, the EP is now involved from the beginning and MEPs interact closely with the Commission. This may have blurred the lines between ex post accountability and ex ante control, but the result is that, for some policy plans, MEPs have a directive put on the table.

With the treaty reforms, a range of ex ante incentives and ex post constraints were introduced and these have resulted in a stronger role in daily policy-making and closer contact between the two institutions. The European Parliament has become a far more vociferous and demanding interlocutor, and this has contributed to the design of a more politically accountable Commission: 'the certainties of the essentially technocratic relationship into which the Commission has bound itself may now be giving way to a more politicised relationship' (Westlake 2006: 277). It is clear that the Commission cannot take its relationship with the EP for granted: it has to work to build and maintain a positive relationship. This, in turn, has generated new expectations about the role of the Commission president.

2. Presidentialization: Strengthening Inner Executive Politics

The formal role of the Commission president, before the Amsterdam Treaty entered into force, was that of 'first among equals'. Some past Commission presidents performed this role with more authority than others. As the first president of a newly founded organization, Hallstein, for instance, led the Commission with political vision (Christiansen 1977: 77; Seidel 2010: 71). Delors used his ten-year period of office to increase the importance and status of the position (Nugent 2001: 63). Yet presidential leadership still relied during this period on personal authority and was not the result of institutional design.

Over time, however, the powers of the president have steadily grown and expanded. As the EU Commission became progressively supranational (Mazey 1996), new demands began to be made on its internal organization, and its external representation gradually became more relevant. A more comprehensive role for the president became critical; one in which 'leadership' was expected, both in external relations, including those with parliament, and internally, in the management of the inner executive.

The Maastricht and Amsterdam Treaties consolidated and institutionalized the elevation of the Commission president. These reforms increased the powers of the president over his fellow commissioners by allowing him not only to decide who was assigned which portfolio, but also to reshuffle them during their five-year term of office; in addition, he may even request an individual commissioner to resign. The president has the power to decide on the internal organization of the Commission and to allocate the responsibilities of the commissioners, both at the time of appointment and throughout the term of the Commission.

The net result of these developments has been an increase in top–down control over the College. The new powers of the president have strengthened his role *vis-à-vis* the individual commissioners, allowing him in principle to run the Commission with greater authority. Enhanced presidential authority

The Commissioners

Table 3.2 Prior Positions of Commission Presidents

Period	President	Highest prior position	**Score***
1958–61	Walter Hallstein (D)	Junior minister (foreign affairs)	0.84
1962–7	Hallstein II		0.84
1967–70	Jean Rey (B)	Minister of economic affairs	1.02
1970–2	Franco Maria Malfatti (I)	Minister of state participation	1.18
1973–6	Francis Xavier Ortoli (F)	Minister of economy and finance	1.92
1977–80	Roy Jenkins (UK)	Chancellor of the Exchequer	1.64
1981–4	Gaston Thor (L)	Prime minister	2.17
1985–8	Jacques Delors I (F)	Minister of economy and defence	1.92
1989–92	Delors II		1.92
1993–4	Delors III		1.92
1995–9	Jacques Santer (L)	Prime minister	2.75
1999–2004	Romano Prodi (I)	Prime minister	2.48
2005–9	Jose Manuel Barroso I	Prime minister	2.2
2010–14	Barroso II (P)		2.2

*Score for Commission president's highest position is based Druckman and Warwick (2005).
Source: Döring (2007).

also meant that it would be easier to coordinate the many tasks of the many commissioners (twenty-seven after the eastern enlargement) and to ensure that the Commission pulled in one direction.

As the role of the Commission president has grown ever more powerful, it has become increasingly essential that this role be filled by a 'political heavyweight'. Experience in the role of prime minister is a distinct advantage for candidates seeking election to the office of Commission president. Consequently, there has been a substantial increase in the importance of the previous political positions held by Commission presidents, as Table 3.2 shows (Döring 2007). Whereas the first Commission presidents were formerly junior ministers, later presidents were formerly full ministers, often with key portfolios. The latest Commission presidents have all formerly served as prime minister of a large EU country.

As a result of these changes, a more presidential role expectation has emerged, which has affected its executive role. Romano Prodi—the first incumbent to enjoy the enhanced powers granted to the office—decided not to retain a portfolio for himself, which enabled him 'to present himself as the political figurehead at the top of the Commission' (Peterson 2004: 17). José Manuel Barroso has adopted a style of control over the Commission that is even more presidential than his predecessors, in order to ensure all the commissioners work together effectively. Using a hands-on approach, he has successfully managed to be personally linked to all major policy initiatives of the Commission; he joins the individual commissioners for press conferences or similar events, when initiatives with a wider public appeal are being presented, and has a much greater media presence than his predecessors Prodi and Santer.

To all intents and purposes, the Commission president has become the 'political boss' of the EU Commission. Not only is he the most prominent commissioner with the most power; he also bears the greatest responsibility.

Presidential accountability: 'to live up to his promises'

As the powers of the Commission president increased, so did the desire of the EP, and particularly the political groups, to acquire more influence over the choice of the Commission's president and the composition of the Commission.

Since the changes made by the Treaty of Nice, the Commission president must be nominated by the European Council by a qualified majority (unanimity is no longer required) and the nomination must be approved by the European Parliament. This provision gave the political parties in the EP considerable power, which they used on the first possible occasion, after the European elections in 2004. After their victory, the parties of the centre-right (i.e. EPP-ED and the liberals) announced that parliamentary approval of the nominee for Commission president was contingent upon selection of a nominee from their ranks.[4] The Lisbon Treaty formalized this situation, but it also reinforced the position of the European Parliament, as it turned the simple 'approval' of the person nominated by the heads of state and government into an election of the president by a majority of the EP's members.[5]

The increased politicization of the role of Commission president is not only evidenced by the emerging party-political congruence between the president and the parliamentary majority, but also by the president's explicit responsibility for the Commission's five-year work programme. Like national governments, the Commission nowadays devises, shares, and defends a common political agenda, which operates as the 'glue' in the collective responsibility of the College (Harlow 2002: 59). In 2009, this led to the president designate being required, before his re-election in parliament, for the first time to present his written 'political guidelines'.

During the hearings in parliament prior to his election as president, Barroso had to make firm commitments to the EP that would be included in the work programme for the new Commission. The EP, in anticipation of the new Lisbon Treaty, had introduced a new presidential appointment procedure. This included asking for this government-type policy programme declaration and insisting on specific priorities before confirming Barroso in office. Several MEPs 'insisted' that their groups' political points be taken into account if Barroso wanted to be sure of obtaining approval for another term as Commission president. In the words of a MEP: 'We wanted to engage with the candidate in a serious and constructive process of consultation on the priorities of the next Commission. We have set specific demands and we wanted to question him rigorously.'

This served to strengthen the trend towards an ever-more politicized appointment procedure. New candidates for the job of Commission president now needed to win and secure the backing of a majority of MEPs, so that the outcome of the elections could be taken into account. This not only represented a stronger political relationship between parliament and the Commission. It also proved how increased parliamentary power has generated new expectations regarding the role of commissioners and that of Commission president. As another MEP phrased it: 'We now expect the newly elected president to live up to his promises to us and be a strong, bold and energetic president who is closely in tune with public opinion, independent of member states' pressure and proactive in seeking common European action where it is so clearly necessary.'

Under the enhanced political accountability mechanisms, the Commission is expected to act as a responsive actor, not only to the member states, but increasingly also to the EP. Responsiveness, defined as the degree of attention to the wishes and demands of elected officials (Putnam 1973), has become an important 'virtue' of the Commission president, emerging from this new set of political arrangements.

The fact that the president is elected and has his own political agenda has also given the president a stronger position in acting as a political figurehead. The establishment of further arrangements underline the president's role as a political player. The introduction of Question Hour in October 2009, for instance, has served to increase the president's answerability to the EP. MEPs from all parties have the opportunity to question the Commission President on any subject, and particularly on the key issues of the day, each time the MEPs meet in Strasbourg.[6] In addition, Barroso's first 'State of the Union' speech in September 2010, a US-style format to outline the priorities of the twenty-seven-nation EU, was delivered as part of a political drive to explain the importance of the EU and the Commission's role in Europe.[7] Moreover, President Barroso represents the European Union as a full member of the G8 at the G8 summits.[8] The evolution of these new arrangements illustrates that the role of the EU Commission president has become more presidential. However, politicization has not only changed the outward role of the president. It has also triggered the need for stronger internal political leadership.

Managing the inner executive

The strengthened political accountability of the Commission president to the EP has served to highlight another aspect, namely that of the expectation of controllability. This is defined as the ability of 'principals' to control their 'agents' (Koppell 2005: 97) and has become visible in the increased powers of the Commission president over the work and policy files handled by the Commission. This has affected his executive role and has been accompanied by a more 'presidential' style of leading the EU Commission. The fact that the president is elected on a political programme has strengthened his capacity to organize the inner executive.

Two elements have made the Commission more presidential in this respect—if we use Poguntke and Webb's (2005: 7) criteria for 'presidentialization'. The first was the growth in the zones of autonomous control for the president, which resulted from the increase in formal presidential powers, for instance over the appointment, organization, and dismissal of other commissioners. In the modern Commission, the president possesses the prerogative power to intervene in any commissioner's portfolio.

Second, there was the expansion of the president's power resources, such as staff and, increasingly, his capacity to set agendas and to define the alternatives at stake. Facilitated by his cabinet and a strengthened Secretariat-General (Kassim and Menon 2004: 100), the president's access to sources and flows of information about developments in other cabinets and other DGs has grown enormously. The president's offices have a huge network of lines of communication. The Secretariat-General has a similar web of contacts, reaching further into the operational divisions of departments. Both enable the president to watch the initiation of policies and inject his views at an early, formative stage. This has allowed the president to become more directly involved in a greater number of dossiers and policy proposals (Kaczyński *et al.* 2008).

The increased power flowing from the combined effect of autonomy and a concentration of resources in the president's office has institutionalized a more centralized way of leading the Commission (cf. Kaczyński *et al.* 2008). Contrary to what many had expected before enlargement, the number of reported disagreements between the twenty-seven commissioners in the current college has not exceeded those among the twenty commissioners in the previous one (Kaczyński *et al.* 2008). As the number of nationalities increased from fifteen to twenty-seven, the opportunity for political leadership of the president has also increased. The Commission president has tended to transact more business through informal meetings of commissioners outside the College, to ensure that all the commissioners work together effectively. This increased informality has strengthened the role of the president. The necessity for the president to set priorities, the reduced room for manœuvre of individual commissioners (and the senior officials under them), and the tendency to centralize policy-making have become, in the words of a Commission official, 'unavoidable' in a Commission of twenty-seven.

Reinforcing the powers of the Commission president—by reforming the mechanisms for appointment, organization, and dismissal in the direction of clearer political control and accountability—has buttressed a more presidential style of leadership. It also has induced expectations of *responsiveness* and *controllability* with regard to the behaviour of the Commission president. One area in which these new expectations have become visible is in the nomination and appointment of new commissioners.

3. Politicization of the Selection of Commissioners

How did the evolution into a more parliament-oriented system of the EU affect the recruitment of the EU Commission's political officeholders? Increased politicization of the selection of commissioners is one of the consequences of a thickening of democratic accountability structures in the EU. The next section will focus on three elements in which this politicization has manifested itself: (*a*) the *process* of selection (and de-selection) of commissioners; (*b*) the *demands* on candidate-commissioners; and (*c*) the *supply* of candidates eligible for the office of commissioner. Figure 3.2 summarizes these elements of the recruitment of commissioners.

The selection process: entrance and exit control

Commissioners-designate, like other political elites, are subjected to formal (and informal) selection procedures. Treaty reforms have changed the selection procedures of the EU Commission, increasing the control of the EP over the access and the exit of this EU executive. The EP is, however, not the only selector in the process. In the recruitment procedure for commissioners, three actors—the member states, the Commission president, and the European Parliament—play an important role divided over two stages of political power play. The first, the nomination stage, occurs behind closed doors; the second, the appointment stage, is more out in the open.

Getting selected: the nomination

During the nomination stage for commissioners, the member states and the Commission president play a dominant role. In the early years of the EU Commission, the approach was an intergovernmental one, and the nomination decisions were set by individual member states, which was crucial in determining the composition of the College. Each commissioner was, in effect, independently appointed on the basis of national governmental choice. For member states, the nomination of the commissioners was a useful

Politicization of Selection

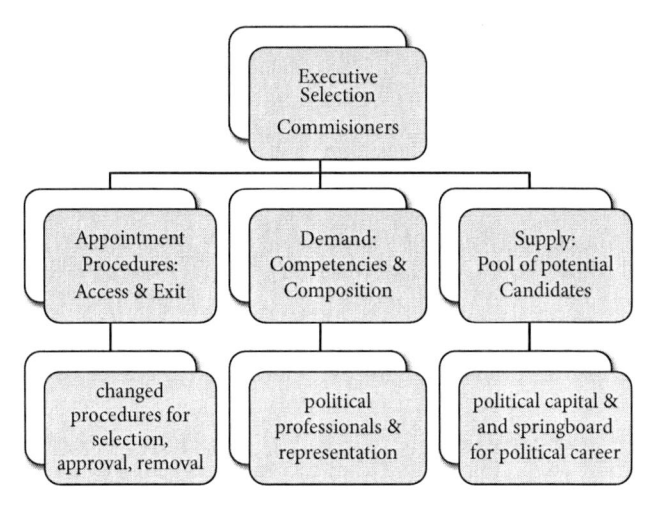

Figure 3.2. Recruitment of Commissioners

piece of political patronage. It could be used to reward loyal service of politicians past their best; or to remove 'political problems' from the domestic scene (Macmullen 2000: 33).

Until the Maastricht Treaty, presidents of the Commission were not able to control the composition of the Commission. The president-designate had no formal involvement in the nomination process; and the political and social balance of the College was the sum of the member countries' choices. Consequently, the cohesion of the College was sometimes problematic. As a result of changes in the treaties (Maastricht, Amsterdam), the Commission president now has a greater margin of independence as regards the selection of candidates. The Commission president is nominated first and then subject to confirmation by a vote of the EP. Nominations are made 'by common accord' between the member states and the president. The Commission president then allocates the portfolios, the distribution of which is entirely at his discretion, and puts the new team forward for the approval of the Council of Ministers and the European Parliament.

This means that the presidential nominee takes part in the nomination of the other commissioners, rather than only being consulted, as was formerly the case. He now has the right to disagree (veto individuals) and bears sole responsibility for allocating his team's portfolios. This way, the president can improve the institution's cohesion and effectiveness; and he can win over the member states to nominate good candidates who are able to serve the institution's external and internal needs. Both Prodi and Barroso have taken the advantage of this strengthened hand by discussing with national capitals the sort of College they wanted and who they would like to nominate to their colleges.[9]

Member states compete for a bigger share of the positions in the Commission, and their influence on the composition of the EU Commission has weakened. Inevitably, a member state's individual bargaining power weighs heavily in the jockeying for positions. The bigger member states expect to be given the bigger portfolios. Several countries place bids for one of the heavyweight economic posts in the Commission—competition, trade, and the internal market, areas where the Commission has strong powers. A second tier of portfolios is prized by some countries because of their impact in particular sectors—environment, information society (which covers telecoms), industry, and transport. Governments will do their utmost to get a high-profile post. The more capable the candidates for the Commission post are, the more likely the Commission president will assign them a powerful portfolio. Several countries have decided that the best way of obtaining a heavyweight portfolio is to put forward a heavyweight commissioner or to put a candidate forward for a second term.

Getting approved: screening and voting

After the line-up of the new team is presented to Parliament, the second stage of the game of political power play begins. According to the rules, the new Commission must be approved by vote of confidence by the EP.[10] Whereas the first stage in the recruitment process unfolds in the seclusion of the backroom where the nominations for appointment are made, much of the second stage, the parliamentary stage, is open to public scrutiny and media attention. The commissioners-designate are subject to hearings at the European Parliament, which will question them and then vote on the college as a whole.[11]

The synchronization of the Commission's term of office with that of the EP (Judge and Earnshaw 2008: 267) has been very relevant. This has enabled the EP to gain more influence over the access to executive office; and to have a greater influence on the screening and censuring of executive candidates. In the screening stage—the hearings—the credentials and past behaviour of potential officeholders are reviewed. The hearings, described by some as 'job interviews', give a taste of what the EU could expect from its new 'employees'. This is also a way of gaining information on the views and priorities of future executive officeholders; and it can serve as a benchmark for the commissioner's subsequent performance (Judge and Earnshaw 2008: 205). The EP has become able to place greater informal and formal constraints on the selection process.

MEPs can only vote to elect the Commission en masse rather than individually, due to a clause barring the European Parliament from singling out any individual commissioner for disapproval. If designate members of the Commission are found to be inappropriate, the President must then reshuffle the team or request a new candidate from the member state, or risk having the whole Commission be voted down. Parliament can also express itself on the allocation of portfolio responsibilities. In the end, there is usually a compromise with the Commission president whereby the worst candidates are removed and minor objections put aside, so the Commission can take office. Once the team is approved by parliament, it is formally put into office by the European Council.

Getting removed: censuring

The political power of the parliament determines how long an executive remains in office. The maximum term of five years limits the length of time the Commission can serve, provided it does not lose the confidence of the legislature. If the EP passes a motion of censure by a two-thirds majority, the members of the Commission must resign. In accordance with the principle of collective responsibility of the EU Commission, however, the EP can only require the resignation of the Commission as a whole. To give the threat of potential sanction more teeth, the Commission and Parliament agreed in 2005 on a democratic innovation that increased the political responsibility of individual commissioners (Judge and Earnshaw 2008: 211, 287). This made it possible for the president of the Commission to ask a commissioner, in whom the EP has indicated that it has lost confidence, to resign. This, indirectly, has contributed to an increase of parliament's power of dismissal. Embedding both the options for screening and censuring by the EP in the appointment procedure has made the (de)selection process of EU commissioners a more politicized one.

The demand side: competencies and composition

There are no rules specifying what sort of people, with what sort of background and experience, should be commissioners, but representation is always an important element. In the early days of the Commission, 'member-state governments, political parties and party networks, industries and trade unions all sought influence on the composition of the Commission' (Seidel 2010: 92). The seats of the Commission were distributed according to these interests governing the member states. An additional 'constant' factor has been the notion that commissioners should be chosen for their general competence.

With the rise of political accountability structures at the EU level, however, there are new expectations to be met by the executive. These are not only marked in the process of selection, but are also translated into the composition of the EU Commission. The College profile indicates that the presence of political competences and representation of parties at the EP level has obviously become relevant. Bit by bit the European Commission is evolving into a 'normal' political body. The handling of its internal balances—political colours, new and old member states, new and old Commission members, and gender—conveys the message that the 'political factor' is increasing in the College of Commissioners, in terms of its internal composition and representation.

Political professionals

Previous political experience has become one of the job requirements for becoming commissioner. In the Barroso II Commission, eighteen out of the twenty-seven EU commissioners held a senior ministerial office at the national level prior to their appointment to the Commission. This ministerial background of commissioners is a significant trend, which has manifested itself since the first Commission (Macmullen 2000: 46; Döring 2007; Wonka 2007); it indicates a move away from the more narrowly technical roles characteristic of a technocratic institution, towards a broader and more political approach. Wonka (2007) argues that an analysis of commissioners' prior jobs in the political arena shows that member states rely extensively on candidates who have a high political visibility. Over time, the number of commissioners who previously served as ministers in their member states, and who therefore are experienced in exercising political leadership over a large executive bureaucracy, has increased. Increasingly, the Commission also includes commissioners who have held a senior ministerial office (prime minister, foreign minister, finance minister, interior minister) or led a mainstream political grouping at the national level.

The box plot in Figure 3.3, based on the data of Holger Döring (2007: 220), provides an indication of how the importance of the previous political positions of commissioners has increased over time. Both the median of the position scores and the highest position held by a commissioner have risen. The frequency of commissioners in the lowest quartile has dropped. In the early years, there was a significant group of commissioners with no previous political experience. But the trend shows that more and more powerful political actors are being appointed to the College of Commissioners. Especially the smaller member states have nominated high-profile politicians as commissioners (Döring 2007: 224).

Representation of interests

Representation of the main political cleavages is a focal point for any 'normal' executive, but also for the Commission. The handling of its internal balances—political colours, geographic, new and old member states, new and old Commission members, and gender—conveys the message that the 'political factor' is relevant in the College of commissioners, in terms of its internal composition and representation.

Politicization of Selection

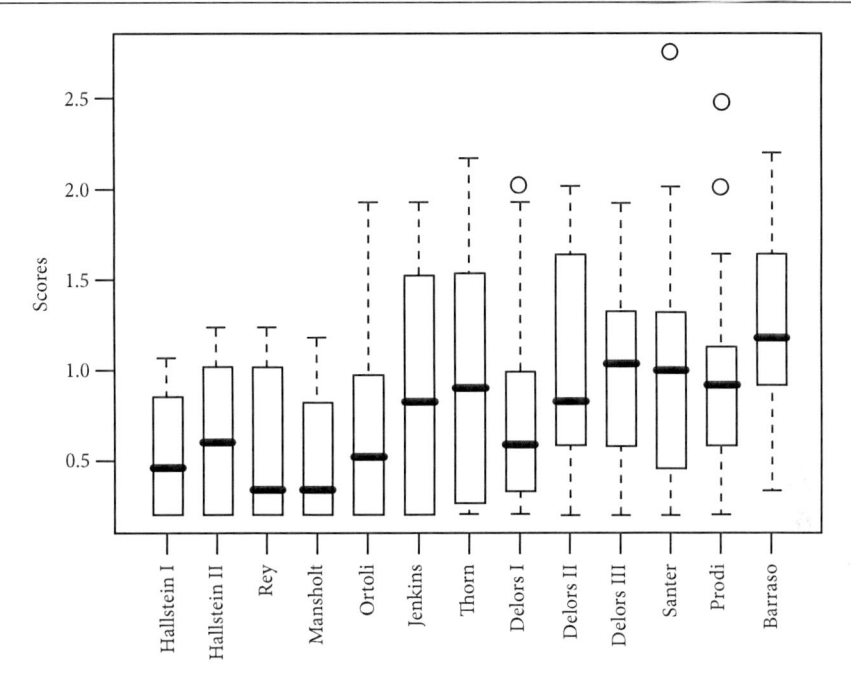

Figure 3.3. Box Plot of Former Positions (Scores) of Commissioners
Source: Döring 2007: 220.

Political party representation and political balances, for instance, play an increasingly important role when constituting the EU executive. Barroso, as a member of the European People's Party (EPP), was appointed by the European Council in response to the victory of the EPP-ED in the 2004 European elections. This was the first time the Commission president was appointed according to the results of the latest European elections, and the change was felt in the political balance of the Commission. The political centre of gravity of the Barroso Commission was more right-wing than the previous two Commissions; both the Prodi and the Santer Commissions contained narrow left of centre majorities (Hix 2008).

This shifting political balance is not simply a function of the changing colour of the member state governments in the Council, but also the result of treaty changes that have turned the EU Commission into a much more 'majoritarian' institution (Hix 2008: 38–9). The introduction of qualified-majority voting (QMV) in the Treaty of Nice implied that a majority in the Council and Parliament is now needed to elect the Commission and that the EU is taking on the characteristics of a 'quasi-parliamentary system of government'—where a particular majority shapes the Commission as a 'coalition' government with a particular political programme.

The Barroso I Commission was also a more partisan college due to the fact that it was the first in which each member state had only one commissioner. After the 2004 enlargement, as the size of the body grew, the larger states lost their second commissioner. The new Barroso Commission was appointed under the Treaty of Nice. Before this treaty became effective, the large member states were allotted two commissioners, which they tended to grant to the largest domestic and the opposition party. Now, with the one country–one commissioner rule, most EU governments selected a politician from their own majority parties as their representative in the new EU executive.

When this change in the structure of representation in the Commission is combined with the introduction of qualified-majority voting (QMV) for electing the Commission president and the Commission as a whole, the result is a significantly more partisan Commission: the Commission president can be elected by a smaller political majority, and he then is able to lead a Commission where his political allies are likely to be in the majority. As for the political balance, the EU executive has become a broad coalition. In the cases of the Barroso I and II Commissions, the strong Liberal presence was ensured by a durable degree of political support from the largest parliamentary groups.

Further, all member states are equally represented in the College. With the eastern enlargement in 2004 of the EU, with 10 + 2 new member countries, the composition of the Commission increased to the size of twenty-seven Commissioners, one for each EU member country. According to the new one-country–one-commissioner rule, a commissioner from each member state is present in the College. Initially there were plans—in an earlier version of the Treaty of Lisbon—that, as from 2014, the number of Commissioners should equal two-thirds of the number of member states, chosen according to a system based on equal rotation among the member states—to make the workings of the college more 'efficient'. But 'political reality' teaches that community interest will be much easier to sell to the member states and its citizens 'if they have a man in' the College (Broin and Kaczyński 2010: 50).[12] This illustrates that, as a political, rather than a technocratic, institution, representation is an important value; particularly, when it comes to one of the main cleavages at the EU level: nationality.

Finally, gender balance is an issue in many modern executives, and the present Commission is no exception. Under pressure of the EP, gender balance became one of the points of special attention in the appointment of new commissioners. During the first thirty-seven years of its existence, the College of Commissioners was an exclusively male club, with the first (two) female commissioners not being appointed until the Delors II Commission in 1989. In the Barroso I and II Commission, nine of the twenty-seven commissioners were women (one in three).

The supply side: political capital and careers

The profile of the College of Commissioners is not only determined by qualifications which are seen as appropriate for executive office, but also by the 'supply' of potential officeholders: eligible candidates in the member states who can be selected for the job. Looking at the career paths of commissioners affords an indication of the political capital (experiences, abilities, and resources) that commissioners bring with them when entering the EU executive. These career paths tell us something about the pool of candidates seeking executive office; and how the experience of working in the EU Commission can facilitate a further career.

The previous career: pathways to power

The social make-up of the European Commission is not exactly representative of society in general. The great majority of commissioners is highly educated and has enjoyed the benefits of university education—often abroad. The 'resources' and 'capital' that they bring to the Commission vary with their career path. Three main career paths are prevalent among commissioners in today's EU Commission: there are the commissioners who have a *'technocratic career'*; commissioners with a *'political career'*; and commissioners who Mattozzi and Merlo (2008) would describe as *'career politicians'*.

Only two out of twenty-seven commissioners in Barroso II come from a *'technocratic'* background—meaning that they have no previous experience in political positions. Both commissioners are from the Central Eastern European member states. Most commissioners come from a *'political career'* background, which means that they have not only held one or more political offices, but have also worked in other sectors, as well. Their professional experience mainly includes work in the public sector or in so-called 'brokerage' occupations (Ranney 1965; Cotta and Best 2007: 14–15). Like political elites at the national level, they have been university professors, consultants, journalists, or lawyers. The conditions in these jobs are conducive to a political career (time available, long vacation periods, professional independence, financial security, social networks, status, and technical abilities that are useful in public life, good rhetorical abilities, knowledge of legislation, etc.). It is a category of jobs that, in Schumpeter's (1984: 362) terms, 'naturally ties itself to politics'.

The route to the more prominent offices in the Commission seems, however, to be reserved for *'career politicians'*, i.e. commissioners such as Barnier, Dalli, De Gucht, Almunia, Rehn, who have spent most of their working life in a political job of one kind or other and have not done much else than politics. Commissioners who followed this career path gained an earlier passage into politics at the level of the member states via a political office or post at the local, regional, or national level—as a parliamentarian or minister. The national level offers many possibilities for participation in formal political organizations. Many systems (particularly the unitary states) are, however, characterized by relatively closed political career paths into the higher echelons of power. Clearly demarcated and 'well trodden ladders' (from party work to local office, from regional government to parliament, from backbencher to junior minister) have to be climbed to reach the pinnacles of power (Norris and Lovenduski 1997). Such a career pathway offers professional and personal resources, and political experiences, and can serve as a springboard for launching an international political career.

Previous experience in politics has become an important resource. Access to and performance in the political profession of commissioner requires progressively specific skills and knowledge that is gained primarily by 'on the job experience' in other political jobs and other political institutions. In the political profession, more than in any other occupation, to quote Borchert and Stolz (2002: 24): 'the whole career represents a kind of on-the-job occupational training and it is during their career paths that politicians acquire the necessary skills and qualifications'. The vertical accumulation of offices across various levels of the political system gives work experience in several political positions and supports a durable political professionalization. This experience provides a 'competitive advantage' over less politically experienced competitors (Borchert and Stolz 2002: 23). It is indicative of the growing relevance of 'political capital' in the EU executive and the diminished transferability of skills between politics and other careers

Moreover, a sizeable group of commissioners can boast of previous experience of active participation in international organizations. Increased globalization has brought about the rise of a class of ambitious career politicians ready to function in international governance positions. The growth of European institutions has multiplied the career opportunities for those relatively highly skilled and mobile individuals who have exploited these new career opportunities. This group thus has experience with working in an international environment through living, studying, or working abroad.

Finally, strengthened democratic accountability in the EU has also brought a certain level of uncertainty to the job of commissioner—a kind of insecurity (the possibility of political defeat, censure) that applies to the occupational arena of politics at large (Borchert and Stolz 2002). It requires a greater subjective willingness of aspirant commissioners to assume the uncertain life, the risks, and costs of taking on a position within the executive power.

Politicization of Selection

It has provided incentives for a further political professionalization of the Commission, because it has brought in a group of 'career politicians' for which the position in the Commission is not a final one.

The posterior career: the Commission as a springboard

The increased politicization of the Commission manifests itself at two other moments in the career path of the commissioner: in the form of 'early departures' and in their post-Commission career. A rule of thumb for members of the European Commission used to be that they were politicians past their prime. Twenty years ago, for two-thirds of the commissioners, membership of the Commission was the last important political position they would occupy (Page and Wouters 1994: 455). Consequently there was 'little political incentive for commissioners to identify objectives which could not have emerged from the normal process of politics and to pursue and sustain them since only a minority can seriously expect to be able to use any success in Brussels as collateral for a resumed political career at home' (Page and Wouters (1994: 457). However, for many commissioners today this office is not their last major public position. More and more, a commissionership in Brussels has become another stepping stone within a political career.

Officially, the Commission's mandate is five years. But there is also an emerging trend for commissioners to leave early before the end of the term. Premature departures (see Table 3.3), either for health reasons, or because a commissioner has died or has taken up a position elsewhere, are usually followed by replacements. Such replacements were rare at the time of the Delors Commission, in the mid-1980s. But in recent Commissions, early leave has become a trend. In the Prodi Commission, six members of the

Table 3.3 Early Leaves, 1958–2012

Period	President	size	holders	died	early leave
1958–61	Walter Hallstein (D)	9	12	1	2
1962–7	Hallstein II	9	10		1
1967–70	Jean Rey (B)	14	14		0
1970–2	Franco Maria Malfatti (I)	9	10		1
1973–76	Francis Xavier Ortoli (F)	13	15		2
1977–80	Roy Jenkins (UK)	13	13		0
1981–4	Gaston Thor (L)	14	17	1	2
1985–8	Jacques Delors I (F)	14+3	18	1	0
1989–92	Delors II	17	17		0
1993–4	Delors III	17	18		1
1995–9	Jacques Santer (L)	20	20		0
1999–2004	Romano Prodi (I)	20	26		6
2005–9	Jose Manuel Barroso I	25+2	34		7
2010–14	Barroso II (P)	27	28		1

The Commissioners

Table 3.4 Overview of Early Leavers in EU Commissions, 1958–2012

Hallstein I (1958–62)	Piero Malvestiti	Elected President of the European Coal and Steel Community
	Giuseppe Petrilli	Became president of IRI—Istituto per la Ricostruzione Industriale
Hallstein II (1962–7)	Robert Lemaignen	Resigned January 1962
Malfatti (1970–2)	Franco Malfatti	Resigned from this post to run for office in Italy
Ortolli (1973–6)	Jean-François Deniau	Resigned 1973 and entered the government of Pierre Messmer as Secretary of State for Coopération
	Patrick John Hillery	Elected President of Ireland in 1976
Thor (1981–4)	Michael O'Kennedy	Returned to the Dáil in Ireland
	Claude Cheysson	Became a member of the French Government as foreign minister
Delors III (1993–4)	Able Matures	Became a member of the European Parliament and spokesman for the Partido Popular at the European Parliament
Prodi (2000–4)	Romano Prodi	Campaigned in Italian election; became later Prime Minister of Italy (2006–8)
	Pedro Solbes	Became Spanish finance minister
	Michel Barnier	Became French foreign minister
	Anna Diamantopoulou	Became member of the Greek parliament; and Greek minister of education
	Philippe Busquin	Became MEP
	Erkki Liikanen	Became Head of Bank of Finland (Governor of ECB and IMF)
Barroso I (2004–9)	Markos Kyprianou	Became Foreign minister of Cyprus
	Franco Frattini	Became Italian foreign minister
	Peter Mandelson	Became UK secretary of state for business in Gordon Brown's cabinet
	Dalia Grybauskyté	Became President of Lithuania
	Danuta Hubner	Became MEP
	Louis Michel	Became MEP
	Jan Figel	Became Slovak leader of the Christian Democrats (KDH)
Barroso II (2009–14)	John Dalli	Resigned because of OLAF report on lobby scandal

twenty-member College left to return to national politics before the end of the mandate. During Barroso's tenure, the Commission has seen seven commissioners leave to fill high political posts back home or to campaign for a post in the EP (see Table 3.4).

These reshufflings in the College are indicative of the political profile of today's commissioners. Commissioners are required to remain above national politics while exercising their duties in the Commission in order to maintain independence. However, that requirement has slowly been eroded as the institution has become more politicized. Commissioners no longer cut themselves off from national politics when they move to Brussels. Politics, at both the national and international level, are important for political professionals, as they provide access to the accumulated resources for a career following their stint in the EU Commission. Prodi and Monti both became

Politicization of Selection

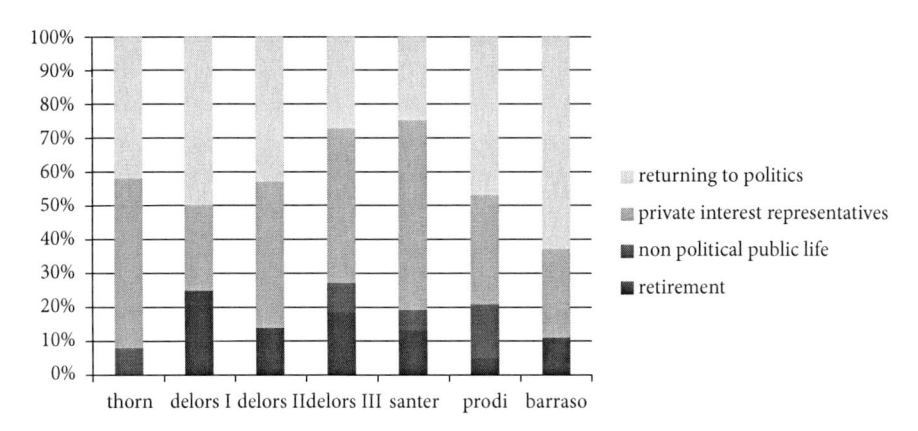

Figure 3.4. Activity After Leaving the European Commission, 1981–2009
Source: Vaubel et al. 2011: 66

prime minister of Italy; Grybauskité became president of Lithuania and Lamy director-general of the WTO.

If not to new political posts, ex-commissioners move to lucrative business and commercial positions (cf. Vaubel *et al.* 2012). They become lobbyists, join pressure groups, or take senior positions with lobby firms and think-tanks. These days, their prestige and experience in European politics, their national and international network contacts, and consequent political leverage and entree to the EU executive, make them very interesting and highly valued after their term of office. In return, they also gain the opportunity to earn the large sums of money denied to them in their careers in government.

The mobility between political and economic areas is a normalized career path for politicians at the level of the member states (Kavenagh and Richards 2003: 192)—but also for commissioners. The percentage of commissioners leaving the Commission in the period 1981–2009 to become private interest representatives varied between 26 and 50 per cent as the data from Vaubel *et al.* (2012: 66) show (see Figure 3.4).

Of the fifteen outgoing commissioners of the first Barroso Commission, eleven took up a corporate executive position or some other activity in the private sector within six months of leaving their Brussels office. The posterior careers of contemporary commissioners indicate that the years spent in the EU executive become a springboard for a next step in a more globalized setting offering new career challenges and opportunities. The connections and political experiences of ex-commissioners have become interesting 'resources' for international companies and organizations. Work experience in the private sector may not be helpful in gaining access to a career inside politics, but experience as EU commissioner apparently does not hinder a new career in the private sector after exiting politics.

77

4. The Commissioners' Executive Leadership

Commissioners, like ministers at the national level, fulfil a range of roles in relation to their policy portfolio, parliament, and the wider public (Marsh *et al.* 2000; Hart and Wille 2006). They must manage upwards to the president, across to their colleagues, and down to the cabinets and the officials. Each relationship is different and creates a different set of calculations about how they should act and for what they should be responsible.

Disentangling the commissioner's roles and relationships leads to a more complete understanding of what is at stake and what political accountability means. The internal role expectations of commissioners, in relation to their policy portfolio, the Commission president, and their colleagues will be explored first, followed by the external role expectations of commissioners—towards parliament, member states, the media, and the general public. The interaction and relationships with their departments and cabinet officials, though an important part of their internal roles, will follow in Chapters 6 and 7. The discussion in this section draws largely on information from the interviews with Commission officials, commissioners, and MEPs.

From personal to political responsibility

'Before the late 1990s the Commission paid little interest to how it might regulate the ethics of its officials and commissioners outside the framework of the Treaty and the Staff Regulations' (Cini 2007: 70). The fierce debate on ethics and integrity that flared up after the high-profile case of commissioner Edith Cresson led to demands for less tolerance, more transparency, and clearer guidelines on commissioners' behaviour. Progressively, commissioners are expected to behave responsibly in their political lives, but also in their personal life and relationships. High travel allowances, unacceptable conflicts of interests, maintaining embarrassing sexual relationships with staff, providing misleading information to tax officers: these are all forms of behaviour which are perceived to be unacceptable. Although the commissioners' personal behaviour may have little to do with their public office and their work in the Commission, they may not only be held to account, but may even be judged on this as well. Today's commissioners need to demonstrate that they have behaved with a 'sense of responsibility' (cf. Bovens 1998: 32–38)—and that they have and will live up to the new 'responsibilities that belong to this office'.[13]

All members of the European Commission are required (according to Article 245 of the Treaty) to swear 'a solemn undertaking' when they take office that they will respect their obligations under the EU Treaties, and be completely independent in carrying out their duties during their mandate. Whereas administrative staff are governed by legally enforceable statutes, it is considered inappropriate to regulate the behaviour of commissioners. There are, therefore, few legally binding regulations that apply to commissioners (Cini 2007: 109). The events leading to the resignation of the Santer Commission, however, exposed a number of structural weaknesses in the Commission that indicated the vulnerability to ethical misconduct (Cini 2007: 70). In response, the Commission has developed a whole set of ethical standards 'to support holders of public office and officials in maintaining high standards of ethical behaviour thereby contributing to the confidence of the public in the functioning of the European Institutions' (European Commission 2000: 3). This range of new initiatives and soft law instruments, part of what Cini (2007: 108–21) calls the Commission's ethics framework, is added to inform and guide (rather than regulate) the commissioners to act in an ethical, accountable, and responsible manner.

On their appointment, each commissioner receives a mission letter from the president that communicates the role and responsibilities of the commissioner. After their appointment, three seminars are organized for the incoming Commission, plus a meeting at which the current president communicates the vision and the working methods of the new Commission. Commissioners receive a Code of Conduct that lays out a compilation of principles and ground rules for commissioners and for their communication with the services. In the declaration of interests that is attached as an annex to this code, each commissioner must declare all the information required to be provided under the Code of Conduct. This includes information on former and current outside activities, financial interests and assets, and spouses' activities. All these documents (mission letter, code of conduct, and declaration) are published on the internet site of the Commission. This ethics framework aims to increase clarity and agreement about standards of appropriate behaviour and to raise the commissioners' awareness that their personal behaviour, too, has become publicly accountable.

From collective to individual accountability

In the founding treaties, the Commission was designed as a uniform political actor, where commissioners had no significant role of their own (Mehde 2009). They were part of the College, a collectivity that, as a group, was responsible for decisions made there. Commissioners were therefore in the first place accountable to their colleagues in the Commission.

Today, collegiality is still the basis of decision-making in the EU Commission, although in a slightly modernized form in terms of its responsibilities. This implies that one of the most important political accountability forums for the

Commission lies, not outside, but inside the EU executive itself—in the form of the College, and not least, the president who manages the dynamics of this collegial accountability. In this inner, closed accountability forum, commissioners have to present, defend, and discuss their policy plans in front of their colleagues. Although this form of accountability remains somewhat hidden, it provides, in theory, an important opportunity to exercise a check on the behaviour of individual commissioners. It is only after dealing with the Commission president, with their colleagues, and all these inner-circle safeguard mechanisms that commissioners face the wider accountabilities of the outside world of parliament and the media.

Collegiality rests on the notion that the executive ought to act as a collective entity, able to maintain cohesion and display political strength. Decision-making as a College, in which all member states are represented, increases the legitimacy of decisions (Seidel 2010: 173). Maintaining a high degree of collegiality is thus treated as synonymous with preserving the supranational character of the Commission (Seidel 2010: 18). Collegiality operates as a 'buckle' that binds the EU executive together (cf. Rhodes *et al.* 2009: 127) and it serves as a shield against accusations of partiality. Although collegiality may give legitimacy to the proposals and decisions of the Commission, it also serves as a security blanket for the EU executive, providing a sense of protection to commissioners and their departments. Collective responsibility of the EU Commission implies that the EP can only require the resignation of the Commission as a whole. Formally, it is not possible to ask an individual commissioner to resign.

The responsibility of individual commissioners became an issue of concern after the resignation of the Santer Commission in 1999. The Commission and Parliament agreed in 2005 on two important innovations that have enhanced the political responsibility of individual commissioners (Judge and Earnshaw 2009: 211, 287). The first, in recognition of the fact that commissioners are responsible for the actions of their Directorates General, explicitly sought to give commissioners more authority over their departments and to be responsible for matters in their portfolio. The second, already discussed earlier in this chapter, made it possible for the president of the Commission to ask a commissioner, in whom the EP has indicated that it has lost confidence, to resign.[14] The fact that the commissioner in question can, in the case of serious political problems, be asked to leave by the president—a personal sanction—has strongly contributed to an 'individualization' of accountability in the Commission. If it comes to 'hang together or hang separately', it has become increasingly clear that in practice, responsibilities have been assigned such that a commissioner will be 'hanged separately'. The agreement with Parliament emphasized the individual responsibility of each commissioner. This 'responsibilization' of commissioners partly addresses the problem of managing collective responsibility.

Collegiality on the work floor

The collegiality principle assumes that 'each Member of the Commission has the right and duty to keep him/herself informed as to the activities of every other commissioner' (Committee of Independent Experts 1999b: 126). Collective responsibility makes 'mechanisms' necessary in the overall accountability structures of the Commission, to ensure that 'commissioners receive information on matters falling within colleagues' portfolios'. In the early years, the Commission used a working-group system. Decisions were prepared in the working groups, but the final decisions on Commission policies were taken by the College, in the weekly meeting. The increasing workload of the Commission demanded a better and more efficient distribution of work. The Commission's meetings were too detailed and time consuming and the members had little time to concentrate on the overall picture. Committed to the principle of collegiality, the Commission decided in the 1960s to apply a more systematic, written procedure and to strengthen the preparatory role of the *chefs de cabinet* (Seidel 2010: 77).

The cabinets and their chefs still play an important role within this collegiality. A commissioner describes it as follows:

> So the challenge for the commissioner is to have the work in the cabinet organized in such a way, and to have priorities established—because you cannot cope with everything—so that when there is something that is important, that I am consulted by my members of the cabinet. So we make a list of priorities. Today we made, we were discussing about the work of the college in the next months and we were discussing what will *not* be our priorities. Of course in the college which is deciding on so many things, the work of the cabinet is so essential and also the system of agreeing con priorities. And also the DG, because we send our priority list also to the DG so that they know in the inter-service consultation what my position is on these issues. So a lot of responsibilities with the colleagues are to be found at the lower levels.

One of the problems in organizing collegiality is that, in the words of a commission official, 'some commissioners have a very large portfolio, but with the same size of cabinets as the others, and thus less time to check the portfolios of their colleagues'.

It is obvious that the organization of collegiality has become an issue in the enlarged Commission. 'As some portfolios have come to be seen as more important than others, the college has grown in size, and also as the power and status of the president had increased, then so has collegiality become less fully attainable' (Nugent 2001: 92–3). But it is not clear if this is solely linked to the move from twenty to twenty-seven commissioners. A commissioner described the College dynamic like this:

> Also before 2004 there were colleagues that learned of most of the decisions through the media. That is also the case because 90 per cent of the decisions are made by the written procedure or by delegation. It is true that if I go through the review of the sheets of information of the decisions that we [the college] have made, then I realize that there are things I have never heard of. It is absolutely true. And we probably don't have to hear about everything, because you can't cope with everything. But what counts for the college is basically that what is still discussed, is that where we have no agreement on, because the previous levels could not do it.

It is the responsibility of the president and his office and the SG that the College act as a body—to give meaning to collegiality and to make it work— to ensure that due process is followed, to manage the collegial decision-making. In the Barroso II Commission, this has resulted in the emergence of a new phenomenon: so-called 'commissioners groups'—in which one commissioner takes the lead over colleagues, with a view to developing cross-cutting policy initiatives—and orientation debates, which help to transact business in the College. A commissioner described this as follows:

> I appreciate the role of the President, who is a good manager and who actually managed to have consensus-based decision-making in this twenty-seven member state college and not to vote; and it has worked, much better than was expected. But it takes a lot of preparatory work and most discussions are held mostly before the college meeting. I cannot say that I am not taking part in a discussion when I don't have the time to discuss it during college meetings. I can go to the regular preparatory meetings and give my opinion. There is sometimes a heavy fight. And I cannot imagine this is working any other way. Perhaps we should have more discussions at the college level. But if you bring all decisions to the twenty-seven member body you will probably end up, very soon, in not deciding anything.

It has meant that the current Commission, in the words of an interviewed official, is 'much more concentrated around the figure of the president and much less collegiate'. The weekly meetings of twenty-seven commissioners are much shorter than in the past: 'So even if the College is bigger, they talk less, with Mr Barroso and a few "engaged commissioners" tending to take the decisions of the moment.' A commissioner explained it like this:

> Of course with twenty-seven, it means that the role of the president is much bigger. By definition, if you have a bigger group, then the role of the leader is much bigger. In a way easier, if you have six then you are obliged to listen to every word. If you have twenty-seven ... fortunately the college meetings are not that long at all. We don't speak that much. So you don't see the size back on the length of the

discussion. But I am aware of the fact of a more presidential system, the bigger the college is.

The five-year political guidelines and the more coherent political outlook of the College may have helped the management of collegiality. And the need for collective endorsement of decisions also made it necessary to tighten 'college discipline'. Voting by simple majority has become less acceptable within the Barroso colleges, and since the introduction of the one-country-one-commissioner-rule, it is felt that 'no legitimate vote could be held in a system where a majority of member states representing only a minority of the population can outvote the rest' (Broin and 2010: 50).[15] In the opinion of a *chef de cabinet*:

> Structurally diluting from twenty to twenty-seven doesn't change fundamentally the dynamic of collegiality. What more has changed is the personal grip of the president, which is a positive thing, and which means that there is a lot more central direction. But that is not a function of the enlargement, but of the style of the President.

Over the past decades the EU executive has demonstrated different patterns in the way it practised collegiality. Collegiality is perhaps an ideal which came closest to being achieved under the EEC presidency of Hallstein. In the current constellation, this principle has been relaxed to accommodate present-day constraints in arriving at a workable solution. The practical difficulty of keeping up with the portfolios of twenty-seven colleague commissioners in the current EU Commission, the evolving presidential style, the increased degree of 'individual responsibility' of commissioners, are all factors that have contributed to a 'modernization' of the *collegiality principle*.

The policy role: from officeholding to political direction

Given that today's commissioners carry a general responsibility for the policy area and the issues that are included in their portfolios,[16] a more politically explicit role is expected of them when it comes to the development of policies in their portfolio.

Commissioners are expected to play a leading political role in establishing priorities, by being actively involved in developing and monitoring the annual work programmes and by directly involving themselves in the preparation of these new proposals (cf. Nugent 2001: 110).[17] Senior officials interviewed almost unanimously attributed this role to the commissioner. In the opinion of a director-general: 'it is normal that when there are choices about policy, the responsibility for the choice is with the commissioner'. Other senior officials appreciated an even more visionary role of the commissioner: 'You have to have somebody who has a clear vision, who knows what he want. Who is political ... You need a politician, more than someone who wants to do a desk officer job.'

Providing political direction was also how commissioners perceived their own role. As one phrased it:

> The Commissioner must have a vision of his portfolio. I have created vision here. This is what is expected from you. You can also call it the political guidelines. It is based on your knowledge, your experience, the reading of books, articles, attendance of meetings.

Another commissioner specified his/her added value along these lines:

> I bring a different perspective on what is being done; and the feeling of responsibility. I bring also the political dimension; and my knowledge that I have acquired through my working life. ... And also what I bring is the capacity and curiosity to learn, to be more open. ... I sometimes make things difficult when I ask: 'can we do it?' I then hear: 'No Commissioner.' And then, I ask 'Why not?' If you come to a place like this it is: 'Mais non, ce n'est pas possible. It is always done like this, so we cannot do it in another way.' So I then ask 'why not?' Why can't we do it in another way? Why is it not possible? And that is my added value too.

New policy proposals allow room for political entrepreneurship and create the opportunity for political profiling. Commissioners are expected to decide on the preferred strategies, to allocate and commit resources at the macro level, and to sell policy proposals externally.

As a commissioner, it is essential to produce 'visible' results, or as one put it: 'if you are only producing ideas and vision and achieve nothing, then you are no good'. But they acknowledge that it is a role that is performed within certain limitations: 'Our role is to be strategic. But having worked a long time in the executive at the national level, I also understand the practical constraints.' Comparing it to his long-standing ministerial experience in one of the national executives, a commissioner described it as follows:

> The scale is different if you compare it to national executives. And the decision-making here is quite complex. But a successful executive is not measured by its declarations but by its achievements. So you must take things as they are and try to promote your vision.

The use of new policy technologies, like policy guidelines, work programmes, and activity-based management, provided a framework that was settled, shared, and accepted by commissioners and senior officials, and that explicitly emphasized a pronounced role for the commissioner in setting political priorities. The materialization of these new style governing arrangements has not only cumulatively highlighted or articulated a more political role of commissioners but, as one of the heads of cabinet noted:

> I think that since the introduction of activity-based management in the Commission, there has been a strengthening of the centralized control in resource allocation and priority setting, and this had consequences for the roles of individual portfolio commissioners. There is now more control from the centre, by the secretary-general and the president.

The five-year political guidelines provide a framework (for the annual work programmes and activity-based management) that has articulated and constrained the policy role of the commissioners. This is not the only aspect that has changed the expectations of the commissioner's role; as the activities of the Commission increasingly come under public scrutiny by the EP, commissioners are expected to retain the prerogative and to bear responsibility for matters in their portfolio.

Parliamentary role: from procedural legitimation to political answerability

What does parliamentary control and accountability mean for commissioners? The EP has played a major role in securing the political accountability of the EU executive.

The link between commissioners and the EP starts with the hearings. These hearings serve as 'rites of passage' and have an ex ante function in parliamentary oversight. Given that nominees for commissioner come from different parliamentary traditions and may have different interpretations of their responsibilities, these hearings offer an opportunity for communicating accountability expectations. MEPs question the commissioners-designate on their views of appropriate behaviour, test their responsibilities and future answerability requirements to the EP, and ensure that the visions of the candidates do not conflict with the views of the MEPs. The new investiture procedures instituted by the EP have contributed to a new form of 'credit' (or legitimacy) of commissioners during their mandate. Today, a commissioner is no longer appointed on the basis of bureaucratic hierarchical rank, but has been vetted by the EP.

Parliament has ample opportunity to scrutinize the performance of the Commission, to become informed, to hear explanations, and to have assurances placed on the public record when the commissioners appear before the EP. This accountability process, in which questioning and explaining play a major role, can help teach commissioners to identify and learn certain key elements and requirements of politically responsible behaviour. By being compelled to address political concerns and priorities by parliament, commissioners become aware of, and can try to live up to, the expectations of these accountability holders.

The growth of new accountability mechanisms means a stronger democratic legitimacy for commissioners but also for their policy proposals. Many commissioners are obliged (as a result of the introduction of co-decision brought about by the treaties) to include MEPs in their negotiating strategies. This can be useful for the Commission, as a director-general explained:

> We need them and it works extremely well. It is an extra source of power for the Commission. It gives our proposal more strength. If we bring a proposal to the Council, we can say we have negotiated this with the European Parliament and they are behind it as well. It is not just our crap, it is crap supported by parliament. That is a good tool.

Apart from gaining the Commission more clout, it also validates its work, as a director-general made clear: 'What we do here in the Commission has become more democratic, and has an increased legitimization attached to it now that it is debated in parliament'.

Even before the Lisbon treaty came into force, commissioners and their officials regularly appeared in parliament and before various committees, submitting to questioning and some degree of scrutiny. Even then, although not always strictly required, commissioners and their officials were prepared to answer and to 'render account' to parliament. As one Commission official said:

> MEPs mostly do not refrain from asking a lot of questions. On our side, we are required to give an answer to every single request (even the stupidest) fast. This is what I call democracy and accountability. It surely happens at the national level in some countries, but rest assured that we are controlled by a democratic body.[18]

Commissioners believed their individual responsibility made it necessary to meet their accountability obligations by subjecting themselves to the regular scrutiny of the EP; they regarded it as a constructive aspect of their duties and as a normal part of their portfolio. Going to parliament also offered an opportunity to explain positions, policy directions, raise issues, attitudes, and operations; i.e. as an information-gathering process it can be beneficial to both commissioners and MEPs.

The empowerment of the European Parliament has thus introduced a new dynamic into the work of the commissioners (and no doubt by extension, the Commission's services). Commissioners meet at regular intervals with parliamentary committees to discuss, defend, and advocate Commission policies. In the words of a Commission official:

> I actually welcome this scrutiny, because it reminds us that policy isn't just a theoretical exercise. It might be harder to work through the politics of the Parliament, but it is much healthier.

This does not imply that the relationship with parliament is always appreciated, or that each Commission official values the new form of oversight.

Commissioners differ in the extent to which they take pleasure in or see the significance of parliamentary work and to which this work complements or offsets (or encroaches on) the other aspects of the commissioner's tasks. Whether commissioners enjoy appearing before a parliamentary committee depends on the type of committee and what is at stake; whether they are merely supplying information, or whether are facing a critical interrogation; and whether their reputation (and that of their department and service) is on the line. As a senior official commented:

> We feel the existence of the European Parliament, mostly, not all the time but most of the time, through its negative effect. Every time we have to go there, I wonder what is the added value. It is democratically correct, but it has no contribution to the substance. In our field MEPs do not ask the right questions; and the end result is a complete fragmentation of our policy; they make our policies worse. It is counterproductive. A parliament is there to control, not to do micro politics.

Some Commission officials question, therefore, the role and relevance of the EP. A senior official described it like this:

> In the EP there are brilliant people, of course. But as a group, as an institution, is there anything new, innovative in that they have proposed? We go there to explain what we are doing, how we are doing it and why we are doing it. We see it as a formality. The place where we really do the cooking is in the Council. There we have high flying discussions.

Other Commission officials are more circumspect in interpreting the influence of parliament: 'Before the EP was not taken seriously. It is now seen as a partner, although there are sometimes large differences, our view is that Parliament is our natural ally. Not on all points but in general. But they are giving us a hard time, by putting the Commission on the edge.'

The Commission can no longer impose its decisions without a fuller consent by the governed. Policies are not struck in isolation inside the EU Commission. As a consequence, commissioners and their officials spend much more of their time explaining situations, setting out the various options and trade-offs, and persuading. Under the Lisbon Treaty, the EP has gradually evolved into 'the institution that aims at protecting the common interest'. This can lead to some frictions and contestation of decisions between the Commission and the EP, but this is the way things work in any government.

Representation of interests: national, sectoral, and party-political

In their solemn undertaking, commissioners swear that 'they shall neither seek or take instructions from any government, or from any other body'. This always gives rise to the question of whether and how far commissioners may take instructions from political parties, or engage in political activities, and if they are allowed to represent views advocated by a political party of which they are perceived to be a passive member, if not an active one (Van Gerven 2009: 122).

The informal norms and culture in the College deem a blatant promotion of national interest to be inappropriate conduct for a commissioner (cf. Nugent 2001: 116; Joana and Smith 2002: 114; Egeberg 2006b).[19] Commission officials have indicated that, by and large, pursuing national interests is deemed unacceptable in the Commission setting. 'COREPER-like behaviour' is considered to be rather counterproductive for commissioners and it would mean an immediate loss of credibility with other colleagues. But that does not mean that articulating the interests or 'feelings' of the member states is illicit. A commissioner phrased it as follows:

> This is a delicate matter. We are not allowed to defend national interests, but you are welcome to express the knowledge of your own country. There has to be a delicate balance. I always try to give information about the opinions in my country. The Commission president has never strongly asked anybody to refrain from doing this.

The increased portfolio responsibility and the enhanced role assigned to the European Parliament in the daily policy-making process compels commissioners to operate more often as defenders of the European, rather than national interests, in their particular portfolio (cf. Egeberg 2006a: 63). The 'political-ness' varies with the nature of the portfolio of the commissioner. Responsibilities for Community policies (agriculture, competition, external trade) can take a more *political* approach. Commissioners that are in charge of more intergovernmental policy-making need to go to work more cautiously and 'technocratically' (Joana and Smith 2004: 30).

As the Commission's relationship to the European Parliament continues to grow, both as regards the appointment of Commissioners and their daily policy-making, there is reason to believe, argues Egeberg (2006b), that more emphasis will be put on their 'political' role in future colleges. Major political groups in the EP have made it clear that they also aimed to improve the coordination of political action inside the Commission. The leader of the Liberal group in the EP indicated that his political party intended to work more closely with its Liberal commissioners. Until now, they had only met once a month in a Brussels restaurant, which he said was 'nice, but you don't make much policy with that'. Meetings with the commissioners will now be more streamlined and more regular, he said. Politicization according to political-party lines can also have benefits for the Commission, as a commissioner pointed out:

> At the national level you always have the support of the governmental coalition; and it is clear which parties belong to the opposition; and of course there is the possibility that in a next election that you will be outvoted. But here in the European Parliament there is so much uncertainty. You never know what kind of attitudes and opinions will rise in parliament. I for myself cannot complain because there are a lot of reasonable parliamentarians dealing with my portfolio. But separate from this personal side, clear coalition politics at the institutional level would make the work easier

Under the leadership of Prodi and Barroso, commissioners have appeared to be cultivating progressively more explicit political roles as members of political parties. According to the Commission, members of the Commission are 'politicians' carrying out a political function, who, while honouring the obligations imposed by their function, 'remain free to express their personal opinions quite independently and on their own responsibility' (van Gerven 2009: 122 n. 22).[20]

External relations: from telling to selling

Commissioners are, in fact, the Commission's main external representatives for the policy areas which fall within their portfolios (Nugent 2001: 111–12). They maintain relations with the Council, the other EU institutions, the member states, non-member states, and a vast range of outside interests that are part of their remit. The Commission's public communication suffered for a long time from the fragmentation of political authority, a pervasive technocratic mindset, and a lack of adequate staffing (Meyer 1999). But the rise of the internet, the mushrooming of news channels, and the changed role of media have turned the Commission, like many governing organization, into a 'fish bowl'. Public accountability, transparency, and public opinion have emerged as the new parameters of executive power. Within these new constraints, selling policy, PR, and media communication have become progressively more relevant to the effective operation of the European Commission.

Some commissioners are very keen on the presentation and public relations of their plans, which can also have positive effects for their departments. As a director-general noted:

> The commissioner has very good political instincts ... She is very effective politician in the way she sells. We now do much more communication and press work than we are doing before. This is in the interest of the commissioner. But this has also positive aspects on what we are doing. We realize that what we do is much more visible, because we are in the press.

The plan to improve the Commission's communication record has resulted in an internally renewed organizational structure, and externally in a more media-driven communication policy. This reorganized communication department works closely with the political centre of the Commission in order 'to allow' commission officials to properly convey the agreed political message. The aim was a 'stronger centralization in the delivery of messages', one of the interviewees explained. Internal reforms have professionalized and centralized the communication function, evidencing the use of professional media-management since 2004 in the Barroso era.

Today's commissioners have their own spokespersons. These spokespersons, who are required to hold a different nationality than the commissioner they work for, communicate with the press, but also with lobbyists and NGOs; they decide which messages to convey, which tools to use, what the emphasis is on, and so on. Apart from the commissioners, the spokespersons are the only persons who speak on the record in respective policy areas. These people have become *the professional mouth* of the EU executive. The spokespersons are not members of the cabinets, but are answerable to the upper Commission spokesperson.[21] This can sometimes cause tension, as one spokesperson noted:

> I have special consideration with the commissioner because I am supposed to speak on his behalf. At the same time the one who decides whether I am promoted or not is the head spokesperson. Being in the structure like this, we have a strong feeling of belonging to a corps. This is very much in the spirit of the institution itself; the Commission is a college, and we do not take individual decisions. I have a special relation with my commissioner, but I would never do something that is contrary to other commissioners. So I consult my colleagues from the service. We do not follow blindly what the commissioner says. That makes it more cumbersome.

It indicates a stronger centralization to convey a coherent and understandable European message and to leave behind 'a past of leaks'. The credibility and the success of the EU project, as another spokesperson said, 'can work only if the Commission is perceived as the EU's government'.

Besides relations with the press, communication with the public at large has become increasingly centralized in a politicized EU Commission. After the talk about the 'democratic deficit' at the start of the 1990s, 'the Commission was confronted with legitimacy expectations appropriate to a political, not a technocratic institution' (Meyer 1999: 635). The idea that the EU should no longer impose its decisions without fuller consent of the governed took hold. It was to widen the scope of its accountability practices by rendering account to a wider public forum. In the words of an official: 'the Commission is making a real effort to communicate with the citizens'.

Especially after the seismic political shock in 2005 (following the French and Dutch referenda), the notion of 'bringing Europe closer to its citizens' was becoming an ever more pressing theme. To narrow the communication gap between the EU and its citizens, the Commission has taken polling—by means of the Eurobarometers—to new heights. The launch of a whole series of citizen-friendly deliberative and participatory initiatives, focus groups, and transnational debates to engage in a dialogue with European citizens was indicative of the search for new ways of developing *responsive* EU policy-making (Boucher 2009) 'to regain the confidence of the public', as a commissioner emphasized. The Commission has been trying to get citizens to be more supportive of the 'European project'.

The Commission's concern with 'external communication' indicates a break with the past, when citizens' consensus on the output side was largely taken for granted. In its new approach, the Commission acts as if it were a representative body of the people, serving the collective interests of the European polity.

5. From Technocrats to Politicians

This chapter has shown how executive political leadership has changed under the influence of EU treaty reforms since the start of the 1990s. In its original design, the Commission was intended as a technocratic body, with a mission to defend the interests of the EU as a whole. Inevitably, treaty reforms in the last decade have contributed to a greater politicization of the Commission. New rules, procedures, and arrangements have allowed for more 'top–down' political control of the EU legislative over the EU executive. These developments reflect the increasing trend towards *normalization* of the European Commission, in which the political level has become more political—both in its institutional design and in its elite behaviour. Table 3.5 summarizes the features of this new normalization of the political executive. Several trends are indicative for the normalization of this part of the Commission.

The normalization of the Commission's political executive

FROM TOP–DOWN TO BOTTOM–UP POLITICIZATION
Politicization of the Commission's political executive (officeholders) is one of the faces of normalization. Giving political direction is the focal point of any political executive, particularly when it comes to policy-making. At the national level, ministers are the ones who 'give leadership to public organization', but in the EU it was long assumed that it was not possible 'to locate any such instance of political control' (Page 1997: 112).

The Commissioners

Table 3.5 Politicization of the Commission's Political Executive

Actor	Governance Demands	Institutional Design	Behavioural Implications
EP	Political control	Increased powers in appointment EU Commission, more powers of scrutiny, greater influence policy-making by Treaty Maastricht, Amsterdam, Nice, and Lisbon	More parliamentary activism and stronger and more politicized relationship
President	Political control	The possibility of the president 'reshuffling' the allocation of tasks in the College during a Commission's term of office	Internal organization more centralized
	Political responsiveness	The Commission president is nominated by the European Council with qualified majority (not unanimity anymore) and that 'the nomination shall be approved by the European Parliament'	Willingness to work with European Parliament
	Political accountability	Question Hour once a month State of the Union	'Presidentialization'
Commissioner	Political control	Priorities and policy guidelines are set at the political level	Overseeing those parts of services and DG that fall within commissioners' remit
	Political responsiveness and legitimacy	President allocates portfolios, confirmation hearings by EP, political guidelines	'Ministerialism' working within political guidelines
	Political accountability	Framework Agreement 26 May 2005, signed by presidents of Parliament and Commission: Political Responsibilization	Personal portfolio responsibilities Increasingly accountability to president and parliament
	Political responsibility	Code of Conducts, oath	Conceptions of integrity and moral responsibility of public office

It would not be correct to say that previous Commissions were not political, as these were also marked by highly politicized episodes. A relatively bureaucratic phase during Monnet's tenure was followed by a more political one under the leadership of Hallstein. After Hallstein's reign, there was a return to the bureaucratic nature of Commission activity, until Jacques Delors introduced new 'leadership' and significantly politicized the work of the Commission (Christiansen 1997: 77). The widely held image of the Commission as a technocratic institution appeared less established in reality.

The huge range of national interests, the system of comitology, the politicized issue networks, and patronage in the appointment system all combined to make politics an integral part of the work of the Commission. This form of politicization in the earlier days of the Commission had a strong 'bottom–up' character. Politicization in its current form is top–down in nature. It is based on the political reforms in its institutional design; and it enables stronger political control over the executive—in terms of appointment and policy-making—a more pronounced emphasis on political representation and responsiveness, more weight being attributed to political guidelines, and an identifiable coalition to govern for a limited period.

INCREASED PARLIAMENTARY CONTROL OVER THE EXECUTIVE
Politicization is also apparent in the relation of the Commission with the EP. Through its augmented powers, the EP has become able to place greater informal and formal constraints on the EU executive. The investiture procedure of the EP has granted a greater say to MEPs regarding the selection of the EU executive. Its changed recruitment procedures and new demands have affected its composition and have resulted in new expectations that have increasingly shaped the executive responsibilities of the Commission. The increased powers of the European Parliament have provided more legitimacy to the office of commissioner, creating a new mix of mechanisms that stressed the political and that sharpened the accountability of the Commission to the EP.

FROM TECHNOCRATIC TO CORE POLITICAL EXECUTIVE
The political level of the Commission is expected to perform an active and effective role in developing its policy proposals.

- The EU Commission president has been increasingly able to mobilize power resources that allow him to govern more independently, which has led to an enhanced steering capacity of the centre of this EU executive. It has made the Commission more presidential.
- The Commission's five-year guidelines define the commissioners' political missions and give a plain indication of the programmatic objectives during the commissioners' term of office.
- Activity-based management—and the Commission's strategic policy planning process—have contributed to clearer expectations of the role and responsibilities of commissioners.
- The responsibilities and obligations of commissioners have been increasingly codified.

The work of the commissioners is increasingly shaped by values such as political responsiveness, responsibility, and answerability, and is highly focused on developing a more pronounced relationship with external actors such as the European Parliament and the European public. Commissioners

The Commissioners

are embedded in a web of accountabilities and different forums—parliament, Court, investigative and audit bodies, but also the media, civil society, and interest groups—all play a part in a continuing process of rendering accountability. Enhanced political professionalism in the EU executive can therefore best be understood in terms of new democratic challenges where the highest political personnel of the EU executive need to address the problems of a modern democratic polity.

This has also placed greater pressure on commissioners to control their administrative directorates. These emerging new political accountabilities, among other things, have fed new demands for structural reforms in the Commission's administration. What the impact of these reforms has been on the cabinets and on the top level in the bureaucracy will be the topic of the next chapters.

Notes

1. European Parliament's Question Hour, 14 Dec. 2010.
2. Graham Bowley, 'EU Commission Chief Vows to Push for Change', *New York Times*, 24 Nov. 2004.
3. The right of MEPs to ask questions was already incorporated into the Treaty of Rome. Since 1973, the Council has agreed to take questions from MEPs as well, though unlike the Commission, treaty law does not require the Council to reply.
4. Still, it was the European Council that decided on the candidacy of the president—at that time, José Manuel Barroso. Basically, then, the election of the Commission president was the object of a kind of co-decision between the European Council and the European Parliament.
5. A campaign, in which European political parties mobilized against Barroso's renewed candidacy in 2009, by means of the 'Anyone but Barroso' website and blog, illustrated how this new provision has given the election procedure more visibility.
6. With the introduction of this Q&A session MEPs were hoping to liven up the parliament's proceedings and add a touch of spontaneity.
7. The address attracts comparisons with the annual speech by US presidents at the beginning of each year.
8. EU is a member together with Canada, France, Germany, Italy, Japan, Russia, the United Kingdom, and the United States. Barroso has attended the summits since Gleneagles in 2005. Since the Lisbon Treaty, he attends these together with the president of the European Council.
9. Barroso pressed member countries to name female candidates when he was putting together his second college.
10. Formally established by the Maastricht Treaty, but building on evolving practice: in Feb. 1981, after the new Thorn Commission had assumed office, the EP, on its

Notes

own initiative, voted on the investiture and programme of the new Commission (Nugent 2001: 83).
11. The European Parliament has codified the practice of hearings for commissioners designate. The practice of hearings does not appear in the treaty but since Jan. 1995 has been political practice between the European Commission and the Parliament (Judge and Earnshaw 2008: 205).
12. The Treaty of Lisbon (copying the draft Constitutional Treaty) states that, as from 2014, the Commission should comprise a number of commissioners corresponding to two-thirds of the number of member states, chosen according to a system based on equal rotation among the member states (Article 17 TEU = article I-26, Constitution). In order to satisfy one of the demands of the Irish people—in view of the second referendum (held on 2 Oct. 2009) on the ratification of the Treaty of Lisbon—the European Council of Dec. 2008 declared that, provided that this treaty entered into force, a decision would be taken to the effect that the Commission should continue to include one national of each member state. Hence, the current situation of one commissioner per member state will remain applicable, despite the wording of Article 17 of the TEU.
13. The fact that Rumania Jeleva, the Bulgarian commissioner designate, faced allegations and accusations about her financial interests, and that she lacked the right experience to be the commissioner in charge of humanitarian aid, made her an impossible candidate in Barroso's II line-up. Any undeclared financial interest would put Jeleva in breach of European Parliament rules and European Commission rules (as a commissioner).
14. EU health commissioner John Dalli resigned on 16 Oct. 2012 in a dispute about tobacco lobbying. The Maltese commissioner stepped down after Commission president Jose Manuel Barroso told him that OLAF, the EU's anti-fraud office, had filed a report on him. A Commission spokesperson has insisted that it was Dalli who voluntarily resigned. Dalli hinted in the media, however, that Barroso made him resign. <http://www.maltatoday.com.mt/en/newsdetails/news/national/WATCH-I-expected-Barroso-to-support-me-Dalli-20121020>.
15. If representativeness of the Commission is judged from the perspective of the numerical width of the member states in terms of population, the current constellation might be thought to fall short and thus lack legitimacy.
16. Commissioners also carry a general responsibility for the work in those parts of the services that fall within their remit. This is responsibility of a general overseeing kind—ensuring that the services are working well and are fulfilling their various obligations. The responsibility for day-to-day affairs lies with the directors-general.
17. In the case of routine matters or the consolidation of existing policies, there often is no need for the active involvement of commissioners. The matter can go through the College meeting fairly quickly or, more likely, be dealt with by a delegated or written procedure, with the role of the commissioner remaining limited. But if a new legislative or policy proposal is at issue, the commissioners and their cabinet staff engage in deliberations with the service before the matter is referred to the College.

18. This and the next quotation stems from a Commission official's blog, posted in Apr. 2009, about the workings of accountability in the Commission. The quotes from this blogpost summarize quite effectively the opinions that the Commission officials and officeholders communicated during the interviews <http://eurotechnocrat.blogspot.nl/2009_04_01_archive.html>.
19. Although there is officially no link between commissioners and member countries, they have always functioned as easy and efficient links between the Commission and the national political circuits of the member state governments. At the same time the main loyalty of a commissioner 'should' lie with the Community interests.
20. Margot Wallstrom, the EU communications commissioner, supported French Socialist presidential candidate Segolene Royal in her blog. Dutch commissioner Neelie Kroes openly supported Angela Merkel in her bid to become chancellor just days before the German elections. During the last Commission, Italian prime minister Romano Prodi actively campaigned in the general elections in Italy while still head of the Brussels executive; and Greek commissioner Anna Diamantopoulou also took a leave of absence for domestic elections and then resigned after winning a seat. Louis Michel, the EU's commissioner for development in Barroso I, took unpaid leave to campaign in Belgium's federal elections. Although he positioned himself so as not to be elected, the European Parliament's development committee asked the Parliament's legal service to assess whether his participation violated the treaties. Michel claimed that politicization of this kind is part of reconnecting the Union with its citizens.
21. The spokesperson for each portfolio is designated by the spokesperson of the Commission, in agreement with the commissioner in charge of the portfolio. The only restriction is that the commissioner and the spokesperson have to have different nationalities. They are appointed according to the Commission rules governing the composition of cabinets.

4

From National Agents to EU Advisers: The Chefs of Cabinet

> Speaking truth to power remains the ideal of the analysts who hope they have truth, but realize they have not (and, in a democracy should not have) power.
>
> (Wildavsky 1987: 12)

1. The 'Europeanization' of Cabinets

Ahead of the confirmation vote of the new Commission in the European Parliament, as the commissioners-designate prepare for their hearings, they also begin to pick and pencil in officials for the key positions in their 'cabinets'—their teams of (personal) advisers. Assembling a cabinet is no easy feat: commissioners must deal not only with a stream of CVs, but also with lobbying by national governments, civil society groups, political parties, and friends keen to get their favourite candidates into the top jobs. All this creates a feverish atmosphere, as Europe's elite competes for the 200 jobs in the cabinets of the new European commissioners. For a hopeful few, it is also an excruciating period of waiting as new commissioners hand-pick the six or seven members of their inner team with whom they will work over the next five years.

One of the most important choices and crucial appointments of the incumbent commissioner is that of his or her closest adviser: the head of cabinet (or *chef de cabinet*). The head of cabinet holds office in close proximity to the commissioner and has various responsibilities ranging from gatekeeper, senior policy adviser, and key political strategist to manager of the commissioner's office; he or she must cope with the political and policy pressures that face the commissioner and often operates as a personal adviser to the commissioner.

Part of a commissioner's success depends on the personnel selected for these key jobs in the cabinets. The rules on putting together commissioners' cabinets are, however, strict. Each commissioner is allowed no more than six advisers, plus one expert.[1] Nationality plays a big role; not more than four members of a cabinet can be of the same nationality as the commissioner, the chef and deputy-chef must have different nationalities, and the spokesman cannot come from the same country as the commissioner. Cabinets were historically portrayed as national enclaves (Michelmann 1978; Cini 1996; Spence 2006c), but since 1999, new rules apply that have forced these to become more 'European' in outlook. These rules were accompanied by a redefinition of the roles of cabinets, designed to draw sharper lines of responsibility between cabinets and services, in response to the accusations of favouritism and nepotism to which the cabinet structures in the EU Commission had given rise.

What did this mean for the work of the *chefs de cabinet*? Did these reforms affect the selection of the heads of cabinets? Did they bring a different perspective to the qualities required to lead the cabinets? The discussion that follows will take a closer look at aspects relating to the backstage leadership of heads of cabinets. The chapter starts by outlining the key features of the cabinet system. Then it describes the new rules for cabinets introduced under the presidency of Prodi (1999–2004). It will take a closer look at recruitment and roles of cabinet heads in the post-reform Commission. And it explains how the evolution of the cabinet system has 'professionalized' the qualities of these top officials in the EU Commission.

Cabinets: the commissioner's inner circle

Cabinets occupy a central position in the Commission's organizational system. They are responsible for a vast majority of decisions taken by the College and perform a crucial role at the political–bureaucratic interface in the Commission. Cabinets are advisory arrangements that aim to enlarge a commissioner's capacity and to extend his or her reach. They are, like the French cabinets, the US spoils systems, the Privy Council Office in Canada, and the Cabinet Office in Britain, important nodes of what Savoie and Rhodes have called *court politics* (Rhodes *et al.* 2009; Savoie 2009). The *court politics* metaphor refers to a differentiation and competition between different (clusters of) advisers to senior executive leaders, as well as to dynamics of the resultant interaction between executive leaders and their advisory groups (Hart and Wille 2012).

The commissioner's need for staff support derives from a situation of 'bargaining uncertainty' (Dickinson 2003). Policy choices emanate from opaque interaction and bargaining among multiple executive actors (Hart and Wille 2012). For a policy plan to gain the necessary support, negotiation is vital. Commissioners are engaged in negotiation and bargaining with other actors whose political resources they need in order to achieve their political and policy goals. Since commissioners cannot do this alone, they require the assistance of 'agents' who can act in their name.

In all cabinets there is an internal division of labour, with each cabinet member being expected to provide general support for the commissioner and also to assume responsibilities for particular aspects of the commissioner's work. They alert their commissioners to issues, problems, and opportunities on the horizon, and they provide the commissioner with advice and information about the relative advantages and disadvantages of different policy options (cf. Meltsner 1976; Wildavsky 1987). At its heart, advice is what Gill and Saunders (1992: 6–7) characterized as 'a method for structuring information and providing opportunities for the development of alternative choices for the policymaker'.

In a real sense, for most commissioners the problem is not too little, but too much advice. Not information, but *attention*—the capacity to process this information—is the chief bottleneck in organizational activity, and the bottleneck becomes narrower and narrower as we move to the top of an organization. The real problem in these advisory groups is, therefore, not so much obtaining information and advice, but structuring it; i.e. reducing the sea of information to a coherent whole, which means organizing and staffing (March and Olsen 1989; Rudalevige 2005). Providing for the bargaining and advisory needs of the commissioner, and managing the internal advisory machinery of the commissioners: these are key tasks for the heads of cabinet.

From private to political offices

In the early days of the Commission, it was agreed that cabinets should consist of two members (*chef de cabinet* and a deputy) plus a secretary and a typist. These officials, acting as personal aides and advisers, were to assist the members in their daily tasks, preparing opinions on policy matters and generally keeping them informed of events elsewhere in the Commission (Seidel 2010: 22). It was not surprising that most heads shared the same nationality as their commissioner: another task was to maintain contact with government institutions in their commissioner's home country and to advise the commissioner on the possible implications a policy proposal could have 'back home' (Nugent 2000; Spence 2006c). Cabinets acted as go-between, and hence the staff of the cabinet tended mainly to have the same nationality as the commissioner. Cabinets constituted 'a quasi-national element in the supranational administration' (Seidel 2010: 22).

The role of the cabinet rapidly gained influence during the 1960s and 1970s (Seidel 2010: 82). Because of the collegiality principle, commissioners were expected to remain informed on other policy areas. As their workload grew, however, they increasingly delegated this task to their cabinet heads, on whom they relied for advice and assistance. The *chefs de cabinet* started to meet before the Wednesday sessions of the College to discuss specific problems, and these meeting gradually increased in importance.

Meanwhile the commissioners introduced two categories of decisions. A-category decisions would appear on the Commission's agenda for the weekly meeting if one of the commissioners wished to discuss the topic further. All other cases were classified as B-category items and it was left to the *chefs de cabinet* to take a decision. Cabinets became responsible for the vast majority of decisions taken by the college, which (in the case of non-contentious decisions) were worked out either during special meetings of the cabinet heads or by means of the so-called written procedure (Spence 2006c: 67). This resulted in an increasing influence of the cabinets and their heads (Seidel 2006: 78).

Concomitant with this growing influence, the number of cabinet members also expanded, both in seniority and calibre (Spence 2006c: 62–5). Commissioners began detaching high-flying civil servants from the DGs to serve in their cabinet, and the cabinets thus gradually acquired a major influence over the day-to-day running of the Commission. Cabinet jobs became top jobs in the Commission. Heads of cabinet do not dirty their hands with resource management and budget. They have the opportunity to work closely with the commissioner on the challenge of defining the European policy agenda, which offers them a chance to test their political skills at a high level, and clear prospects of 'parachutage' into a managerial post in the services when their period in the cabinets comes to an end.

Shadow bureaucracy: 'too many pimply boys with too much power'

Gradually, the central function of the cabinets came to resemble that of their national counterparts, namely to serve as the *political eyes and ears* of their boss (Donnelly and Richie 1997: 43; Nugent 2001: 123). They became the gatekeepers to the commissioner's desk; they provided an additional source of and channel for policy advice; they were responsible for monitoring, on behalf of the commissioner, the activities of the other departments in the Commission to coordinate policy development; and they controlled the work of the administrative services attached to their boss—in other words, they were meant to act as a bridge between the Commission's political and administrative layers.

Under both Delors and Santer, complaints were rife in the Commission's permanent services that the cabinets had become outposts for member governments and that the cabinet system had the features of a parallel bureaucracy. Cabinets interfered far too aggressively and meddled directly in the work of the services and the DGs (Nugent 2001: 129; Peterson 2004: 24). Relations between cabinets and permanent Commission officials are 'inevitably delicate' writes Spence (2006c: 71, 73) because: 'Cabinet members, including the most junior of them, often reworked and rewrote the work of the services.' As a result, 'the distinction between policy guidance and interference is not always clear-cut' and 'the risk of conflict between cabinet and permanent officials is real'.

The burgeoning power of cabinets was partly the result of the weakness of the Commission's administration, which was growing increasingly fragmented (Seidel 2010: 83). Policy proposals were often prepared and discussed in one DG without consulting other DGs and a cabinet meeting was often the first occasion on which a proposal was discussed across different DGs. Skilful cabinets became 'shadow cabinets' for their commissioners' administrations, undercutting the autonomy of the services. As a former cabinet member during the Santer Commission related: 'too many pimply boys had too much power'.

Cabinets also played a pivotal role in the Commission's staff policy: they monitored the national balance of staff and put forward candidates especially for the senior positions (Seidel 2010: 83), and they began to interfere in appointments, down to the most junior management levels of the Commission. The influence of the cabinets and the exclusiveness of the relationship between the commissioners and their cabinets triggered problems and jealousies, as some cabinets attempted to control access to their commissioner to the detriment of the directors-general.

Discontent with the cabinet system led to criticism from parliament, from the secretary general, from the Committee of Independent Experts—whose report triggered the mass resignation of the Santer Commission in 1999. In this report, cabinets were saddled with much of the blame for the Commission's 'distant, needlessly hierarchical and bureaucratic approach'.

A cap on cabinets: new rules, new roles

One of Romano Prodi's injunctions on taking office—after his appointment as president—was to reduce the powers of the cabinets. He reduced the maximum number of cabinet members from nine to six per commissioner. He insisted that each cabinet had to be staffed multinationally and include at least three nationalities, apart from that of the commissioner. This marked a significant break with the past, when each cabinet was required to include only one non-national (who would then often be marginal players within cabinets) and cabinets were often national enclaves.

Prodi also believed that the cabinet–service relations were unsatisfactory (Nugent 2001: 129) and that a clearer definition of the roles of cabinets and services was needed. The Prodi Commission introduced a 'code of conduct', which was already in the making in the Santer Commission. This code of conduct set out the responsibilities and reporting requirements for Commission staff, including political advisers. Prodi also handed back some powers to the secretary-general—the head of the Commission's services.

This new allocation of the roles of cabinets was designed to draw sharper lines of *responsibility*; to constrain the possibilities for favouritism and nepotism to which the cabinet structures gave rise; and to achieve 'a clear distinction between political responsibility and the managerial function' in order to clarify the relationship between the advisers and the permanent staff. The aim was to avoid the excesses of the cabinet system, 'by keeping them in the political process and out of the day to day running of the services' (Spence 2006c: 71), and to limit 'parachutage'—cabinet members from outside the Commission were to be treated on the same footing as regular applicants. The goal was to achieve cabinets that were reduced in size and multinational in composition.

The new rules were embedded in a broader package of political and administrative reforms with regard to the functioning of the Commission. What, precisely, was the impact of these new rules and the broader changes on the recruitment and the role expectation of *chefs de cabinet*?

2. From Political to Professional Offices

As indicated earlier, the first and perhaps most important appointment which commissioners make is that of their head of cabinet. How political leaders put together their advisory teams and set them to work usually reflects their personal leadership style (Herman and Preston 1994; Preston and Hart 1999; Burke 2007: 176–7). We know, however, very little on how commissioners appoint their close advisers. It seems, therefore, best to assume that the selection and appointment of heads of cabinets and deputy heads, like the recruitment for other executive positions, may be understood as a marketplace determined by the rules and *procedures* that govern the appointment process, by the *demands* of the 'selectors', and by the *supply* of candidates that are eligible for this office (cf. Norris 1997). Figure 4.1 gives a schematic representation of the three elements that are relevant in the hiring choice of commissioners for their (deputy) heads of cabinet. A comparison of the interview data with earlier studies indicates that the demand and supply of heads of cabinets can be progressively characterized by an emerging professionalism.

The selection procedure: personal handpicking

From the early years on, the recruitment of *chefs de cabinet* by commissioners was marked by a number of unwritten rules and a good deal of leeway with which to interpret them. Who was nominated as close adviser, what tasks

From Political to Professional Offices

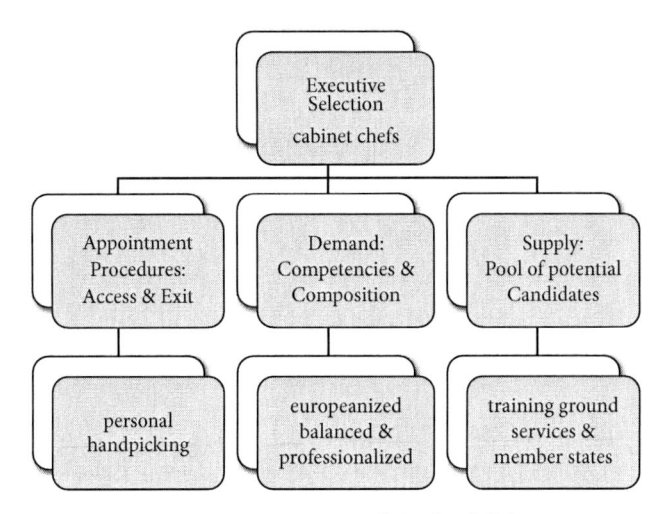

```
                    Executive
                    Selection
                  cabinet chefs
      ┌───────────────┼───────────────┐
  Appointment      Demand:         Supply:
  Procedures:   Competencies &  Pool of potential
  Access & Exit  Composition      Candidates
      │               │               │
   personal      europeanized    training ground
  handpicking     balanced &      services &
               professionalized   member states
```

Figure 4.1. Recruitment of Heads of Cabinet

were expected of them, and what balance to strike between national and Commission officials, depended on the commissioner's approach to leadership (Joana and Smith 2004: 32–6).

Today, commissioners' hands are tied by the rules that are set by the president of the Commission. The commissioners 'handpick' the heads of their cabinets within the confines of these rules, often helped by recommendations of others. But there is still a good deal of leeway in the selection of cabinet heads.

'Basically how it [the selection] works, is that it is very much up to the discretion of the commissioner' says one of the heads of cabinet; 'the only criterion is, that it is a person that has the commissioner's full trust'. Compatibility with the commissioner is an obvious condition for the selection of (deputy) heads of cabinet—given the close working relationship. In the past, commissioners could rely on a cultural connection of compatriots which served as a source of trust, leading the choice of their heads of cabinet. Today, the candidates for the post need to gain the confidence of the commissioner on their own, unfettered by their nationality.[2] The cumulative effect of the denationalization of the cabinet system is that 'personalization' has become a clearer hallmark of the selection process than in the past.

The demand side: European and balanced

In the new post-Prodi regime, all commissioners were required to appoint a *head* or *deputy head* from a member state other than their own. Most commissioners appointed one of their own nationals as head and a non-national as *deputy* (see Figure 4.2). The new regime, in place since 1999, has led to a considerable

103

The Chefs of Cabinets

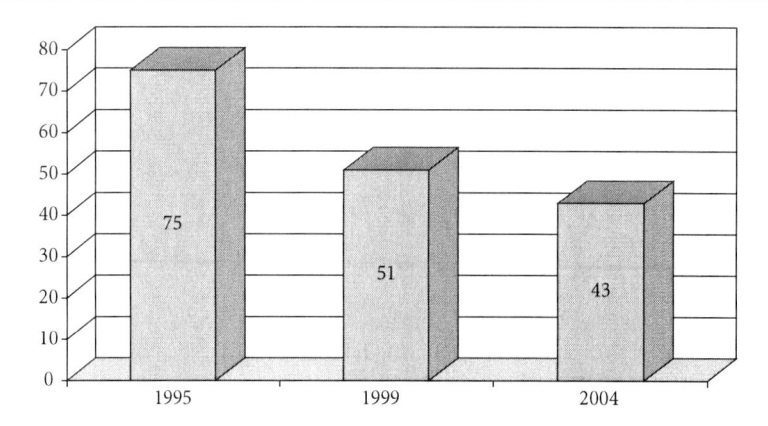

Figure 4.2. Cabinet Members having the Same Nationality as the Commissioner
Source: Egeberg & Heskestad 2010

'denationalization' of commissioners' cabinets as empirical data from Egeberg and Heskestad (2010), displayed in Figures 4.3 and 4.4, reveals. The composition of the cabinets is shown to be highly multinational, marking a significant break with the past. In 2004, 96 per cent of the cabinets were made up of more nationalities than prescribed by the rules. For the first time, the cabinets were staffed by a majority of non-compatriots of the respective commissioners.

These changes in composition made the cabinets more diverse and increased the legitimacy of the cabinets, as a former chef of cabinet indicated:

> To be effective, a commissioner must be able to work with, and learn from, colleagues with other nationalities, to take account of the susceptibilities of others. If the commissioner and the cabinet are all of one nationality, it will probably be easier to agree among themselves, but they will be unlikely to convince everyone else. ... The reason for having deputy heads of cabinets or deputies of the same nationality is not to influence the Commission, but to communicate back with the country of origin. Commissioners who try to lock themselves up, usually find themselves locked out.

The appointment of a *chef de cabinet* or deputy of a nationality other than that of the commissioner, and the achievement of a gender balance are the formal constraints modern commissioners have to comply with when staffing their cabinets.[3] The strong assumption underlying the 'denationalization' was that a cabinet cannot be effective in its work unless it contains a geographical balance in its staff composition. An adequate geographical representation is necessary to provide the cabinets with credibility and to assure a sense of Union ownership of the cabinets.

Does this mean that nationality has become irrelevant, since this denationalization of the cabinets? One of the unintended consequences of

From Political to Professional Offices

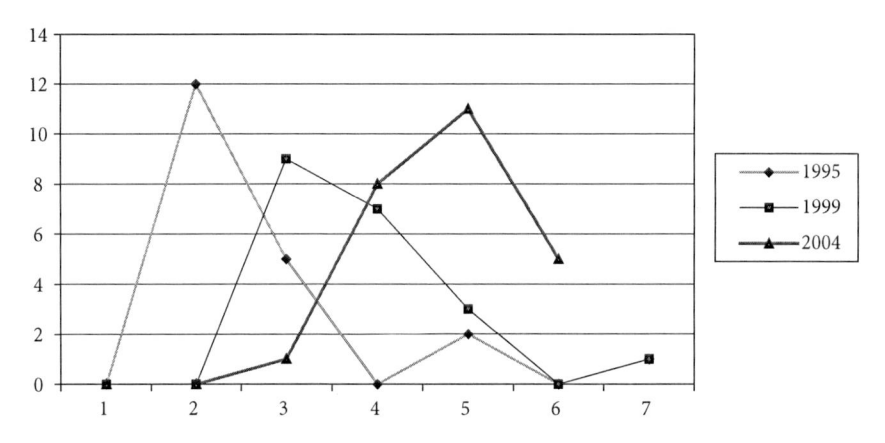

Figure 4.3. Number of Nationalities Represented in the Cabinets
Source: Egeberg & Heskestad 2010

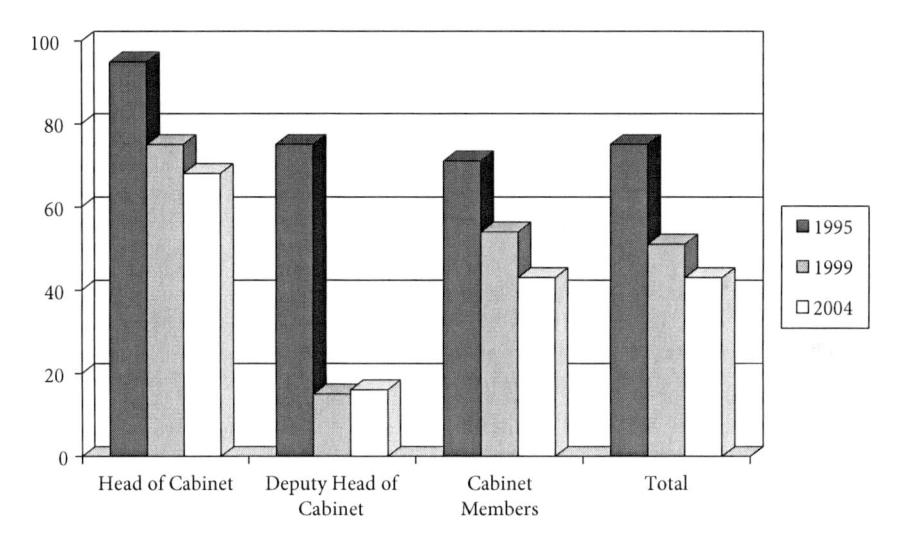

Figure 4.4. Cabinet (Deputy) Heads and Members with the Same Nationality as the Commissioner

'denationalization' was that 'national balance' has become a far more relevant factor. These days, after the lists of new cabinet members and spokesperson have been published, the first assessment immediately gauges the heads of cabinets, the deputies, the cabinet members, and the spokespersons in terms of nationality (and gender) balance: how many French, German, and UK names are represented in the cabinet ranks, and are the numbers representative of the EU population and the political weight of each member state?

Respecting national balances in the cabinets has become an issue. A serious disequilibrium would lead to distrust of the cabinets. A wide geographical spread is a means of maintaining the Commission's independence, a shield against partiality and patronage.

The demand side: professional qualities

Professional qualities and competences of cabinet members have today become a focal criterion for selection, especially because of the caps on cabinet size. Given the restriction on the number of staff, and the need for commissioners to implement the political guidelines of the Commission, it is important to be supported by *chefs de cabinet* and staff professional enough to ensure that the commissioner can 'deliver'. Competency requirements have, thus, become progressively important. Relying on experienced advisers in the cabinets puts commissioners at an advantage in the backbiting world of Brussels deal-making. Cabinet heads must, therefore, be able to advance their agendas in a complex political environment and be effective. A cabinet head clarified: 'You need to be fast and clear and most of all emotionally intelligent. Like in any management position, you have to be able to identify trends, be able to motivate people, to make things happen, to drive change.' And a colleague chef specified the necessary professional profile of a head of cabinet as follows:

> It has to be someone who is a generalist, who can—whatever the situation is—quickly analyse what the situation is, what the challenge is, what the positions should be, how best to tackle it. What is essential is a bit of analysis and negotiation, because you have to defend the commissioner's position; ... And you are going to need interpersonal skills. You need to have good management skills, good communication skills; and a good way of knowing how to use the available resources to get the best possible result.

Commissioners need staff who have a good understanding of how the Commission works (cf. Nugent 2001: 122) and who can help to form a bridge between political aspirations and practical realities. Also, in the pre-Prodi cabinets, 'inside' knowledge played a significant role in the selection of cabinet heads and deputies. But since Barroso ruled that the commissioner's cabinets were to include at least three permanent officials, the group of *chefs de cabinet* and deputies drawn from the Commission's administration and seconded to the cabinet for a five-year term has increased. The new recruitment provisions aimed to limit the extent to which outsiders were 'parachuted', over the heads of existing civil servants, into senior posts of the Commission bureaucracy.[4] And the emphasis on 'insider' recruitment was an indication of the significance attached to professionalization in the handling of policy issues. As a head of cabinet noted:

> It makes a lot of sense for a head of cabinet to know the 'House' very well. The Commission is a big animal with a lot of intricate ways of doing things. And it is

good if your head of cabinet knows that and (and is someone) who can play the system to the advantage of the commissioner.

Another cabinet head described it like this: 'a varied cabinet drawn from different sources and with experience in the Brussels machinery is the best way forward'.

The supply side: cabinets as training grounds

The selection of cabinet heads is not only determined by demand, but also by who is available for this office. From the two pools that were traditionally important—the member states and the Commission services—the number of cabinet staff recruited from outside the Commission has declined in favour of officials who have been seconded from within the services of the Commission. The movement between cabinets and services was already an established practice in the earlier days of the Commission (Nugent 2001: 122) but has increasingly gained in importance, since certain posts in the cabinets are regarded as development positions, and are used as 'stepping stones' to (senior) management posts in the services.

Cabinets have become a training ground, since they give a broad overview of the operations of the Commission on both an administrative and political level. Officials who have been seconded and who have worked in key positions in the cabinet possess a better chance of reaching the top of the bureaucratic hierarchy than their colleagues in the services. Their time in the cabinet is an important springboard on their way to heading a section or subdivision or direction in the services. As a director-general indicated when asked about the competencies and experience required for his position: 'you need to be an "old hand" in the Commission. Exposure to the cabinet level is essential, because you need to have experience at the political level.'

Multinational staffing and an increased emphasis on internal recruitment are the two trends that summarize the personnel policy of heads of cabinet. The secondment to cabinet units of Commission officials has a dual effect; it brings insiders into the cabinet system, on a temporary basis; and it allows personnel recruited from within the Commission to become acquainted at first hand with the political aspects of the work of the EU executive. What is more, personnel drawn from the Commission administration usually have weaker ties to any particular national constituency. The flow from central positions in the bureaucracy to central cabinet positions, and vice versa, has promoted institutional integration between the political and administrative levels (cf. Egeberg 2003). It has given the Commission a more markedly supranational structure. But what are the implications of the changes for the roles cabinet heads are expected to perform?

3. The Art of Shadow Management

Chefs de cabinet remain largely invisible and function 'as the commissioner's shadow', as one of the cabinet heads described his role during the interviews. Several roles entail crucial responsibilities: these officials function as 'omnibus advisers' to the commissioner; they lead the commissioner's cabinet; they are instrumental in setting the commissioner's policy agenda; and they often act as brokers. The success of the commissioner depends to a large part on the 'shadow management' of the heads of cabinet. Comparison of the material from the open-ended interviews with descriptions of the work of cabinet heads in the literature in the pre-reform period makes it possible to conclude that the basic role elements of cabinet heads have not changed radically, although there have been some interesting small shifts in the way these executive officials perform their roles.

'The power to be all things to the commissioner'

Cabinet heads are expected to brief the commissioner on a range of issues, to provide a link with the director-general, to coordinate proposals going to the commissioner from civil servants in the services, and to help the commissioner to perform his or her parliamentary role, including debates and answering questions. They may sit in on Commission meetings and need to represent their commissioner in all sorts of forums inside and outside the Commission. They maintain links with the other heads of cabinets. Some commissioners travel a lot and the heads of cabinet need to 'keep the shop', as one of the heads phrased it, while the commissioner is away.

'I am the right hand of the commissioner and we have to be like one' noted one of the cabinet heads in an interview. The relationship between commissioner and their head of cabinet depends upon a high degree of *delegation* and on the knowledge and competencies of those to whom responsibilities are being transferred. A cabinet head must, therefore, have standing, experience, and sway.

'Being all things' to the commissioner, most cabinet heads are likely to have a good knowledge and understanding of their commissioner's views in order to successfully pursue the commissioner's agenda. This implies a *personalization* of the relationship between the head of cabinet and the commissioner. To understand how the commissioner's mind works, the *chef de cabinet* meets and communicates with the commissioner on a regular basis. A head of cabinet described the relationship with the commissioner like this:

> We know each other. And I think I understand her mind very well. To get a reliable sense of what she really wants requires an investment in terms of explaining the commissioner the issues. And that does take time and effort.

The Art of Shadow Management

Such skilfulness can only be sharpened and polished through ongoing interaction. Some *chefs de cabinet* meet with their commissioner every morning for thirty to forty-five minutes—when the commissioner is in Brussels—to review the day's agenda, to brief the commissioner, to bounce ideas around, and to consider emerging issues. Other heads snatch short moments with their commissioner between meetings, when they move round the building, conducting business in brief unscheduled chats.

Even more critically, acting as the commissioner's closest adviser entails more than simply reading the mind of the commissioner well. The cabinet heads must also know which information needs to be 'surfaced up', when it is time to pull the boss in, and when to raise the caution flags, or red lights, if necessary, to urge the commissioner to rethink some options. 'Speaking truth to power' demands timing and diplomatic skills. It also calls for a sense of candour, readiness, and requires adroit use of the right moment and awareness that that disagreement may well be equated with disloyalty. But as one of the heads declared: 'loyalty to a person and whatever they say or do, that's the opposite of real loyalty, which is based on telling someone what you really think and feel—your best estimation of the truth instead of what they want to hear'.

Loyalty is often thought to be a hallmark of the relationship between political officeholder and adviser, and in the past sharing the same nationality was considered to be an important indicator of this. But in today's multinational administration, this type of loyalty seems no longer to be the most important credential for appointment. Personal allegiance is difficult to measure in a job interview; and competence and commitment seem to have become more essential qualifications. Candidates with demonstrated credentials for backstage leadership, and who are expected to deliver outcomes consistent with the preferences of the commissioners, are considered better qualified for this position than those with nothing other than personal loyalty going for them.

In the course of mapping the roles of a head of cabinet, it became clear from the interviews that certain standards for doing a professional job were broadly shared. A premium was placed on interpersonal trust and staying in the commissioner's shadow, being practised in the art of conversation and regularly listening to others, remaining calm under pressure, and working long hours.

Managing the inner circle: personalization and pluralization

The organization of the 'inner circle' has important implications for the role the heads of cabinet play and for the quality of the advice commissioners receive. Some cabinets operate on a fairly hierarchical basis and have a cabinet head closely directing the work of other cabinet members. Most communications between cabinet members and the commissioner are channelled through the head, and perhaps the deputy head as well. Although orderly, such a hierarchy can isolate a commissioner, with a key aide such as the head of cabinet serving as a powerful gatekeeper, controlling the access and filtering (limiting) the flow of information and advice to the commissioner. Other cabinets operate with a more open structure in which the position of the head of cabinet is less overbearing. A head of cabinet noted: 'It is teamwork. We meet every day, unless the commissioner is travelling. We have a flat hierarchy and I am very proud of it. That of course depends also on the commissioner.' The way commissioners articulate their agenda, or have a personal interest in particular policy dossiers, sets the tone of relationships with the cabinet (and also the service). In such cabinets the commissioner and staff enjoy regular and direct access to discussions on all policy issues. As a head of cabinet explained:

> This cabinet is very informally organized. If they want to see me, they come to see me. If they want to see the commissioner, they go to the commissioner. Very informal, very direct, non-hierarchic.

The advantage of a flat organizational structure over the hierarchical approach is that the commissioner is directly in touch with the relevant policy people; it creates an opportunity to obtain information from a variety of different people, who, moreover, do not suffer the frustration of being denied direct access to the boss. This can be taken too far, however: in an open matrix model that allows an almost constant channelling of controversy to the commissioner, the decision system will not be able to perform its most crucial function, that of preventing overload. It is forging this balance that is perhaps the most critical test of the head of cabinet's management abilities.

Due to the multinational staffing, the cabinet heads also have to deal with a wider diversity and pluralization of advice. The views in the cabinets have become less monolithic due to the 'denationalization' of the cabinets. Insiders have observed that a more diverse range of views tends to be reflected within individual cabinets than in the past as result of the reforms. A head of cabinet pointed it out as follows:

> It is our strength that we have more nationalities in the team. It allows more flowers to bloom within the cabinet: more ideas, more perspectives. And that is a generally positive thing ... it has enriched primarily the diversity of the internal discussion; you got more perspectives, more sensitivities you can test out. We have a Spanish member in our cabinet and a French. When an idea comes along, without going outside the cabinet, we immediately have a pretty good sense of how it is going to play with a larger group of member states. That is good. But what you lose is the homogeneity of administrative culture. In the old days there

was a very focused team all schooled in the *member state* administrative culture. They all had the same expectations and they fit together from day one.

Diversity within the cabinets increased concomitantly with a growing pluralization of advice. The key challenge for heads of cabinet is to integrate these multiple sources of advice and information to give coherence to the commissioner's policy priorities.

Managing policy vertically and horizontally

Preliminary negotiations related to the decisions to be put to the College mainly take place at this level. Process management, policy coordination, creating opportunities, and building political support to back a policy proposal, both inside and outside the Commission, are the main functions that were and still are performed at the level of the cabinets. In one of the interviews, a head of cabinet described this policy role as follows:

> There are two main functions of the head of cabinet. One is the portfolio issue; there you have to help the commissioner to formulate a policy and a policy line. And you have to work with the director-general. You act as a go-between. There is a direct relationship on a day to day basis as a go between, to make sure that the director general is implementing the policy line laid down by the commissioner ... The other is the non-portfolio issue to follow everything that is happening in the College, everything that is being decided, to help the commissioners formulate positions, and to defend these positions in all the preparatory meetings.

Formally, the College has to approve each legislative proposal, decision, or opinion that emanates from the Commission, a process that, at least in theory, gives each commissioner a right to influence European Commission proposals. It is, however, the preparatory work of the heads of cabinet that largely maintains this principle of collegiality.[5] Ahead of the weekly meeting of the College, the heads of cabinet come together. At the very least, these meetings ('Hebdo' in Commission-speak) expose the areas of conflict and disagreement, and frequently result in a decision. During these meetings, the collegial meeting for the current week is prepared down to the tiniest detail so that as many contentious issues as possible between the commissioners can be cleared out of the way. As an integral part of this 'editorial work', a commissioner's cabinet frequently interacts with other cabinets in order to register disagreements and pre-empt objections that might be raised at the level of the College (cf. Nugent 2001; Spence 2006c).

Heads of cabinet and their staff are, therefore, key in shaping this collective responsibility. They must inform their commissioner about the activities and plans of his/her colleagues; and they have to make sure that the colleagues of the commissioner are informed about the commissioner's plans. They play a coordinator role by ensuring that a policy initiative does not conflict with the interest of other commissioners. If it does, they may need to sort it out and find a resolution. They must stop proposals of the colleagues that are either inadequately prepared or politically unacceptable. And they must send inadequate policy proposals back into the administration for modifications, whether polishing or substantive change. On the other hand, an agreement at the level of the heads of cabinet (point B) is virtually equivalent to a full Commission decision. 'In a whole range of areas it is, therefore, the *cabinet head* or staff, on behalf of their Commissioner, who actually settle the decisions that the College then formally endorses, or for which the College has given them delegated powers' (Stevens and Stevens 2001: 235).

Head of cabinets have an important role in the policy process. Horizontal coordination remains one of the central concerns for today's cabinet heads, especially as policies have become increasingly 'cross-cutting'. Actual involvement in non-portfolio issues depends, however, on the workload of their own portfolio. Commissioners and heads of cabinet of large portfolios complain that they simply do not have time to get involved in the portfolios of others. With the importance that is attached to realizing their commissioner's policy agenda, the heads of cabinets increasingly assign priority to vertical coordination, that is, the making and monitoring of proposals that fall within the remit of their commissioner's portfolio.

Managing the twilight zone: blocking, brokering, and bargaining

In their work within the 'horizontal' dimension of policy, where various players interact across organizational boundaries, heads of cabinet play an important *brokering* role. This involves bargaining positions among cabinet offices in cases of policy overlap and policy conflict, with the aim of resolving differences before an issue is taken to College. Heads of cabinet must, thus, be able to sustain relationships and negotiate successfully in a terrain of multilateral ties with shifting responsibilities and fluid roles.

Cabinets remain twilight zones—areas of ambiguity between the political and administrative level, usually containing some features of both. In this form of 'court politics' there is a shift from formal hierarchy and decision-making (in the College and the civil service) to informal process. Formal meetings are supplemented by informal and casual meetings with other cabinet members, civil servants, and a variety of other persons involved in policy matters. This informality includes such features as irregularity, lack of agenda, no minutes or even the chance of a clear outcome, and changing membership. Elusiveness is a common feature of these informal processes, which are all about providing quick and inventive access to the levers of power, with the aim to get things done, to see results, to predigest, to concert, to bypass; i.e. to manage the political-bureaucratic environment.

Cabinet heads need to be good at making things work. They need to bring it all together and get it through the process. As a former cabinet head related:

> It is often thought that Cabinets block the work of the Commission. But the whole idea of blocking is misplaced. To get ideas accepted, commissioners usually do not have to build a majority, it is the opponents that have to mobilize opposition, and the time to do that is usually not available. The key to success lies in anticipating, and taking account of possible objections, and incorporating acceptable solutions in the proposal from the start.

The location of the *chefs de cabinet* gives them important resources: information and relationships. They have access to information about agendas and policy opportunities, as well as knowledge of the positions and interests of stakeholders. They are linked with key players both within the executive and the wider political environment. In their dealings with others, they carry not only the authority of the commissioner but also the power to control information flowing to the commissioner. With sufficient skills, expertise, and delegation from the commissioner, they may be very effective players within the executive interactions. In the words of one head of cabinet: 'It is a very powerful role.'

Managing accountability: power without responsibility?

The heads of cabinet undertake innumerable informal executive activities linked to the formal work of running the college. It is in this area of the Commission that politics is visibly invisible. They head what is called the 'private offices' or the commissioner's 'team' and have no authority and no power and no justification for exercising or wielding executive authority. Despite increased accountability for the Commission as a whole and a thickening of political–bureaucratic accountability arrangements in and around the Commission, the commissioner's cabinet, in terms of these formal arrangements, appears to form an 'accountability-free zone' that is premised on the notion that the cabinet staff is an extension of their commissioner. But does this mean that heads of cabinets belong to a class of 'untouchables', one that bears power without responsibility? To whom are heads of cabinet accountable, and for what?

The pattern of accountability relationships for heads of cabinet appears to be a function of the nature of their task. The nature of the heads' task is fairly non-routine. Their work is relatively fluid, affording extensive autonomy and little structure or formalization in terms of accountability. They face diverse, changing, and occasionally contradictory performance expectations, which complicates the accountability picture for the heads of cabinet. In the interviews, they are clear about the priorities that need to be assigned, and about the commissioner–head relationship being the paramount source of their authority. *Chefs de cabinet* feel first and foremost answerable to their 'political' bosses. As 'surrogates' of the commissioner, they act on their authority and within the parameters authorized by them. All expectations are weighed against this primary focus.

Consistent with this alignment, the interviews refer to a mixture of professional and informal types of accountability. The work affords a high degree of autonomy and is subject to the discretion of heads of cabinet who are expected to base their decision-making on internalized norms of appropriate practice. These norms of accepted practice are derived from professional socialization, personal conviction, organizational training, or work experience. A head of cabinet worded it like this:

> There is a lot of autonomous action that has to be done by the cabinet and the head of cabinet. The trust element is crucial. If I had to ask the commissioner about everything that I do, things would not work. You have to have agreed parameters with the commissioners within which you have to work autonomously.

Informal expectations among commissioners and their heads of cabinet regarding the organization of advice, their working relationship, and the administrative practices are key factors in fostering what Romzek and Utter (2012) have called informal accountability. This accountability emerges from the unofficial expectations and discretionary behaviours that result from repeated interaction among heads and commissioners. A head of cabinet explained it like this:

> In any working environment you need to have 'rapport' with your superior. What is important is a professional match of expectations—even though the commissioner comes from a country I did not know very well. But the fact that s/he worked in an international organization helps. We have a shared understanding of the limits of delegated responsibility.

Hence informal accountability operates as a means of organizing the cooperation and maintaining accountability to another. The challenge, like in formal accountability systems, is ultimately linked to a system of rewards and sanctions (Bovens 1998; Romzek 2000). Consequences refer to what happens to cabinet heads as a result of reviews of their performance (whether formal or informal). This concept can embody both rewards and sanctions. Staff can face negative effects to their reputations, decreased job mobility, less involvement in policy deliberations, and less access to informal meetings because of poor performance. One long-time cabinet chef emphasized: 'There is no doubt if the commissioner wants to sack me tomorrow, this could happen.'

4. From National Agents to Professional Advisers

Commissioners rely, during their time in Brussels, heavily on their political advisers, and especially on their heads of cabinet. These individuals can, to some extent, counterbalance a commissioner's shortcomings and can be used to strengthen their performance (Nugent 2001; Spence 2006c: 68). 'It is no coincidence', observes Spence (2006c: 61), 'that the most effective commissioners have traditionally been those with the best staffed and organised cabinets'.

The role of the heads of cabinet has traditionally been to organize advice in terms of personal and portfolio demands. This role has evolved as a response to the wider institutional and policy imperatives facing the Commission as a whole. New governmental demands for a more democratically accountable, effective, efficient, and less fragmented EU executive, with clear policy priorities and coordination, have been translated into reforms and new rules. New patterns in recruitment and role expectation of cabinet heads have become discernible. An overview of these trends is summarized in Table 4.1. These trends allow the following conclusions about the commissioner's closest advisers to be drawn.

The normalization of the Commission's cabinets

For a long time, commissioners' cabinets were viewed as exotic arrangements, institutionalized forms of political influence, comparable to those found in the Napoleonic systems of Belgium, France, and Italy, that acted as 'the eyes, ears and possibly also voice of the politician within the bureaucracy' (Page 1997: 13).

The commissioners' cabinets have evolved in line with a trend in many Western executives towards the development and greater use of advisers, ministerial staffing, and political or policy advisory arrangements. The seemingly inevitable general tendency to park small, easily manageable, and personally loyal groups of personal or political advisers outside mainstream bureaucracies has become an increasingly common characteristic of governance in the member states (Spence 2006c: 61 Eichbaum and Shaw 2007; Savoie 2008). It has caused the cabinets of the Commission to become less abnormal compared to the operation of national executives.

Two developments have contributed to an increased normalization of the cabinets and a shift in the role of cabinet heads. First, denationalization rules have directly influenced the organization of the cabinets. Second, the wider suite of institutional reforms targeting other sites in the Commission indirectly had a spill-over effect on the operation of the cabinets and their heads.

Table 4.1 Modernization of the Cabinet System

Demands in Governance	Institutional Design	Behavioural Implications
Denationalization of the cabinets	Cap on number of 'nationals' in cabinets;	Personalization of selection Pluralization of advice
Clarified political–bureaucratic responsibilities	Code of conduct	Awareness raising of restricted role of the cabinets: supporting the policies developed by the president and the commissioner
Stronger capacity to provide political direction over policy-making	Major political programme focusing on key priorities Instruments for exercising control	Politicization
Professionalization of services Demand for integrated and high-quality policy advice	Administrative reforms Increased coordination of strategic areas within Commission	Professionalization Hybridization: internal recruitment of cabinet heads from the services

BEYOND NATIONAL CLUSTERS AND CLAIMS

Originally, heads of cabinet were personal collaborators of the commissioner and the cabinets were intended as private offices and a vital point of contact for the member states. Cabinets were national *clusters* within the Commission, staffed by fellow nationals of the commissioners, and access point for *claims* from the member states. The introduction of denationalization rules has made the composition of cabinets more permeable, less captive of seconded officials from national capitals, and more diversely 'European'. As a result, finding an advisory structure that *personally* suits the commissioner has grown to be relevant. The inner circle of the commissioner has become more heterogeneous since the denationalization of the cabinets. This *pluralization* of advice has been a new challenge in the backstage leadership of heads of cabinets.

HYBRIDIZATION OF THE CABINETS

Denationalization of the cabinets has gone hand in hand with the emergence of a Commission that is more focused on 'delivering' a Europe of results. This focus on a more effective management of the policy-making process implies that the cabinets were expected to concentrate their work above all on supporting policies developed by the commissioner. The task of implementation was to be left to the departments. The role of cabinets was to be fulfilled with a stronger professional focus on increasing the policy capacity of the political level—but without direct political involvement in the services.

As the scope, pace, and complexity of the advisory task has increased under the pressures of modern policy-making, so, too, has the need for professional support—and thus the appointment of professionalized staff to key cabinet positions. Advisers who are both qualified and committed to their commissioner's policies have become vital to a commissioner's pursuit of policy objectives in the Commission. The political complexity of policy problems and the more demanding political context asked for more *political management* on the part of the heads of cabinets. Political management, including the relationship with the European Parliament, with the member states, and the major lobby groups, monitoring public opinion, and media management, has continued to gain importance.

Crunched between a more politicized college and a more professionalized administration, there was an increased need for heads of cabinet boasting both political and professional skills. A large part of the cabinet head appointments were drawn from the existing ranks of the Commission's civil service, which ensured that commissioners could rely in their cabinets on skills and established bureaucratic networks that could increase their politically effectiveness. In many ways, the best credentials for working at the political–bureaucratic interface, is someone who understands the detailed workings of the Commission, but is fully attuned and sympathetic to the College's political and policy objectives. This practice has contributed to what Peters *et al.* (2000: 13) described as a *hybridization* of advisers, referring to the increased blending of political and professional spheres. The leadership of commissioners, like that of many political executives, is grounded in the advisory arrangements woven around them, and particularly in the role of their heads of cabinet. Sometimes the latter are even more influential backstage than are the commissioners in the front lines. Both need, however, the input of *director-generals* to achieve their goals. Their role and responsibilities will be the subject of the next chapter.

Notes

1. The European Commission president can have twelve members in his/her cabinet that must represent at least three different nationalities.
2. Not surprisingly, many of the heads of cabinet from the Barroso I Commission followed their commissioners to their new posts in Barroso II. Of the fourteen commissioners from Barroso I who remained in their Brussels office, many kept most of their previous team in Barroso II. Of the former twenty-seven heads, twenty-four returned from existing cabinet positions, and fourteen were already heads. In many ways, the high number of returning heads, and other returning cabinet officials, is an indication of the value that is attached to receiving advice from people they trust.
3 The ingenuity with which these new restrictions are evaded by commissioners makes it clear that considerable determination and alertness on the part of the president of the Commission is needed to ensure that the rules result in a long-term change. An internal note distributed in 2009 by the services of the Commission president

underlined for the new composition of cabinets in Barroso II that men outnumber women and many cabinets were too nationally oriented, with an all-too-evident predominance of officials from the same country as the commissioner who selected them. Commissioners were being asked by the Commission president to make their cabinets more multinational and gender-balanced.
4. Cabinets served traditionally as stepping stones for rapid advancement of national officials to senior post in the Commission's services. Parachuting was criticized by staff unions for causing demoralization down the ranks of the services.
5. The principle of collegiality necessitated the cabinet system (Ross 1994, 1995; Seidel 2010: 74).

5

From Mandarins to Managers: The Senior Civil Service

> We will make merit the absolute precondition for promotion.
> (Neil Kinnock, 19 January 2000[1])

1. Professionalization of the Administration

Leadership successions are high-stakes processes (Hart and Uhr 2011: 5) and this also pertains to the Commission's management merry-go-round. The periodic decision to reshuffle batches of its senior management from one department to another is preceded by periods of speculation among top officials in the service willing to solve the unknowns in the equation. Who is going to be appointed at the head of what department? Which senior managers are up for a transfer to fill the vacant posts? And what positions will be unaffected by the scores of new management transfers?

The system of job rotations is in line with the Commission's mobility rules, under which senior managers are required to rotate jobs after spending five years (or in exceptional cases, seven) in a particular position. The creation of this 'musical chairs' system for senior management positions allows the Commission more flexibility in hiring, firing, promotion, and demotion of senior managers. It was part of Kinnock's earliest internal reforms package and was followed, between 1999 and 2004, by a broader set of renovation measures. These implied an overhaul of the administrative systems and procedures, a change in the management of financial and human resources, and the reorganization of the way in which the Commission plans and programmes its activities. The reforms are generally perceived as one of the most radical and comprehensive programmes of internal modernization since the Commission was established in 1958.

The Commission's senior service not only experienced firsthand the multiple efforts to change the workings of the organization.[2] It also had to do much of the 'heavy lifting': confronted with new work routines designed to bring performance and accountability to the Commission, this cadre of senior officials was charged with executing the new appraisal procedures, implementing financial controls in their units, and overseeing the shift to management by objectives.

This chapter will take a closer look at the implications of these reforms for the Commission's senior service leadership. It will first outline the key problems of administration in the European Commission of the pre-reform era. Then, it will discuss how the Kinnock reforms have transformed the senior services. It assesses how the reforms have changed the criteria for appointment to the senior services and the professional leadership qualities required; and it points out in what respect recruitment and role expectations of senior officials have changed.

Pressures for change: less power, more professionalism

The Kinnock reforms resulted in a radical reform of the Commission's management. However, a closer look at the institution's administrative history reveals that, since the 1960s, an uninterrupted series of reviews and reports have appeared, commenting on the administrative weaknesses to which the Commission was susceptible and giving rise to incremental adaptations to the Commission's administration (Cini 2007: 9; Schön-Quinlivan 2010: 13–55; Seidel 2010: 101). These constituted small remedies, to cover 'many of the worst impacts of ... the "efficiency problem"' (Dimitrakopoulos and Page 2003: 330), which explains the lack of substantial change in the first fifty years of the institution—despite its organizational difficulties.

One of the problems was the role that nationality played in the organization. The Commission, as an international bureaucracy, was organized along sectoral lines (Egeberg 2006c, 2012), but territorial lines also remained important in the Commission organization. Several conditions in its recruitment and organization have compelled the Commission to remain sensitive to member-state interests and to introduce intergovernmental elements into its functioning (Page 1997; Christiansen 1997). Failures to meld the different cultures of which the Commission bureaucracy is compounded, and which has proved hard to unify, impeded the internal cohesion of the Commission (Harlow 2002: 59–60).

A second major problem of the Commission administration was its fragmentation. Each DG was an organization in itself, developing a different administrative culture, including a 'mission', values, and working methods that were closely related to the policy area in question (cf. Cini 1996). 'There is no civil service, but civil services having too much autonomy' reported a commissioner as early as the 1960s (quoted in Seidel 2010: 154). Coombes (1979) called the Commission a 'porous organisation' and Cram (1994) described it as a 'multi-organisation'. Lack of political control served to reinforce this fragmentation (Page 1997).

A third problem was expansion. The EU has expanded in all ways since the 1957 Treaty of Rome; but the most obvious has been the increase in number of member states. An effective streamlining of the Commission was hard to address—efforts in this direction were frustrated by the enlargement of the EU and the desire of member states for 'fair shares' of their nationals in the Commission (Dimitrakopoulos and Page 2003). As more members joined the Union, more important jobs needed to be found and were created for these nationals, which led to a proliferation of organizational divisions within the EU administration.[3] At the same time, several enlargements and new incoming 'national' traditions were slowly helping to reshape the 'culture' of the administration. As a result, the European Commission has started to drift away from its Franco-German parent models (Balint *et al.* 2008). Membership of the British and the Scandinavian countries brought a greater commitment to openness and performance in the Commission. But where nationality is important, it is nearly impossible to hold to merit, organizational simplification, audits of efficiency, performance measurements and targets, and operational autonomy.

The Commission's inability to say no to new tasks and responsibilities was a fourth problem, which lay at the root of many of its management deficits. In the 1980s and 1990s, the Commission had taken on an ever-expanding repertoire of activities without a matching of resources. The Commission prioritized policy-making; the flipside was its 'management deficit' (Metcalf 1996). Also, the mismanagement of EU funds had become a frequent theme of auditors' reports on the EU budget (Dimitrakopoulos and Page 2003: 318). The Commission was simply not equipped to spend large amounts of money: it lacked both trained personnel and reliable accounting systems. The absence of effective financial and management controls led to a series of fraud allegations and corruption scandals, in which the Santer Commission became mired. This transformation from a policy innovator to a spending bureaucracy was one of the reasons that contributed to the fall of the Santer Commission in 1999 (Murray 2004: 39).

By the end of the 1990s, European politicians and the member states had become convinced that 'Eurocrats' had too much power, that they were poor managers, and that their recruitment was mainly the result of patronage. Comprehensive reform was urgently needed for several reasons. One was to promote performance and efficiency. The other was to establish that it was the political level, and not bureaucrats, who should have power. The third was that the problems of nationality, recruitment, and career planning required a radical restructuring of the Commission. And a fourth reason was that the Commission's bureaucracy was also faced with the institutional impact of its most drastic enlargement.

The accession to the EU of Bulgaria and Romania in 2007 would mark the completion of the '10 + 2' enlargement. The Commission had to integrate the nationals from the twelve new member states. Recruitment of a significant number of new staff from the new member states, officials from Central and Eastern Europe, made an important mark on the Commission: new nationalities, an increase in the number of official languages used inside the Commission, and the arrival of new administrative cultures would challenge the modus operandi in the Commission's administration. As with every previous enlargement, the Commission needed to reserve a number of posts for nationals of new member states. The enlargement to twenty-seven, and ensuring that the new member states were allowed 'their' share of the senior jobs subsequent to accession, would affect the internal workings of the Commission in a number of ways and represented a serious challenge to the aspiration to modernize the EU bureaucracy (Ban 2013).

Kinnock reforms: new rules, new recruitment, new roles

The appointment of the Prodi Commission launched a new stage in the administrative history of the Commission. This Commission issued two *White Papers*—one on 'European governance, and the other on a 'reform strategy'—which announced an ambitious agenda for reforming internal management to enable the Commission to perform its core functions efficiently. 'Reform of the European Commission should ensure that it never again faces the scandals that brought its humiliating collapse in 1999', Neil Kinnock, the new commissioner of Administrative Reforms, said when he announced a new set of specific proposals in March 2000.[4] Amongst the reforms were a new personnel policy, the introduction of more efficient and performance-oriented working methods, the creation of a new system of financial management, and new ethical rules. As these reforms have already been well documented and a comprehensive review of their implementation has been carried out elsewhere, I propose not to discuss these in any detail here (Kassim 2004*a*, 2008; Bauer 2007*b*; Cini 2007; Schön-Quinlivan 2011). The major changes are summarized in Table 5.1.

The Kinnock reforms aimed to realize a more efficient and well-managed bureaucracy that could improve the Commission's standing.[5] The modernization of the Commission and the need to integrate most of the 3,900 officials from the new member states who were set to join the EU's institutions were both, each and of themselves, major challenges. By buttressing New Public Management (NPM) and neo-Weberian principles in the organization, the Commission's administration was expected to become a better managed and unitary organization, with a far more flexible working culture and room for a new professionalism. What did the administrative reforms mean for the

Table 5.1 Overview Administrative Reforms in Commission since 2000–4

Professionalizing Personnel Policy	
A new career structure	• recognizes and rewards proven ability and performance
A new appraisal system	• a closer link between objective assessments and career evolution
New mobility rules	• senior managers change their positions every two to five years.
New appointment procedures	• new rules for selection, appointment, and appraisal of top officials
Reforming the Financial Control System	
'Responsibilisation'	• managers are responsible for the financial decisions they take and are personally liable for their actions;
Audit	• at departmental level a separate Internal Audit Service
	• externally by the Court of Auditors
Detailed, formal procedures	• to ensure that the accounting system, the management and the financial control are responsibly conducted.
Compulsory transfer in 'sensitive' posts	• compulsory transfer anyone who has occupied one for more than seven years
Central Financial Service	• Central Financial Service gives central professional support
Accrual accounting	• the Commission moved to accrual accounting on 1 January 2005
Establishing an Ethical Infrastructure	
Clarification of rules	• Staff Regulations
	• a code of good administrative behaviour.
	• internal rules on potential conflicts of interest
Awareness-raising	• ongoing awareness-raising activities
	• a network of ethics correspondents
	• a communication on standards of professional ethics for its staff.
Creation of an ethical infrastructure	• ethics correspondent to act as a first contact point
	• established a disciplinary office (IDOC)
	• report suspicions of irregularities
	• administrative inquiries and disciplinary procedures

cadre of senior officials in the Commission, for their recruitment and role expectations?

2. Senior Appointments: From Nationality to Merit and Mobility

Many of the recurring problems with hiring the Commission's senior staff and the appointment of its top echelons were related to a fundamental point: the EU Commission's civil service was not just about personnel rules and regulations, it was an integral part of the EU intergovernmental system; as such, it was also the product of political, economic, and social demands and decisions.

In the 1980s and 1990s, recruitment and career patterns of senior officials were marked by a high degree of *politicization*. The recruitment and selection of senior staff was poorly formalized and heavily influenced by individual commissioners, cabinets, and member states (Egeberg 2006a; Seidel 2010). Senior (A1 and A2) posts were qualified as 'political posts'. This meant that the recruitment procedure—which was regulated in the staff regulations—did not apply, and that candidates external to the European administration could be appointed or 'parachuted in' to take these posts (Seidel 2010: 83).[6] Hooghe (2001: 59) asserts that, at the time of her study in the 1990s, nearly half of senior appointments in the Commission were recruited through parachutage. There was also an informal system of 'flagging' where certain director-general posts were expected to be held by nationals of particular countries (DG Agriculture was French and DG Competition German, for example). Directors-general who had been working at the same post for a long time contributed to the establishment of particular working habits, characterizing the 'administrative culture' of a DG that was partly nationally coloured (Page 1997: 52–54; Georgakakis and de Lassalle 2007: 5–6). Nationality represented both a condition and a limit to the accession to posts of directors-general.

Within this politicized system, having the right political and national connections were often more valuable for promotion prospects than a good performance record. The lack of a serious staff management system undermined confidence in the independence of the Commission. Frustrated high-performing staff saw their options for career development blocked as the director and director-general posts remained de facto unattainable steps in the career of European civil servants (Stevens and Stevens 2001: 74; Balint et al. 2007). Meanwhile, the institutional framework was not conducive to cultivating a homogeneous, cohesive, bureaucratic elite, possessing a strong common identity and *esprit de corps*. Weakly institutionalized recruitment procedures contributed to a fragmented civil service (Page 1997; Seidel 2010).

Making merit and mobility within the EU civil service a prerequisite for a senior career path was one of the main priorities of the Kinnock reforms. New *demands* on the Commission administration were translated into changes in the recruitment and career structure for senior officials. Also, the call for objective and standardized assessment *procedures*, together with the need to integrate the *supply* of internal candidates and new senior managers coming from the twelve new member states, contributed to a professionalization and standardization of the recruitment of the senior civil service. Figure 5.1 summarizes the main demand and supply factors playing a role in the appointment of high-level senior management in the Commission.

The demand side: from politics to merit

MERIT INSTEAD OF NATIONALITY

As a part of the Kinnock administrative reforms, more weight was to be assigned to quality, motivation, and performance of senior officials in the

From Nationality to Merit and Mobility

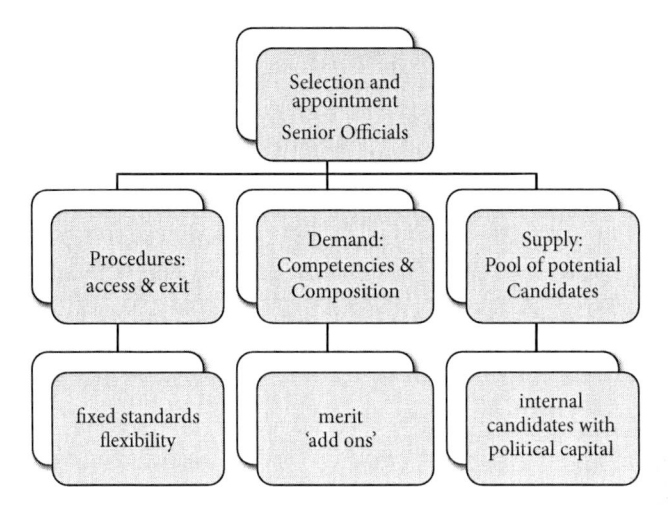

Figure 5.1. Recruitment of Senior Officials in the EU Commission

Commission. From then on, the primary criterion for the appointment of senior officials was *merit* and *competence* relevant to the function. The reforms underlined internal recruitment and the development of career opportunities for senior officials. Nationality is no longer allowed to be the main determinant in appointing a person to a particular post. But, as an international administration, abandoning this principle was easier said than done.

ADD-ONS COMPLICATING THE MERIT SYSTEM

As attractive as the idea of employing the best person possible for senior positions in the Commission may be, in reality the issue of representativeness, along important political cleavages, remains an important dimension in the recruitment process. Moreover, two additions to the system, or 'add-ons' (cf. Ingraham 1995: 56), which throw up obstacles to the merit system, must also be taken into account by the Commission when appointing senior staff.

The first add-on is that the Commission needs to maintain a measure of balance when it shares out the top posts. The Commission's policy is 'to seek a broad geographical balance' in the appointment of senior officials, to ensure a fair spread of all EU nationalities across its DGs and services.[7] In 2000, when the changes in senior appointment were introduced, Kinnock stressed that 'Merit must have primacy, even though the Commission should strive to have senior managers of all EU nationalities in this multinational institution. We are not prepared to run a sort of Eurovision contest for which nationality holds the greatest number of posts—and we do not think that the European public would want us to.'[8] But with respect to the senior posts, the national balance is still observed with a particular strictness. Moreover, as a general rule, the commissioner and the director-general responsible for the same

125

directorate-general may not to share the same nationality, in order to counterbalance national influence. At the same time, the Commission must also promote and achieve a better gender balance. These geographical and gender 'add-ons' may complicate the merit system, but are considered necessary for a fairer and more broadly representative sharing out of the top posts.

A second 'add-on' that detracts somewhat from the merit system is the demand for a 'match' between a director-general and the responsible commissioner. The approval of the Commission is required and the views of the responsible commissioners are very important. They are consulted in the selection procedure and usually have a clear idea or feel about what they want from their director-general. As one of the commissioners explains the choice for a new director-general:

> I didn't know him before. I met him when he came for the interview. I collected a lot of information, I spoke to many people and his name was mentioned by many people as somebody very good. I talked to him. And from day one, from moment one, it was clear. ... It is this having a good feeling about somebody that is important.

A director-general commented:

> The candidates are asked to sit for a daylong interview. This was introduced recently—it was not there when I became a director general. Then the advisory committee draws up a shortlist of who is technically suitable for the job. And then the commissioner and the Commission as a whole make their choice out of this shortlist. You must have the formal requirements in terms of seniority and formal experience and titles. Then you must go through this two step process to get on the short list. And if you are on the shortlist, then it is a purely political personal choice of the commissioner.

These officials may be selected primarily on the basis of their qualifications; eventually, it is the Commissioner's consent and personal preferences that override the objective standards, yielding the ultimate choice for an appointee to be a form of 'personal politicization'.

The selection procedures: from poorly formalized to fixed and flexible

MERIT THROUGH STANDARDIZATION

An important aspect of the merit reforms was the establishment of straightforward standards for senior managers and a transparent procedure for selecting them for the posts. The emphasis on merit in the recruitment process not only involved taking into account the candidates' qualifications, competences, and past record, but also evaluating their capacity to carry out future senior management tasks. The selection procedure had to include tools to assess these qualities and had to be primarily based on an objective assessment of the respective merits of the candidates.

Not only were the criteria standardized, but also the selection procedure was formalized. It was largely the EU enlargement, expected to bring in new directors-general and directors from the accession countries, that sparked these procedural reforms. Allowing the new member states to have 'their' share of the senior jobs subsequent to their accession generated concerns about the future quality of the services after the enlargement (Egeberg 2006a: 42). To safeguard a merit-based recruitment system, external candidates had to meet strict objective criteria. The Commission introduced an additional layer in the selection procedure: the 'assessment centre method' for senior staff coming from the new member states and for external candidates. This 'standardized' quality control mechanism, originally established for new senior managers, was eventually extended and applied to all senior management posts.

In the new procedure, a crucial role was reserved for the *Consultative Committees of Appointments* (CCA), which were charged with assigning and evaluating the quality of the candidates for the positions of higher management (European Commission 2004). This meant that now, whenever a senior management post fell vacant, a selection procedure was started. Today, the CCA serves as an 'interviewing and evaluation board' and prepares a short-list of candidates from which the commissioner may choose (Egeberg 2006a: 38–9). All candidates short-listed for an appointment to senior management for the first time, whether coming from within the Commission or outside it, are now required to undergo this independent external assessment. Figure 5.2 gives a schematic representation of the new selection procedure.

The adoption of standardized and transparent procedures and clearly specified requirements that have to be met, contributed to an 'objectification' of the recruitment process. The assessment centre process is now applied to all senior management posts.

FROM FIEFDOMS TO FLEXIBILITY

To promote merit and to allow staff to build their careers upon broad experience, the Commission decided to introduce compulsory rotation for its most senior officials (and for posts with significant financial responsibility). By introducing compulsory mobility for senior officials, posts could be opened for competition, the Commission's management capacity could be reinforced in specific areas, and posts that are no longer justified could be abolished. Moreover, since reshuffles reduce the opportunity to build up personal or national fiefdoms, it enabled the Commission to break the link between member states and certain posts—a process known as 'de-flagging' in EU jargon.

The Senior Civil Service

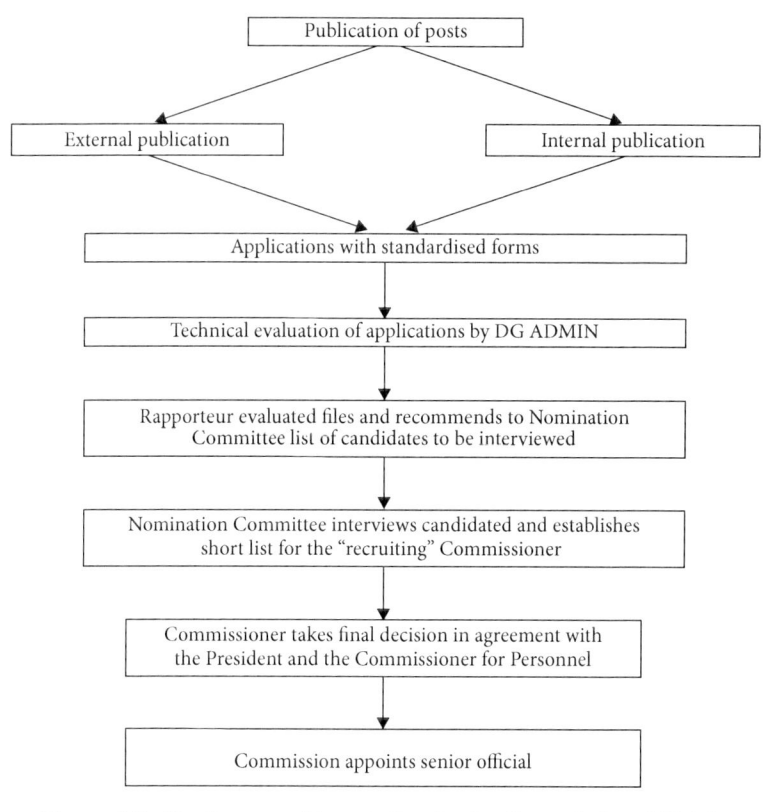

```
                    Publication of posts
                    ↙              ↘
       External publication      Internal publication
                    ↘              ↙
            Applications with standardised forms
                           ↓
         Technical evaluation of applications by DG ADMIN
                           ↓
         Rapporteur evaluated files and recommends to Nomination
              Committee list of candidates to be interviewed
                           ↓
         Nomination Committee interviews candidated and establishes
               short list for the "recruiting" Commissioner
                           ↓
         Commissioner takes final decision in agreement with
              the President and the Commissioner for Personnel
                           ↓
              Commission appoints senior official
```

Figure 5.2. The Process of Appointing Senior Commission Officials

The increased mobility is crucial from the perspective of personnel management and is designed to bring new and innovative approaches to its top-level management. It was introduced with the intention to professionalize the services by promoting merit and fresh thinking, and to allow senior officials to build their careers upon broad experience. President Romano Prodi commented:

> Not only do we want senior managers to change jobs with reasonable regularity so that know-how and experience circulate in the institution, we also want our senior staff to have the widest possible experience. Finally, we want to confirm the primacy of the political dimension of this Commission.[9]

The rotation of top officials has weakened the influence of member states on the process of selection and recruitment. Member states have publicly supported the reforms, but privately continue to battle over the senior appointments. The positions of director-general and deputy director-general are jobs in which national governments have traditionally taken a keen interest. To institute a successful job rotation system, a strong, centralized personnel structure must be in place. The Commission tries, therefore, to prevent particular posts from 'belonging' to particular nationalities. Making decisions on top appointments that stick in the face of national pressures is also a matter of the Commission's credibility.

The system of compulsory transfers intends to contribute to an improved and more flexible management. It prevents long-serving directors-general from becoming too powerful. The system also provided that the senior managers could be removed for poor performance. Senior managers who received unsatisfactory ratings could be transferred or removed. A director-general commented:

> It is very good thing. Then you had those great dinosaur figures that worked for ten, fifteen years on the same policy. It must have been quite difficult for commissioners to define and change something, because then you get the 'no we have tried that 15 years ago'. This new policy is healthful. You keep senior staff motivated and it is positive for the organization. You don't have these well established baronies.

The new mobility system has clearly favoured the generalist over the specialist. Specialization tends to diminish promotion aspects, as it restricts departmental mobility. Generalists are a lot more likely to be considered for a wider range of senior positions than officials with a highly specialized technical background.

Rotation implied a regular transfer of senior officials. It explicitly introduced the 'time' element into the management agenda of 'permanent' executive officials, making it more difficult and costly to embark on projects that require a medium- to long-term perspective. As one director-general described it:

> It introduces one of the conditions of a political life into the life of the civil servant. If you got elected like a politician, you work like sting in the first two years because you can get unelected. Or if you are a minister you might move from one ministry to another ministry. Politicians and ministers are always aware that their life is short. That is why they are impatient to do things. Now when you are director-general you are going to be there for five years, you have to think also in terms of a five-year programme. If you are too slow about the five-year programme, by the time you have thought up the five-year programme, you have to move to the next job. It does bring in the *time*-element. It sharpens all sorts of motives, which are there anyway, because you can get moved for all sorts of reasons. You don't internalize to the same extent, if someone is telling you are going to do the job for five years. It takes you some time to understand what is going on. And there are a number of things you want to change. And that is very much political.

The introduction of the new system has brought a new dynamic into the existence of top officials. Directors-general perceive the prospect of moving to another position every now and then as an attractive option 'to experience other ways of doing things'. Whenever a new round of 'musical chairs' is planned, with senior officials anticipating moving between key management positions, the lead-up to formal replacement decisions is characterized by a period of intensive lobbying. Senior officials who have already spent five years as a director-general and who are therefore scheduled for a move, need to 'advertise' their personal career to increase their chance of and to accommodate their wish for a good transfer. 'Getting noticed' has become a more pressing concern for senior officials. But it also has created 'a situation where too many well-qualified officials are chasing too few jobs' (Kinnock, cited in Peterson 2004: 37).

The intensified mobility also has introduced competition and a certain risk and unpredictability in the career of senior civil servants. Fitting the right person for the right vacancy has become one of the main puzzles of the job rotation. Some officials may have been instrumental in a particular sector, but lack the skills to function at the same level in another policy sector. And what happens if a senior political post is filled by someone who is not technically able to carry out the tasks expected of him or her? To avoid difficult conversations, senior officials who cannot be assigned to another post that corresponds to their grade can also be retired 'in the interests of the service' (the so-called Article 50-exit). Such retirement is not regarded as a disciplinary measure, and provides an easy solution for the Commission to deal with and remedy cases of incompetence, or officials who have outgrown the skills or experience of the organization. Interviewees mentioned the regular use of this Article 50 to get rid of unwanted personnel, comparing its application to the difference between an easy exit and a messy divorce.

Supply side: from outsider to insider recruitment

EUROPEANIZATION OF CAREERS

The appointment depends, for an important part, also on the pool of potentially qualified job candidates from which judicious selection can be made to fill vacant senior management posts. This refers to the supply side of executive selection. Examining the educational background and the career paths of senior officials gives an indication of the type of candidates from which the Commission is likely to recruit for this position, and of the kind of professional capital that is available and relevant.

First, senior managers are recruited from a group that has completed a university education (it is one of the formal qualifications). In most cases, they have training in law, economy, or political science; and increasingly, they are drawn from a group with an international degree. Figure 5.3, which is based on the data of Didier Georgakakis (2010: 124–5), portrays this increased internationalization of the educational profile of the Commission's senior management.

From Nationality to Merit and Mobility

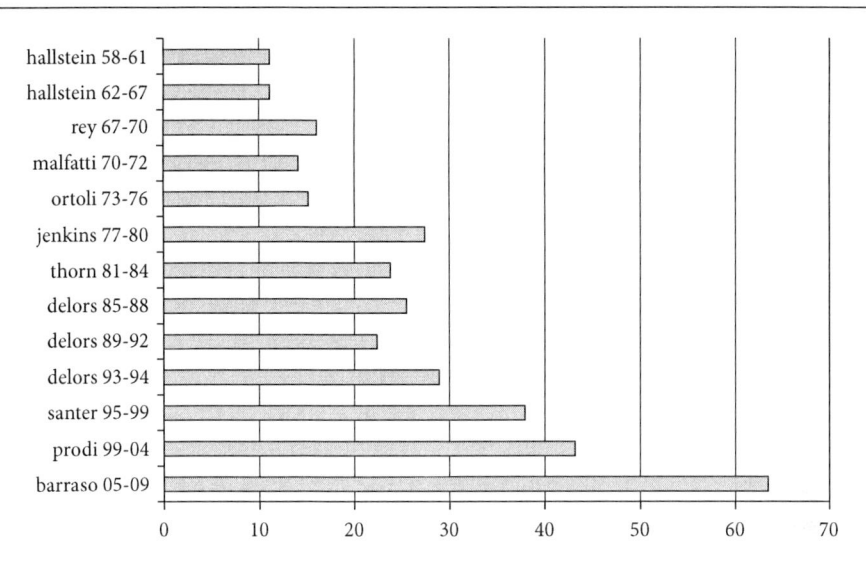

Figure 5.3. Senior Managers with Studies in Foreign Countries
Source: Georgakakis 2010

In the Hallstein Commission only a tenth of the directors-general had followed (some part of) their studies abroad; in the Barosso I Commission, this had swelled to two-thirds.

Second, there are, generally, two pools to recruit from for these posts: *insiders* and *outsiders*. Whereas in the past a considerable part of the senior service was parachuted in from the outside, today's senior officials are increasingly recruited from inside the 'House'. Officials indicated in the interview that the internal route to office has become the dominant one. Didier Georgakakis's study (2010: 124–8; cf. Georgakakis and de Lasalle 2007) confirms this trend: a long-term career among senior managers in the EU Commission has become progressively more prevalent. There is a growing group of senior managers who have spent their entire or most of their professional life in the European institutions. Nearly four out of five senior officials had held a previous position in the Commission before they were appointed director-general (see Figure 5.4). The number of employees pursuing a career in the EU institutions has grown, while the percentage of senior officials with a background in national politics has decreased. It is an indication of an emerging 'Europeanization' of careers (Georgakakis 2010).

Most senior officials who took the inside route to the top position have worked in the Commission administration for nearly half their life—over twenty-five years is no exception; hence, most have long-standing experience in this institution. By serving in the Commission, preferably in several positions, from the top to the bottom, and across different policy areas, these 'home-grown' leaders

131

The Senior Civil Service

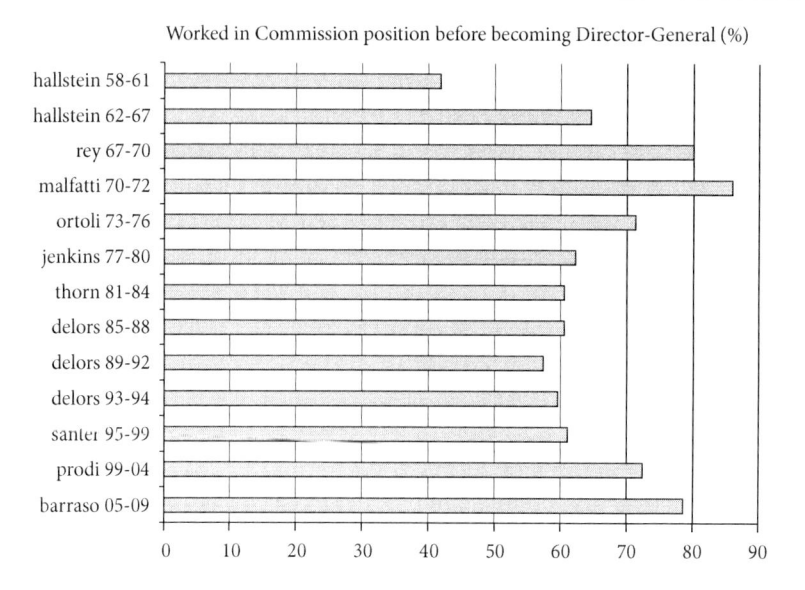

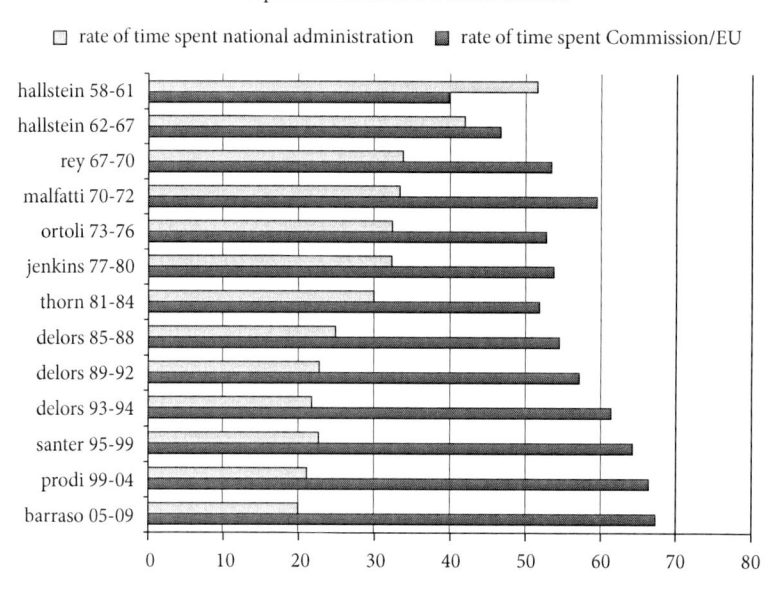

Figure 5.4. Europeanization of Directors-General
Source: Georgakakis 2010

have built up intellectual 'European' capital and accrued the experience that is needed to become qualified for a top position.[10] A director-general pointed out:

> Increasingly you need cross-sectoral knowledge and you need cross-institutional knowledge in order to have the package of qualifications that are required.

> Previous experience with work with the political level or political experience yourself, or working in the cabinet or assistant of a minister. With this package you would have the qualifications. I am not talking about languages and formal qualifications, because it goes without saying that you have to speak three or four languages. You have to be knowledgeable both in economics, legal, or political science. But this goes without saying because these days you also need these in the national administrations. You must be able to build alliances across, for example, agriculture, internal market and environment.

Filling positions through external publication of job vacancies mostly happens for two reasons; in order to recruit senior managers from the 'new' member states; or to recruit for a post with qualifications that cannot be met through internal recruitment, or for which a serious internal advertisement has not yielded a suitable candidate. In the latter case, the commissioner for personnel, together with the 'recruiting commissioner' and the president, may decide to extend the search and open the post to external candidates. Recruiting from the outside occurs in open competition but, as a director-general indicates, is

> a less frequent path, and I have to say so that it is not always successful. It is very difficult for people to come in late in their career, mastering the game in the Commission and among the institutions. Not because it is particularly complicated, but it is when you become in a national administration a top boss from another planet. You simply don't have the levels to operate at this level and I have seen that it takes these people two or three years to make their mark. Some of these people are very intelligent and capable.

A director-general talks about an outside candidate

> who I have hired myself; and I said come back to me in eighteen months. And he said 'no, no I will find my way' and we spoke a couple of months ago and he said: 'I still haven't learned my way. And he was recruited three years ago. So it really is quite complicated.

POLITICAL CAPITAL

Officials who have worked for a commissioner, and who have demonstrated political experience, preferably in the cabinets, have a clear advantage for a leading post in the Commission. Membership of a cabinet, as previously indicated in Chapter 4, is good for one's career in the Commission's administration. Longitudinal data from Georgakakis (2010), presented in Figure 5.5, shows that the share of directors-general with previous work experience in a commissioner's cabinet has progressively increased across time. In the pre-reform Commission, membership of a cabinet was also a relatively important means for political promotion in the administration (Seidel 2010). But these officials

The Senior Civil Service

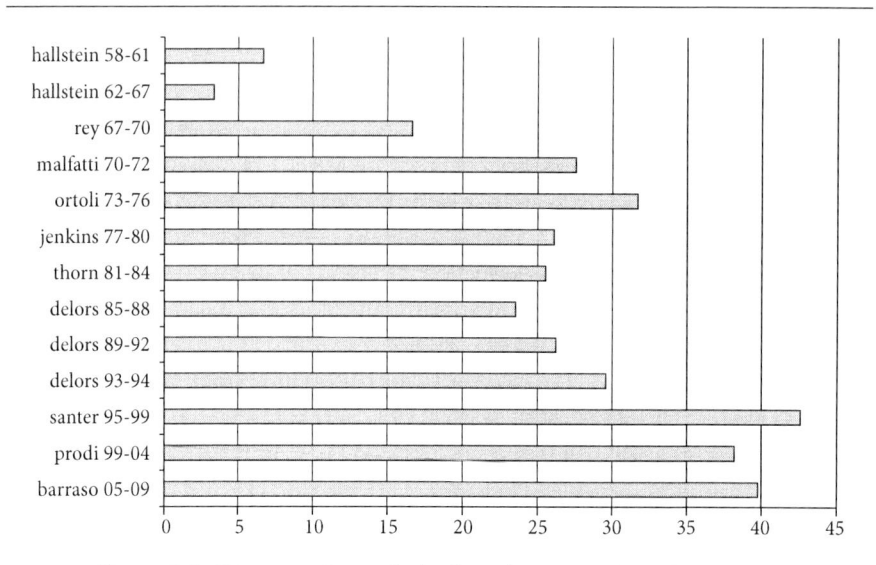

Figure 5.5. Directors-General who have been Member of a Cabinet
Source: Georgakakis 2010

coming from the cabinets were then often 'parachutists' (Page 1997: 80–1). The pool now consists of aspiring Commission officials who were seconded at a commissioner's cabinet, and who use this experience to join the higher echelons in the Commission.

Conclusion: depoliticization of senior appointments

The shifts in senior appointment policy in the Commission indicate, all in all, a 'depoliticization' of the appointment process. This does not mean that political factors are completely removed from the selection process. Senior appointments in the Commission will always be politically sensitive. The system of geographical balance has not been abandoned and still serves as an add-on to the merit system. Depoliticization means that professional norms and transparent procedures have now come to dominate the recruitment process. The tendency to attach national flags to top posts has significantly decreased (cf. Egeberg 2006*a*: 39). The recruitment of senior personnel has become relatively insulated from the pressure of national governments, with priority being given to internal candidates, insiders. In particular, by introducing clearer rules and better defined responsibilities, the aim was to raise the level of management skills and create a common management culture across the Commission. It has resulted in an administrative top that is more flexible, more oriented to merit, and more European in outlook. What the implications are for the role conceptions of the senior service is the topic of the next section.

3. Senior Service Leadership: From Politics to Performance

Senior officials in the Commission were, and in a way still are, easily associated with the stereotype of the intractably obstructive mandarin, as the complaint of Verheugen at the start of this book illustrates. When Neil Kinnock unveiled the proposals for the Commission reforms in 2000, he told the European Parliament that he wanted to create a 'modern public service' in which 'the best in the Commission would be typical of the Commission'. Given that the Commission was pictured as an essentially autonomous and uncontrolled bureaucracy that had failed to develop an effective 'management culture', and was saddled with a senior service with the reputation for being resistant to control and change, it is no surprise that the reforms were announced as 'drastic' ones.

The enlarged array of accountability mechanisms that have emerged as a consequence of the administration's reform package provides an increased number of opportunities for holding senior officials answerable for how they perform. They were also translated into new expectations for the styles and substance of senior civil service leadership in the Commission. What were the role expectations that emerged in parallel with the changes in the recruitment and accountability framework?

Between the autonomous administrator and the responsive adviser

Providing advice and recommendations is perceived as the predominant element of the competences of senior officials. They agree that it is their role to help commissioners reconcile the political commitments of the Commission, and they provide assistance at two points. They possess a good grasp and judgment of how the policy arena operates, and they offer advice about the substantive issues. Most perceive this role as one that is carried out in interaction with the political level. A director-general explained it thus:

> You start giving ideas to the commissioner, and receiving ideas, and you have a more constructive discussion of where could we be in five years time. You outline your programme, this can be done and that. A good director-general has to provide the politician with options. This will mean this and this; this is the middle road and this will mean this; what are the upside risks and downside risks. That will be the intelligent way. A bad director-general tries to manipulate the commissioner into a particular line, but in my view this is risky, because there can be a backlash, because the politicians at the end of the day are responsible.

Directors-general indicated that their role pertains to managing policy advice in their department rather than being involved in day-to-day development of policy. They are expected to organize the information flow upon which policy proposals and programmatic decisions must be based; they know which middle managers in their departments to approach for expert knowledge on the application of particular programmes; they know which groups are to be reckoned with. Senior officials believe that their departments must play a strong role in policy development, and that their task is to contribute an organized mixture of professional competences and expertise. Responsiveness, defined as the capacity to respond rapidly and effectively to the demands and needs of the political level (cf. Putnam 1973: 257–8), is pivotal here. Directors-general indicated that they believe that they are responsive to the commissioner's political agenda, as noted by one director-general: 'I have to help the commissioner to translate what she has in her mind into something that can fly, with the other commissioners, with the public at large, with the parliament, and the member states.'

But responsiveness also requires the political side of the relationship to deliver an appropriate performance. Directors-general worry about some of the policy aspirations articulated at the political level. As a director-general put it:

> Here the political instruction is very diverse. Very often you get instructions from your political commissioner, which you know are not feasible, because you know the commissioner has not formed the adequate alliances at the top of the system, which means that, when you try to execute the order, you will go nowhere ... In a way, you have a mix of policy decisions that are constantly questioned when you go to the lower echelons, also because the political level has not performed its task.

In these cases when commissioners do not fulfil their political role, some senior managers feel that they have a part to play, particularly when the necessary consensus at the political level is not achieved. It is clear that the 'Sir Humphreys' (from the BBC parody *Yes, Minister*) have also found their niche in the Commission bureaucracy. As one director-general commented on the input of commissioners:

> It is not easy to shape a political programme with a left-wing social democrat from a Nordic country and a right-wing Catalan politician. It is very complicated. But that is what has to happen, when you want to be sure. That is why a lot of the compromising is actually done between the DGs. We try to find out what can fly, what is possible knowing our political masters, and then we have the political responsibility of checking with our political masters that they can accept that kind of orientation.

There may be some tension between responsiveness and competence in the advice of senior officials, and much depends on the ways in which the political–bureaucratic relationship is organized, as we will see in Chapter 7. But professional standards and technical expertise guide the recommendations of senior officials, and it is not the role of the political level, in their view, to become involved in the detailed choices in the policy process that are associated with administration. A director general explained:

> We do what the commissioner wants. He can have visions and make speeches, but it is not his job to know how to do that in an area like this. It is not his job to know anything about the technical details. We are the multiplier of his vision. First, we interpret it. Secondly, we make it happen on the ground. We are the executive that he leads and guides. Sometimes we add vision to the information. It is not that all the ideas are coming from the head of the commissioner. We can propose, we can advise; but above all we can multiply and execute.

The responsive competences of administrators are developed and adapted in light of the political needs and preferences of the commissioners. But directors-general seek to maintain their autonomy to act on the basis of their professional perspective. They are there to provide technical input; they have their own view of the European interest; and they want to advocate both in making recommendations. Senior officials act as the political agent of the commissioner, but not in a passively loyalist manner. They are aware that they wield immense resources for the commissioner.

Running the department: towards effective management

Management has become an important ingredient in the role of the senior service. The wide use of the term 'senior management' for the top civil service highlights the belief that it has become a basic skill of these officials, crucial to the ongoing success of the organization. It means running departments, motivating staff, crafting policy advice, and managing political–administrative boundaries. Or as a director-general summarized the core competencies required for his own job: 'strong strategy making, convincing, negotiating, to set objectives and achieve them, also managerial skills, and the capacity, in addition to the standard things, to manage in a multicultural environment'.

The development and introduction of a systematic programme of management training for managers at all levels in the Commission indicates that management skills are regarded as a key condition for operating successfully in the Commission's senior services. A director-general described this 'change of seasons':

> All the management posts in the Commission suffered from a paradigm shift. In the past, the director-general and the heads of units were recruited because of substantial knowledge. The head of the legal service was the best lawyer. Now we

have discovered that you can be the best lawyer in the Commission, but an awful director-general, because you have to manage a team.

Along with the new emphasis on the need for managerial skills, the policy role of the senior civil service has changed as well. The focus for most senior officials has shifted from a professional policy advisory role, with a clear focus on content, to a role of 'process' management. They still need to know 'the system' in their policy sector, but they no longer need to be technical experts. Senior officials move from position to position in order to develop skills in a range of policy areas. Departing from the idea that generic management extends across policy domains, managerial leadership qualities were increasingly preferred over policy-oriented professionalism in the job of the director-general.

Policy delivery: performance-oriented

Performance-based management has caused a cultural shift within the Commission, as routines have changed from input focused to output focused. A focus on management by objectives, as well as the use of planning, monitoring, evaluation, and reporting, have helped the Commission to (re)structure its work and to 'rationalize' the policy process. In this context, it is one of the jobs of the director-general to participate in the Strategic Planning and Programming (SPP) cycle—the Commission's variant of activity-based management (ABM).

This cycle has run since 2003. The basic concepts are prioritizing, planning, executing, and reporting. Directors-general are expected to translate the political priorities set by the College, the Annual Commission Strategy, into specific objectives for the service in an Annual Management Plan, and to report progress made in the Annual Activity Report.

The managers interviewed were decidedly mixed in their reactions to the impact of these new accountability systems. Some indicated that the entire reform process and SPP in particular have contributed positively to a change of culture, turning the focus to the actual results of EU policies. This form of output management makes it, generally speaking, clearer what senior officials are accountable for and the performance plans provide the standards against which they can be judged. It has made senior officials subject to regular review and questioning and it has contributed to a very concrete conception of accountable behaviour: that of performance. The implementation of these arrangements was said to have made management more effective, results-oriented, and transparent. As an official pointed out:

> The reforms have caused a lot of moaning and groaning, and things take incredibly longer; that is true. But the quality of the output is better, there are new systems of

planning introduced and people have become aware that we have to perform on time. The discipline in the organization has been improved immensely.

A number of advantages were also mentioned, i.e. that the new system has enhanced the transparency of the organization; and that it can help to make the Commission's performance more visible. The fact that these forms of 'performance agreements' have grown into a well-established management tool, and have become an integral part of many modern managed governments, has also contributed to the acceptance of this system by senior officials.

Activity-based management has also bureaucratized the Commission, in the eyes of senior officials. The annual drafting and reporting process is considered costly and time-consuming and, in combination with the great number of rules and regulations for financial management, is perceived as terribly burdensome. The proliferation of arduous and demanding rules and cumbersome procedures, and the heavy reporting burdens, have induced a sense of frustration among the staff.

The SPP cycle serves, in most departments as an additional instrument through which political priorities—set at the political level—are 'cascaded' down. The senior service is expected to link the goals and performance measures for each organizational level. The introduction of management-based objectives and performance-based incentives has contributed to increased steering power from the centre. One of the officials described it as follows:

> I think that since the introduction of ABM, there has been a strengthening of the centralized control, in resource allocation and priority setting, and this had consequences for the roles of individual portfolio commissioners. There is more control from the centre, by the secretary-general and the president. My experience with activity-based management is that it began and remains to a very large extent a largely mismatched attempt to generate much more bureaucratic bottom–up approaches with a rather authoritarian centralized political orientation without actually joining them up. A huge amount of generated activity for the service!

The changes in strategic planning may not have left the senior service indifferent. They are less contested than the modernization in financial management

Financial accountable

The Santer Commission became caught up in allegations of fraud and mismanagement because of the absence of effective financial and management controls. Under Prodi, the Commission has sought to repair its financial accountability structure completely. It has abolished centralized 'ex ante' spending controls—i.e. the requirement of each directorate-general to seek prior approval for spending requests—and revised its budgetary and financial management rules.

Detailed, formal procedures were created to ensure that the accounting system, the management of contracts, and the financial control of the Commission's services are responsibly conducted, so that it is clear who is answerable for what. Internal audit capabilities were set up at departmental level, largely in order to help the directors- general deal with this new responsibility. A central financial service, based inside the DG Budget, was established to provide support to the rest of the Commission and help to maintain common financial standards. A new intern audit service now acts as the Commission's watchdog, ensuring that the DGs spend budgets in a proper fashion. Under the new financial regulation, directors-general (and sometimes directors as well) act as so-called 'authorizing officers by delegation'. In this role, they are responsible for 'sound financial management'. They must also ensure that the 'requirements of legality and regularity' are complied with.

At the end of each financial year, each director-general completes an 'annual activity report' and a 'declaration' specifying the expenditures for the year. The declaration attests to the accuracy of the information contained in the activity report, and also records any reservations the director-general may have about the quality of financial controls.[11] The director-general also figures as one of the possible contacts for officials with concerns about possible wrongdoings.[12]

These changes in the financial management of the Commission's resources (decentralization of financial responsibilities, introduction of audit and ex post control activities at department level) were meant to give directors-general more autonomy and flexibility in their work, as well as more responsibility. This emphasis on the individual responsibility of directors-general, combined with the yearly reports, created new notions of liability: senior officials personally had to face the consequences attached to their performance. They were 'responsibilised'.[13] The guidelines define the personal financial responsibility of officials for mismanagement or fraud. They detail in what circumstances officials can be held liable for financial losses to the EU budget. The guidelines also provide for the recovery of money when an official has caused financial loss as a result of gross negligence.

Senior officials underlined the importance of the new checks and controls, and they emphasized that these new standards have increased the reliability of the organization. But they also expressed their concern with this displacement of responsibility onto senior officials; overly detailed definitions of responsibility limit flexibility and result in risk-avoiding behaviour. As an official observed: 'The introduction of personal responsibility has made that a lot of people here do not have the guts anymore to take a decision, let alone, to take any risk.'

Almost all senior officials expressed their dissatisfaction with the extra bureaucratic red tape resulting from the new internal and external regulations and complained about high costs of the new system in terms of time and energy, arguing that well-intentioned reform measures have placed a heavy burden of requirements on them. Interviewees felt that the balance has been lost: there are now, they claim, too many legalistic procedures, too much reporting, and too much supervision.[14] A director-general put it as follows:

> There was an enormous cramp in the organization after the Santer resignation which has led to overregulation, containers full of auditors and controllers within the organization, everything has become strictly regulated, nothing can be done spontaneously, we are controlled by DG Legal and Budget, and it is nearly impossible to change this.

The imposition of a more demanding and strictly enforced system of rules, reporting, controls, and the growth of central auditing, inspections, and 'excessive monitoring', as a Commission official called it, means that directors-general have a somewhat ambiguous task. These officials gained greater freedom to choose their means and to deploy their inputs; but, at the same time, they have become less free to define the goals themselves and feel they are under closer scrutiny than ever before. They complain that, in some cases, the overly rigid system of accountability in the Commission does more harm than good; it has stifled creativity, while the increased culpability has led to decreased risk-taking. Accountability mechanisms that are experienced as overly controlling and intrusive may lead to accountability being experienced as a negatively felt necessity.

Political management as part of professionalism

Senior officials operate in a political environment and are expected to be tuned in to the realities of their political bosses. Taking stock of the role expectations linked to the work of directors-general, it is clear that one of their major assets, in order to maximize the chances for the realization of the commissioner's substantive objectives, is that they know how to navigate the policy-making process, that they consider the likely political implications of policy proposals, and that they are able to perceive these in the broader context of the Commission's programme; that they know how to anticipate and, where necessary, influence the reactions of other actors in the policy-making process, particularly, the EP, the member states, and organized interests. Given their long-standing experience in the institution, this is usually not a problem. Sometimes the political professionalism of senior officials even outweighs that of their political bosses, as can be read from the opinion of a director-general:

> Because I have the knowledge where we are in the European integration process, I have to explain to the commissioner, if you want this as a policy line, then we have to do it hand in hand with the parliament. They want it also, but you must not go into a conflict with the parliament. In the national context this would not be a problem, because you have the well grounded institutions, and it is not a problem. But with the Euro-parliamentarians, who have been sniped by the national politicians, who have just been voted, it is not the same story. The commissioner did not understand this in the beginning.

Directors-general also represent their DGs in dealings with other DGs, the other institutions, governments, outside agencies, in conferences, and at other events. Powers to adopt the definitive text of any legal proposal may also be delegated to the directors-general by the Commission or the commissioner. The growing emphasis on consultation and partnership in developing proposals also compels senior management to negotiate with interest groups and all kinds of political stakeholders. The increased role of the EP has made Commission operations and programmes more sensitive to external politics. As one of the directors-general, working in a policy field in which the EP was powerful, indicated: 'In my field we are in the hands of the EP. I have to work hand in hand with the EP. My life insurance is the good relations with the EP.' Senior officials in the Commission still belong, when it comes to policy work, to Putnam's (1973) category of 'political bureaucrats'.

4. From Mandarins to Managers

In the context of European politics, senior officials in the pre-reform Commission were commonly perceived as powerful *mandarins*. Due to their influence on the policy agenda and their responsibility for a vast majority of policy initiatives, the Commission's bureaucracy was associated with what Putnam (1975: 87) calls 'the rule of officials'. They knew their departments well—the policies, the programme, the staff, and outside groups with a strong interest in the area. It was an ideal setting for 'stove-pipe' management and to protect one's turf. The Commission bureaucracy was characterized by politicization and organizational fragmentation, and by the limited cohesion of its bureaucratic elite. It was not sufficiently skilled in management; and was accused of being insular, self referential, too powerful, obstructionist, and unresponsive to political demands.

In the Brussels of today, this image of the Commission's senior civil service may safely be regarded as a relic of a bygone age. The Commission has been subject to the same processes of reform and 'reinvention' as many other Western bureaucracies. The administrative reforms were needed to create

Table 5.2 Professionalization of the Administration

Demands in Governance	Institutional Design	Behavioural Implications
Merit	Formalization and standardization of selection procedure	Clarification of competences, basing staffing on merit and relevant experience
Representation	Broad balance of nationalities and gender	Maintaining a broad geographical balance
Flexibility	Compulsory Mobility Policy Exit option (Article 50)	Corporate consciousness (*esprit de corps*)
Responsiveness	ABM, job rotation	Political sensitivity
Responsibility	Administrative norms and ethical infrastructure	Professional behaviour
Effectiveness and efficiency	Activity Based Management	Managerialism Performance-oriented
Financial accountability	Decentralization of financial controls	'Responsibilisation'

a modern, efficient, and well-managed international administration based on the principles of 'efficiency, performance, transparency and accountability' (Commission's *White Paper on European Governance* 2001). The European Commission has evolved from an international organization, arranged along intergovernmental structures, into a normalized core executive, in which the administrative level has become more 'professionalized'—both in its institutional design and its elite behavior. Table 5.2 summarizes the features and impact of this normalization on the Commission administration.

The normalization of the Commission's administration

FROM POLITICIZED TO DEPOLITICIZED

The reforms can be read as an attempt to 'depoliticize' the Commission bureaucracy from a number of 'bottom–up' political influences. Depoliticization does not imply that politics play no role in the services. Depoliticization means that merit has become a salient dimension in the recruitment process; and that the professionalization, formalization, and regulation of recruitment and the new administrative responsibilities have de-emphasized the political. By reinforcing a mixture of 'Weberian' and NPM principles in the organization, the Commission's bureaucracy has moved away from structures characterized by national quotas and responsiveness to national interests. Although the national balance principle has not been eliminated fully from appointments and promotions criteria, it has been downgraded, while the introduction of standardized personnel policy, reforming appointment and promotion procedures, awarding talented staff, and reducing the proportion of officials on temporary contracts or secondments, have contributed to an upgrading of the meritocratic principle (cf. Nugent 2001: 327). It has resulted in a more flexible, more European, and more professional senior service.

THE POWER OF PERFORMANCE MANAGEMENT
Reforms in the Commission's organizational design not only prompted change in the characteristics of the senior civil service, but also a transformation in its conceptions of and approach to leadership. Internal administration reforms delineated the 'proper' roles of senior officials and made more explicit what was expected. Expectations have also evolved from 'input focused' to 'output focused'. Performance and quality of outputs are the new values that infuse the working practices of the Commission. Today's senior officials are expected to be able to navigate the policy process, to make things happen, and to manage. A reconfigured policy role, performance demands and managerial skill requirements, and new accountability expectations are now emphasized in the roles of senior officials. The emphasis on the individual responsibility of directors-general, combined with new promotion procedures and the annual activity plans, has marked the beginning of a shift to a management culture.

STRENGTHENED POLITICAL CONTROL
The general tendency of the reforms examined here has been towards *controlling* the influence that the Commission's bureaucracy exerts over the design and execution of the EU policy-making process. Changes in civil service leadership should, therefore, be seen as part of a broader changing executive leadership of the Commission at large, in which a stronger 'top–down' tendency, stronger political direction, and increasing demands for political responsiveness have become evident. Evolving principles of democratic governance and political control are complemented by evolving notions of professionalism, management, degrees of independence, merit recruitment, and professionalization of the executive. A public service staffed independently of political concerns on the basis of merit has long been a feature of the normal model of core executives.

Senior officials recognized that, for the Commission to continue playing a significant role at the European level, it must turn into a more credible and capable organization in terms of its agenda-setting responsibility and policy leadership role. The reforms brought to light the need for a new type of senior service leadership, one in which the requirements are more that of a *manager* than a *mandarin,* with a greater orientation to the achievements of results and an improved financial accountability.[15]

This new expectation of leadership may have consequences for the division of roles between commissioners, *chefs de cabinet,* and their senior officials. To this dividing line between politics and administration, I will now turn.

Notes

1. <http://news.bbc.co.uk/2/hi/europe/609880.stm>, 25 July 2012.
2. All the director-generals belong to the AD 15 or AD 16 grades, the highest levels in the EU civil service hierarchy. Directors-general heading a Directorate-General are the top-level EU civil servants reporting directly to the Commissioner responsible for the policy area covered by their Directorate-General (DG).
3. The effects of enlargement were especially noticeable in the top grades of the Commission.
4. Kinnock in *Guardian*, 19 July 2000.
5. Kinnock pledged to build the 'best multinational administration in the world' (*Guardian*, 20 Jan. 2000).
6. After the staff regulations came into force in 1962, the lower officials (A8 to A3) were in principle recruited through a competitive entry examination, the concours.
7. Although there are no official quotas, this rule of thumb had been fixed in the staff regulations since the 1960s and still applied to the overall number of staff appointed in all categories and to all DGs.
8. Source: IP/02/124, Brussels, 23 Jan. 2002.
9. Source: IP/02/124, Brussels, 23 Jan. 2002.
10. The Commission's staff rules for appointment are quite restrictive: officials can only be considered for senior management positions if they have been in the grade below the senior post for at least two years. Thus, except for recruitments from outside the Commission, senior officials are usually already in their fifties when appointed.
11. The declaration may contain 'reservations' designed to highlight risks which may have been run in using appropriations or to report any malfunctions.
12. Officials should inform their direct superior, the director-general, the secretary-general, or OLAF (the independent European Anti-Fraud Office) directly in case of malfunctions.
13. Responsibilization means that senior officials have been required to become active in securing the protection of their DG from risks, knowledgeable about their circumstances, and be prepared to act accordingly.
14. Discontent among top officials about the growing body of rules and regulations, which is thought to be burdensome, frustrating, and demotivating, emerges from other studies as well. The findings of Schön-Quinlivan (2007) and Ellinas and Suleiman (2008) indicate dissatisfaction among officials in the Commission about the tendency towards bureaucratization brought about by the reforms, especially with regards to financial rules; and a view that the reform had over-hit the mark and significantly increased the level of red tape in the institution.
15. Cf. Dargie and Locke 1998.

6

An Emerging Political–Administrative Dichotomy

> I am firmly convinced that increasing the efficiency and accountability of the Commission in the future largely depends on greatly reducing the grey areas which currently tend to blur demarcation lines of autonomy and responsibility between those performing more *political tasks* and those more involved with *administration*.
>
> (Romano Prodi, 4 May 1999[1])

1. The Ecology of Political–Bureaucratic Differences

In May 1999, the European Parliament voted overwhelmingly to approve Romano Prodi as the new president of the European Union's Commission. After the twenty outgoing commissioners of the Santer Commission resigned, Prodi pledged to restore the Commission's battered image by rooting out mismanagement, improving efficiency, and increasing the accountability of the Commission. Parliamentarians told Prodi they would watch closely to see whether he would carry out his promise to shape up the Commission: 'After today, Mr Prodi, you and what you do will be scrutinized as never before', said the Socialist Group leader in the EP.[2] One of the central issues that Prodi had to address was a clearer definition of the relationship between politics and administration in the workings of the Commission.

The idea that there is, or ought to be, a clear distinction between the sphere of politics and the sphere of administration is one of the cornerstones of the 'normal' model. In this model, separate roles are assigned to politicians and bureaucrats. The degree of distinctiveness between politicians and bureaucrats depends on the extent to which careers and roles are differentiated and norms that are appropriate to each position are followed (Mouritzen and Svara 2002: 25).

Table 6.1 Politicians and Bureaucrats: Evolving Roles

	Image I	Image II	Image III	Image IV
Implementing Policy	B	B	B	B
Formulating Policy	P	S	S	S
Brokering Interests	P	P	S	S
Articulating Ideals	P	P	P	S

B = bureaucrats' responsibility; P = politicians' responsibility; S = shared responsibility
Source: Aberbach et al. (1981: 239).

Several authors, however, have argued that a clear division is impossible, and a number of empirical studies show varying intermeshings of the two spheres (Putnam 1975; Aberbach et al. 1981; Mouritzen and Svara 2002). In their seminal study conducted in the mid-1970s, Aberbach et al. (1981) outlined four 'images' of the relationship between bureaucrats and politicians. Table 6.1 recapitulates these four images.

These interpretations of the political–bureaucratic division of labour are arranged according to a steady progression of bureaucratic influence in policy-making from Image I to Image IV. Image I upholds the political–administrativen dichotomy of the normal model, with its emphasis on politicians making decisions and bureaucrats implementing them. According to Image II, officials are allowed to involve themselves in policy-making but must confine themselves to imparting relevant facts and knowledge. In Image III, top bureaucrats engage in politics—although they respond to a narrower band of concerns and with less passion or ideology than do politicians. Finally, there are the 'pure hybrids' of Image IV where the line between policy-making and administration essentially vanishes, producing a seamless partnership between politicians and bureaucrats.

Politicians and bureaucrats in the Commission: separated or shared roles?

Image IV (a blurring of roles) would seem an apt description of political–administrative relations at the time of the Santer resignation. Politicians and administrators at the top of the pre-reform Commission had roles that overlapped each other and shared influence. Commission bureaucrats looked like quasi-politicians and were politically involved in a broad range of policy matters. Commissioners looked like quasi-bureaucrats: they had a limited link to an elected body and the simple line of political control from parliament through political executive to bureaucracy did not apply (Page 1997: 21). This fragmentation of authority complicated the notion of political control and accountability.

Political and administrative reforms in the Commission gave rise to changes in the responsibilities and in the roles and behaviour of executive officials.

Have these political and administrative changes resulted in a clearer separation between the political and the administrative levels? Which image is the most appropriate to describe the contemporary division of labour between politicians and bureaucrats at the top of the EU Commission?

To answer these questions this chapter focuses on the elements that form the backbone of executive relationships: rules and responsibilities, recruitment, and role expectations of political executives and senior officials. As conceptualized in the first chapter, key to the normal model is a situation in which rules allocate discrete responsibilities to politicians and bureaucrats and in which each group has a distinct set of accountabilities; in which the recruitment of both groups is established and grounded in distinct systems of appointment: a politicized procedure versus a professionalized one; and in which the role expectations for political executives and their senior bureaucrats are distinct.

2. Rules and Responsibilities: The Politicization and Bureaucratization of Accountability

Accountability mechanisms in the pre-reform Commission consisted of a mixture of intergovernmental, judicial, and technocratic arrangements. The picture that emerges from earlier studies of the Commission was that the answerability of commissioners and senior staff was a hybrid practice (Page 1997; Harlow 2002). Legal means, comitology, and a wide variety of informal methods were used to exercise institutional controls over the EU Commission. Faced with an institutional context that granted legitimacy to multiple sources of authority, EU commissioners and their senior officials encountered diverse, changing, and occasionally conflicting expectations. Some of these expectations were formalized and explicitly stated in treaties, staff regulations and codes of conduct. Some were unstated and became only explicitly formulated during the Santer crisis, in the process of calling the Commission to account.

As a reaction to the ambiguous array of expectations over authority, mandates, responsibilities, rules, standards, and expectations (March and Olsen 1976; Olsen 2008: 196; 2013),[3] political actors in the EU have, in the past decades, developed a range of accountability arrangements to hold commissioners and their officials answerable for their performances. In almost every regard, the recent changes in these arrangements have, in effect, focused primarily on the accountability at the political level and on the accountability of services. Parliamentary committees have considerably increased the political exposure of commissioners. The internal administrative reforms, the expanded mandates of internal and external auditors, and the open access to information regime have had a similar effect at the administrative level.

The new political–bureaucratic accountability arrangements are meant to reduce ambiguity, uncertainty, and conflict regarding who is accountable to whom, when, and how. Yet, as the standards of accountability have risen, so have expectations. The thickening of accountability arrangements has resulted in a significant redefinition of the expectations regarding the behaviour of commissioners and senior officials—one that clearly suggests a dichotomy between politics and administration.

The newly established parliamentary political accountability arrangements have had important consequences for the political role of commissioners. They have not only strengthened their 'political' role in daily policy-making, they have brought about a closer contact between the Commission and Parliament. Treaty reforms have gradually enhanced the power of the Commission president to take and impose collective responsibility over this EU executive. Increased media coverage has emerged as an 'additional' forum for accountability for commissioners. Hence their accountability encompasses a wide range of forums, while commissioners inform and are informed by a broad array of actors, embodying different sets of standards and political values. All this has contributed inevitably to a greater political control over and accountability of the Commission, an increased number of opportunities for holding officeholders and officials answerable for their use of authority and for their performance. Numerous examples in the day-to-day policy-making, noted by those interviewed, illustrate the significance of a political definition of accountability and responsibility.

While the treaty reforms largely changed the Commission's political accountability structure, with the Kinnock reforms the Commission also moved towards result-based reporting in ways that better met administrative accountability requirements. The internal reforms had important implications for the jobs of senior officials. Increasingly, they were expected to assume more 'managerial' roles. Changes in the Commission's financial management tended to give senior officials more autonomy and flexibility in their work but also more responsibility. Performance demands and result-based reporting made it, generally speaking, clearer what top managers were accountable for, and performance indicators provided criteria against which they could be judged. The emphasis on the individual responsibility of directors-general, combined with new promotion and grading procedures and the emphasis on results, marked the shift to a professionalized management culture.

The changes in the political and bureaucratic accountability arrangements had a 'spill-over' effect on the operation of the cabinets. *Chefs de cabinet* were faced with a strengthening of (political) accountability of their political bosses. They also needed to deal with the institutionalization of the new norms and incentives of accountability, professionalism, and a clear code of conduct—to ensure cabinets would simply serve as an instrument to support the policies developed by the president and the commissioners.

Multiplying and strengthening accountability mechanisms alone did not automatically lead to an effective system of executive accountability, but did constitute the basic blocks of political and bureaucratic accountability, which were 'properly' linked and put in place to determine the organization and the workings of the accountability system in the European Commission. Subsequently, the chain of 'delegated authority and accountability' has become more closely tied together to form an 'organizational' structure of assigned responsibilities, in which the loose coupling between the different parts has been tightened.

The result is that the political–bureaucratic relationship at the top of the Commission has evolved into a relationship resembling that between a principal and an agent. It implies a political level that places restrictions and checks on the use of bureaucratic authority, and that disciplines or sanctions those found responsible for shortcomings or wrongdoings. The transplantation of these conceptions of accountability and responsibility from the national context to the EU context was the anchor (or base) for the management of a redefined set of expectations for EU commissioners and their officials. It introduced new dynamics into these relationships, giving political principals the right, and the obligation, to check and control those to whom authority is delegated, and to respond with corrective action if appropriate. This element of hierarchy ensures that democratic control over the institution is not lost or compromised.

The considerable shifts in the accountability expectations of commissioners and their senior officials have led to a greater demarcation of responsibilities. As a consequence, it is possible to discern different dimensions of political and managerial accountability for the commissioners and their top officials, as Figure 6.1 shows. The lines in fan-shape formation mark approximate 'zones of responsibility' of commissioners and their top officials (cf. Barberis 1998: 466) and indicate approximate demarcations of accountability. Some areas were largely reserved for either the political level or the bureaucratic level. The top part of the diagram lies mostly within the political accountability system. The bottom part of the diagram contains accountabilities that lie mostly within the bureaucratic accountability system.

There is also a large overlap and sharing in the areas of responsibility of the commissioners and their directors-general, as the interviewed officials indicated, with the responsibility of commissioners being more of an open-ended or residual type that embraces most of the 'zones of responsibility' of their directors-general. Enhanced transparency and disclosure through performance management and reporting regimes for managing outputs and outcomes

Rules and Responsibilities

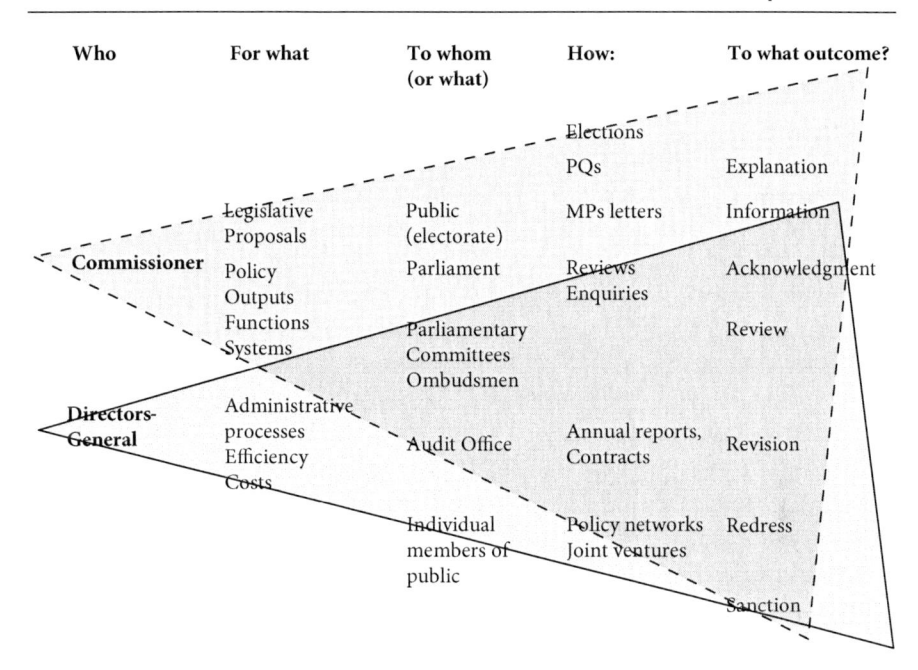

Who	For what	To whom (or what)	How:	To what outcome?
			Elections	
			PQs	Explanation
	Legislative Proposals	Public (electorate)	MPs letters	Information
Commissioner	Policy Outputs Functions Systems	Parliament	Reviews Enquiries	Acknowledgment
		Parliamentary Committees Ombudsmen		Review
Directors-General	Administrative processes Efficiency Costs	Audit Office	Annual reports, Contracts	Revision
		Individual members of public	Policy networks Joint Ventures	Redress
				Sanction

Figure 6.1. Zones of Political and Administrative Accountability
Source: Adapted from Barberis (1998).

have not only strengthened managerial, but also political accountability mechanisms. Managerial accountability has become embedded in political accountability.

The interviews with commissioners, their heads of cabinet, and directors-general revealed an implicit division of responsibilities between the commissioner's office and the departments. But not one that is completely blatant. A rearrangement of accountabilities and formal responsibilities, among institutions and officeholders, not only affects the formal distribution of responsibility; it also makes responsibility contestable. Reorganization of accountabilities and attempts to clarify the question of 'who is responsible' for certain outcomes, also reinforces incentives to avoid or limit blame by adopting various strategies in times of heated political criticism of Commission decisions. From a blame avoidance perspective, a strengthened and linked political–bureaucratic accountabilities architecture induces a risk-averse strategy that limits blame if outcomes are adverse (see Hood 2002, 2007). A director-general describes his blame-generating strategy if his commissioner neglects his advice:

> I prefer to say this doesn't work. It doesn't work for these and these reasons. If you do it, then I will write a note and I warn you. I have that note and if it goes wrong, then it is your mistake.

An Emerging Dichotomy

Another director-general pointed to the risk of crossing the borderlines between the zones of responsibility:

> The commissioner's cabinet doesn't work efficiently. It is full of people that go for details. They should go for the policy line and get their bloody hands off the details, because if they get into the details they go over that borderline between politics and administration. Then they try to micromanage. Micromanagement is death for a cabinet. What they don't realize, because a lot of them are young and idealistic people, is that they actually incur a disciplinary risk, because if they interfere and it can be proven, then if something goes wrong, then they will have to take the blame. They are putting the commissioner at risk, unnecessarily. Why should the commissioner take an administrative risk? That is stupid. They shouldn't do it.

One of the implications of this embedded responsibility is that accountability has become an area of contestation and that blame avoidance has become part of normal institutional politics at the top of the Commission.

3. Recruitment: Politicized, Personalized, and Professionalized

The recruitment process and decisions of appointment were, in the first decades of the Commission history, marked by a lack of formalized criteria. The lack of tangible criteria left open the possibility for basing recruitment decisions on informal rules, personal preferences, or political concerns (Seidel 2010: 91–2). The posts of the most senior category of officials in the Commission (directors-general and directors) were qualified as 'political posts',[4] which meant that a candidate external to the European administration could be appointed or 'parachuted in'. Likewise, member-state governments, political parties, interest groups, industries, and trade unions all sought to influence the selection process of the key political and bureaucratic positions in the Commission. They wanted to ensure a high representation of their nationals by the use of claims on 'reserved posts' within a Directorate General—the 'national flags' system (cf. Coombes 1970; Cini 1996; Page 1997: 68). This all contributed to a highly contentious and politicized picture of the recruitment of officeholders and officials at the top of the EU Commission.

Over the past decades, recruitment patterns for both commissioners and senior officials alike have altered in such a way that the progression of a demarcation between the political and the administrative spheres can be observed. There has been a change and a 'thickening' of procedures and actors involved in the appointment process. For commissioners, the Commission president and the EP have become significant actors in the selection process; for directors-general, the recruitment procedures have been standardized. For cabinets, new rules have been formulated that gave the cabinets a more markedly denationalized structure. The changes have been translated into new

Recruitment and Appointments

```
                    ┌─ Commissioner ──── investiture & ──── political skills & ──── career
                    │                    censure            representation          politicians
Executive ──────────┤
Selection           ├─ Cabinet Chef ──── personal choice ── matching & ──────────── internal and
                    │                                       professionalism         external
                    │                                                               candidates
                    └─ Director-general ─ formalized ────── managerial ──────────── internal
                                          procedure         competences              candidates

                                          procedure         demands                  supply
```

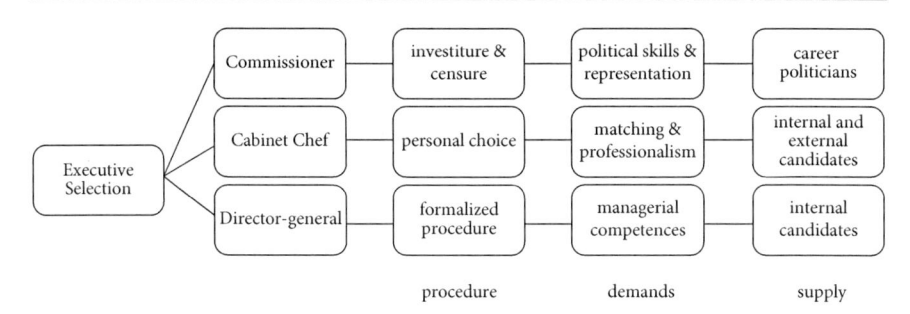

Figure 6.2. Executive Recruitment in the EU Commission

procedures, demands, and supply factors in the appointment process. These are summarized in Figure 6.2, and reveal distinct recruitment patterns for the three key actors at the top of the Commission

The procedure for appointing commissioners has become more 'politicized'. The new commissioners are vetted by the EP before taking office. This has contributed to a new form of 'credit' that commissioners can accrue for their internal and external leadership during their mandate; commissioners can claim a legitimacy that is not simply based upon bureaucratic hierarchical rank, but reflects the fact that their appointment is a political one, supported by a parliamentary procedure. The growing number of commissioners with a ministerial background indicates a move away from more narrowly technical-based roles, in the direction of a broader and more political approach. After a career at the national level, commissioners tend to come in with pronounced political role conceptions. As a director-general noted about the behaviour of commissioners: 'The President comes in and behaves like a prime minister in a small country; my commissioner comes in, and she acts as if she is a minister in her country.'

As the selection of commissioners has become more 'politicized', the appointment of top officials has been designed to become more standardized and more guided by professional criteria. In the procedures for recruiting senior officials, general managerial competencies have become increasingly relevant. Denationalization of the cabinets has contributed to a stronger personalization in the recruitment of the heads of cabinet. New rules have resulted in smaller and more European cabinets. Professional norms now weigh heavily in the selection process. An enhanced 'float' of officials who work for the commissioners in their cabinets, and go back after a while to work in the services, has not only increased the informal and formal interaction between the political and administrative levels; it has contributed to a further professionalization of the cabinet system.

The recruiting procedures for commissioners and their senior staff have become more clearly differentiated in terms of selection, demands, and the supply of candidates, becoming more openly politicized for the commissioners, professionalized for the directors-general, and mixed professionalized–personalized for the *chefs de cabinet*. This has resulted in stronger demarcations between the people in these positions.

In two areas, however, an increased congruence between the recruitment at the political and the administrative level has occurred. First, there is a convergence between the political and administrative groups in their training and educational backgrounds. Commissioners, their cabinet heads, and senior officials all belong to the categories with the highest level of education. They tend to hold degrees in law, economy, or political science, and have often enjoyed the opportunities of an international education. On both the political and the bureaucratic sides, the number of specialist career patterns continues to dwindle. Most of the commissioners in Barroso's College have a general political and not a specialist background; and if we look at the top of the administration, we see a parallel tendency towards the development of generalist career patterns among senior officials.

Second, the temporal dimension has become, not only for commissioners and their heads of cabinet, but also for their senior officials, a relevant factor in their appointment (and management). As incumbent commissioners remain in office for the length of their mandate, the non-permanency of the post means that directors-general and cabinet heads, too, serve for relatively short periods. The dynamics are therefore similar for managers and politicians alike. All groups have an interest in delivering output and showing off the successes of their programmes before the end of their terms are reached. Likewise, towards the end of their term of office, the next step in their career becomes an issue of concern for all categories.

A comparison of executive selection at the political and bureaucratic levels reveals two central values in the appointment process: merit and representation. There is an increased emphasis on merit and competence in the recruitment procedures—even for appointments at the political level. Ideas about democratic politics and good governance provided a justification for replacing patronage by merit. The close interrogation of nominated commissioners in individual hearings by the EP and day-long interviews of candidate senior managers by the recruiting officer symbolize this increased value of meritocratic or competency assessment, in which qualification must override affiliation.

But affiliation remains relevant. The desire to maintain a geographical balance in which all nationalities are represented persists. As an international organization, the Commission tries to ensure a wide spread of nationalities in cabinets, senior positions, and even in the College. Add-ons of 'representation', along the lines of relevant political cleavages (and nationality continues to be a significant cleavage at the international level), remain a practical value in the appointment process, despite its merit character.

To ensure a national balance in the composition of the Commission top is, therefore, an operational guideline. However, the member states have lost control over the selection process with regard to all three positions—commissioners, cabinet heads, and senior managers. The new staff regulations that came into force during the administrative reforms of the Prodi Commission aimed at avoiding institutional clustering according to nationality, and thus eliminated 'flags' from the posts to diminish the impact of national networks. Hence, although the principle of nationality still plays a role in the executive selection process, the process itself has been transformed from a system of recruitment dominated by patronage into one that is characterized by standardized political and professional procedures. The increased role of the president and the political say of the EP in the appointment of commissioners, the introduction of standards and formalized appointments for senior officials, the introduction of job-rotation for senior managers, the denationalization of the cabinets: all underline the increased autonomy of the Commission and a stronger control over the EU executive that is situated at the supranational level.

In the pre-reform Commission, the top executive posts were filled by external recruitment. Commissioners, their cabinets, and the parachuted senior officials were 'outsiders'. Today, at the level of the Commission's senior management, insider recruitment is the dominant strategy. At the political level (among commissioners and their cabinets) outsider recruitment still fills a substantial portion of the positions. The commissioners are outsiders and so are some members of their cabinets. The flow from central positions in the bureaucracy to central cabinet positions (and vice versa) has increased the number of insiders working at the political level and contributed to institutional integration between political outsiders and bureaucratic insiders. Given the emerging divide between commissioners and senior staff, in their responsibilities and recruitment, the next question is: has it also led to distinctions in the way they are expected to perform their roles?

4. Role Expectations: Overlapping Roles, Distinct Perspectives

Policy roles: authority versus advice

There are clear contrasts between the roles of today's commissioners and those of their senior officials. Commissioners are expected to set and legitimize the policy agenda; i.e. to make choices concerning the political mission and priorities. And commissioners need to seek sufficient support to assure acceptance for new policy proposals. A director-general gave his view of the role of commissioners, saying: 'they take the principal decision, and they have to take the torch into the College and get acceptance'. To win political consent for plans and proposals is perceived as a key aspect of the commissioner's policy-making role. It enables officials to perform their part of the policy-making: advising, planning, coordinating, and budgeting. A director-general described it as follows:

> If you want to have a role as a commissioner, then you have to work for the compromise. So you bring in your political analysis and bring in your national experience, but you have to translate it into something that fits with the general. The sooner you do that, the better you can further your own political desires. And then you have to say to your director-general: 'provide me with the tools and the instruments to carry this out. And give me political advice and help me in translating in what I have in my mind, in something that is operational in the college or *vis-à-vis* the broader public.'

Commissioners are expected to perform this role proactively in order to make a difference. The introduction of activity-based management has assigned a more strategic role to the political executive in the policy process. Likewise, in an increasingly complex and fragmented policy-making arena, the commissioners—and the political level in particular—have to take greater action and become more directly involved in the policy process in order simply to maintain some semblance of control. Gone are the days when commissioners and their senior public servants worked in relative isolation, developing policies. Shifts towards more collective policy-making (EP, Council, member states, OMC), but also the growing dominance of the Commission president and its office in that process, and the pervasiveness of public opinion polling have combined to render policy-making progressively more complex, which requires more political salesmanship to become effective.

The *senior service* is increasingly attuned to an administrative role in the policy process, emphasizing the more managerial aspects of their role. Senior officials described their role as pertaining more to managing policy advice and their department, rather than being involved in day-to-day development of policy. The role of the *heads of cabinets* is that of a personal adviser to the commissioner, politically sensitive, operationally active, appointed to further the aims of the commissioner, and acting in the commissioner's name. They can function as a counterpoint to the Commission bureaucracy.

For commissioners, it means that they receive advice from at least two sources: the director-general, who is primarily responsible for policy development, and the head of cabinet, who is responsible for the operations at the political–administrative interface. Each source provides the commissioner with advice, but from a different perspective. Directors-general are more likely to be advocates for their DG, whereas heads of cabinets are more likely to represent the 'Berlaymont view'—the horizontal view from the political level. Heads of cabinets try to maintain a level playing field for 'their' commissioner. Their position and role is a more politicized one, their focus and activities are much more oriented towards the political sphere. They are the right hand of the commissioner, and are expected to handle matters as the commissioner would prefer. Directors-general, on the other hand, work from a more technical position and see their role more in terms of providing a professional input to the development of the commissioner's proposals. They have access to greater expertise, but advise the commissioner more from a vertical sector-related perspective. They have a more distant position from the political level, with a commitment to professional values and competence, and advocacy of European integration. Both these advisers strive for responsiveness in their policy roles, but their responsiveness extends to different dimensions of the commissioner's work. As a director-general notes:

> And the head of cabinet is really the political adviser. The head of cabinet is a sort of junior minister as a political adviser. You see that because the head represents his boss in the college of commissioners. So it is much more political. It is also depending on the head of cabinet. It is not technical. He is not expected to know of the details, but to do politics, whereas I am expected to know enough of the details, and to have some political sense. It is a different role, but a complementary role.

Commissioners, senior officials, and heads of cabinet perceive clear and distinctive contributions of their own role to the policy process. But the boundary line between their roles can sometimes be blurred, especially when it comes to politics.

Political roles: broad versus specific

Commissioners and their senior officials both work in a political environment and both perform political roles, but their roles differ as to the kind of politics in which they are involved. Commissioners, who are expected to steer policy proposals from the department through the College and parliament, need to win support for policy plans by convincing different stakeholders of the benefits of a particular policy proposal. Commissioners also need to interact successfully with actors outside the department: their colleague-commissioners, the president, MEPs, their own political party, and key interest groups. In these encounters and arenas political judgement, experience, and crafts(wo)manship are crucial assets that a commissioner can bring to the political–bureaucratic relationship. They are expected to defend the department's interests in political struggles over policy and budgets.

In this political role, commissioners deal mostly with broad ideas, parliamentary politics, member states, and the politics of parties, whereas most of the time, heads of cabinets and directors-general deal with the politics of bureaucracies, advising commissioners and so on; they deal with the specifics of the political issue at hand. Senior officials try to defend their own turf or work out alliances with other departments to push departmental policy plans through, or to keep other departments off their turf. It is in their interest to build the commissioner up to wage political battles over the policy plans, with both substantive and tactical advice. In this they fulfil important political roles—although not in a party-political sense—and in this they are highly influential in terms of policy-making, but more in the sense of Putnam's political bureaucrat.

5. Normalization: 'Politicized' Commissioners, 'Depoliticized' Officials

There is evidence of both *separation and sharing* in the role interpretations, as became clear during the interviews, but the differences in perspective of commissioners, heads of cabinets, and directors-general clearly stand out. Their *responsibilities, careers, their aims and actions*, and their ways of thinking about public policy, were very distinctive across the different positions. Table 6.2 summarizes the essentials of the three positions. The contrast between the political and the bureaucratic leadership extends to their key functions in the policy process. Commissioners are expected to bring political vision and authority by mobilizing political support, whereas the key functions of the bureaucrats are believed to be management and delivering policy proposals. The key function of heads of cabinets relates to fostering horizontal coordination, communication, brokering, and the monitoring of the policy process. There is a clear demarcation of political and bureaucratic leadership roles. Commissioners, heads of cabinets, and top officials have contrasting 'perspectives' on their leadership, not only according to the roles they are expected to fulfil in the policy process, but also in their core aims, their values, and in activities undertaken to accomplish their goals. The conception of the Commission as a 'pure hybrid', in which commissioners and bureaucrats act as in Aberbach *et al.*'s (1981) Image IV, is gradually disappearing.

On the other hand, a strict division of labour in which officials stand apart from politics, as depicted in Image I, is considered an unlikely form of the political–bureaucratic divide, one not to be found in reality. Commissioners and senior staff share a belief that the department must be involved in policy development. Directors-general recognize that they share the role of providing advice with the cabinet heads. They expect that they will be at the table offering policy input and that their advice will be respected and often, though not always, heeded. Thus, in the Commission, the bureaucracy has a

Table 6.2 Separate and Shared Elements in Executive Relationships at the Top of the Commission

	Separated			Shared
	Commissioner	Cabinet Head	Director-General	
Accountability	Political	Informal and professional	Administrative	Principal–agent like relationship Overlapping 'zones' of responsibility
Appointment	Politicians by background Investiture procedure (EP) Politicized appointment	Float between cabinets and services 'Personalized' appointment	Flexibility Merit as basis for selection prior to geographical balance. Professionalized appointment	Time element Background and training Representation— geographical and gender balance
Key function in policy process	Authority Mission, strategy Initiate policies Mobilize resources Sell policies	Advise Horizontal and vertical coordination policy proposals Facilitation	Advise Initiate and develop policies Deliver policy proposals	
Actions	Building coalitions, consensus, find political support	Managing Advise Brokering and Bargaining	Management and administration	Doing politics
Values	Political guidelines Control Responsibility	Serve and deliver Professionalism	Serve and deliver Professionalism Autonomy Responsibility	Responsiveness

clear role in policy formulation, and this role is shared with the political level. When asked, the interviewees tended to endorse something approximating Image II, in which directors-general concern themselves with technical matters and the feasibility of the policies, specifically contributing technical and administrative capacity to the policy process, but leaving the political values and the organization of consensus to the politicians.

In sum, the division of labour, between politicians and bureaucrats in the EU Commission, is generally shifting in the direction of Image II and Image III. These two images from Aberbach et al. (1981: 241–3) are a good empirical approximation of the distinct orientations to political–bureaucratic leadership observed at the top of the EU Commission. Heads of cabinets have a position in between. They function more and more as a professionalized 'third force' between these distinctive political–bureaucratic worlds. Much depends on the sector and the persons involved in this political–bureaucratic relationship. Normalization has pushed the key political and bureaucratic actors towards a more clearly demarcated executive. The general tendency of the political changes examined here has been towards controlling the influence that the Commission exerts over the design and execution of the policy-making process. The thickening of accountability arrangements and the changed arrangements with regard to appointment and policy-making have produced new behavioural expectations. It has made politicians and bureaucrats tune in to different incentives (cf. Aberbach *et al.* 1981: 254). The more structured the policy process is, with separate incentives for each category, the clearer the political–administrative division is. The desire to 'reduce the grey areas which blurred the political-administrative demarcation lines' (in Prodi's words) has thus brought a significant redefinition of the role of commissioners and their senior officials.

Furthermore, several developments have served to reinforce one another. Politicized recruitment procedures have, for instance, brought in a group of commissioners with extensive political experience acting in a more politicized way. Merit recruitment has resulted in a more professionalized service with managerial role conceptions. This all has contributed to the emergence of a clearer demarcation of the political and the administrative parts of the Commission.

The Commission politics and administration division seems to have evolved to a modified version of the politics–administration dichotomy inspired by Wilson and Weber. The Prodi Commission actually acted on such a dichotomy when designing reforms to increase political control over the bureaucracy. After the fall of the Santer Commission, the Prodi and the Barroso Commmisions became more critical of the management, which they viewed as a cause of the governance problems in the Commission.

The establishment of distinct boundaries between the respective roles of the commissioners and senior officials and heads of cabinet has promoted awareness and an understanding of their own responsibilities. The roles that political executives and senior officials have adopted for themselves, and see for each other, depend on the way their relationship is organized, and this can have important consequences for the manner in which core executives are managed; and for the way they cooperate—as we will see in the next chapter.

Notes

1. Speech to EP, 4 May 1999.
2. Pauline Green quoted in *Guardian*, 5 May 1999.

Notes

3. Van Gerven (2009: 121) explains that the position of commissioners is ambiguous. They are not civil servants, but holders of public office: 'Since they are not subjected to staff regulations, one has to rely on the Treaty provisions to know their obligations.'
4. These posts implied that the required recruitment procedure for Commission officials, through the competitive entry examination (the concours), did not apply (Seidel 2010: 83).

7

Executive Relationships in a 'Normalized' EU Commission

> Government depends not only on a supply of able politicians and bureaucrats, but even more on a successful interaction between these two ... groups.
>
> (Heclo 1977: 3)

1. Politicians and Bureaucrats: Reassessing The Relationship

'The ability of politicians to oversee the ever-increasing influence of the bureaucracy doesn't grow in line with that influence. It can't—after all, human capacity has its limits. There are 27 commissioners, which means 27 directorate-generals. And 27 directorate-generals means that everyone needs to prove that they are needed by constantly producing new directives, strategies, or projects', said former European commissioner Günter Verheugen, in *Der Spiegel* in 2010, a few days after he left Brussels, having completed his ten years in office.[1] Verheugen's view of commissioners railing against an out-of-control bureaucracy fits the common perception of the Commission as a runaway bureaucracy. According to this view, technical expertise, bureaucratic activism, the inherent desire for autonomy, and the command of information enable bureaucratic professionals to dominate the policy process.

The question of political control and administrative responsiveness remains a pervasive theme in the analysis of political–bureaucratic relationships also in the Commission. In the *normal* model, politicians are expected to dominate policy- and decision-making, while administrators perform a compliant role. In this model, the administration is not only *separated* from politics, as argued in Chapter 6, but also *subordinated* to politics. This has become a standard way of conceptualizing political–administrative relationships and is also the groundwork of many democratic structures

Table 7.1 Continuum of Political–Bureaucratic Relationships

Normal model	Weberian state—clear separation between politicians and the administration exists, whereby senior officials are 'on tap' rather than on top.
Village life	Senior officials and politicians became mutually cooperative elites with a primary interest in maintaining the State and promote its efficient and appropriate functioning.
Functional village life	A certain degree of integration in civil service and political careers. A politician and civil servant from one government department may have more in common than a minister with his political cabinet colleagues heading different governmental portfolios.
Adversarial politics	A significant split between the two groups (politicians and bureaucrats), with no clear resolutions to their struggle for power.
Administrative state	A clear separation between policy-makers and administration, but in which civil servants (bureaucracy) are the dominant force.

in which politicians occupy formally superior positions to administrators. Diametrically opposed to this model is the runaway bureaucracy that Guy Peters (1988) calls the administrative state model, in which the concentration of expertise and specialized knowledge undermines political control and administrative responsiveness.

Using the framework presented by Peters (1988), these models can be viewed as being ranged at the extreme ends of a continuum of political control and administrative responsiveness, with, in the middle, three other ideal-typical modes of political–bureaucratic relationship. Table 7.1 displays this continuum of possible relationships.

In Peters's typology, there are three intermediate categories between the two extreme ends of the continuum: 'village life', 'functional village life', and 'adversarial politics', in which the relationship is more equal. The notion of 'adversarial politics' refers to a strongly politicized relationship in which politicians and bureaucrats compete for control over public policy. In the village life model, cooperation rather than conflict characterizes the interactions between the 'players', each seeing that their most important goals will be achieved by working together instead of attempting to 'win' the game. While the village life conception conceptualizes government as a single entity, the 'functional village life' model views government as being divided among a number of competing policy sectors. Within each sector there may be a good deal of integration, but across those policy areas there may be more competition than cooperation.

An additional intermediate model that characterizes contemporary political–administrative relations is Jim Svara's (2001, 2006) notion of 'complementarity', based on the presumption that politicians and administrators are highly dependent upon each other for getting their respective jobs done.

Svara (2001) argues that most current interactions among politicians and officials resemble the win–win situation of complementarity, in contrast to those concerned with bureaucratic power.

Branding the political–bureaucratic relations at the top of the Commission as a prototypical runaway bureaucracy, as Verheugen does, makes good press. But does the shoe still fit the Commission? Political and administrative reforms in recent decades have introduced several devices that have tied the administration more closely to the political level and have given the European Parliament powers to monitor the Commission more closely. What model is an adequate approximation of the executive relationship in today's Commission? A more systematic reassessment may throw new light on this question.

Normalizing the political–bureaucratic interface

At the end of the 1990s, the Commission was viewed as a typical example of a runaway bureaucracy operating without much democratic control (Page 1997; Pollack 2003). As the report of the Committee of Independent Experts revealed in 1999, many of the difficulties leading up to the resignation of the Santer Commission were classic political–bureaucratic relationship problems that can be briefly summarized under the following headings:

- *Political control and administrative responsiveness*: Unclear and tenuous linkages between the political and the technical level inhibited effective steering and supervision of the administration by the political level.
- *Communication infrastructure*: The increasing power of the cabinets made it difficult to forge cooperation and steering. The CIE observed that the cabinets often acted as screens and fences, impeding direct communication between commissioners and departments, which resulted in a distant, needlessly hierarchical, and bureaucratic approach.[2]
- *Norms and expectations:* Different values and contrasting perspectives between the political and administrative level in the Commission nourished tensions and animosity that produced difficulties in working together.

The introduction of new arrangements that placed greater emphasis on the accountability and performance of the Commission bred also new expectations about the behaviour of commissioners and their senior officials, and their interaction. In a way, they were projected to achieve a 'normalizing' of the interaction between the political and the technical level in the EU Commission. The innovations were:

- Centralization in the EU Commission and a strengthening of central coordination mechanisms steering the Commission's wider agenda and policy issues. This was also intended to keep political–bureaucratic conflicts in line.
- The use and development of a number of result-oriented managerial tools, including mission statements, strategic plans, and performance measurement, in order to mitigate the natural tensions between politicians and bureaucrats by creating common ground around achieving results.
- The use of working agreements and codes of conduct, intended to gain greater clarity and precision in political–bureaucratic responsibilities.
- A 'revolving door' policy, under which officials occupying central positions in the bureaucracy spend time working in the cabinets, after which they return to the services. This facilitates the development of informal networks stretching across the political–administrative divide.
- The easy exit option, which provided the organizational suppleness to move executive officials to other posts, to find convenient alternative places for those who are considered ill-suited for a 'cooperative' working relationship.

These arrangements were meant to bring the bureaucracy in line with the political level. Setting clear political goals, as embodied in the political guidelines and the SPP, could give executive officials a better sense of the overall aims. For commissioners, cabinets, and senior officials it was no longer possible to operate within their own parallel universes without interacting much with one another. Temporal asynchronies between politicians and bureaucrats were synchronized with these new arrangements, which had the added benefit of clearly and publicly establishing the Commission's policy objective and time frame. Moreover, an orderly policy process was introduced to promote cooperative management and collaboration. When people know their place in the system, the division of labour may be exploited more efficiently (March 1991). Formalization can in many instances decrease conflicts, and it makes it easier to reach consensus within a shorter time frame. But did it change the political–bureaucratic relationship?

Reassessing the Commission's executive relationships

The chief aim of this chapter is to arrive at a systematic assessment of the normalization of the political–bureaucratic relationship among the *triads* working at the Commission's apex. The idea of a triad emphasizes that most of the communication and provision of information occurs not simply

A 'Normalized' EU Commission

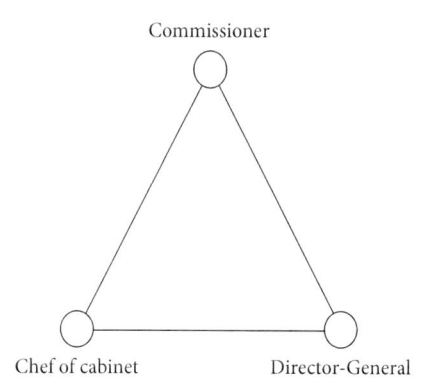

```
                    Commissioner
                         ○
                        ╱ ╲
                       ╱   ╲
                      ╱     ╲
                     ╱       ╲
                    ╱         ╲
                   ○───────────○
             Chef of cabinet   Director-General
```

Figure 7.1. Political–Bureaucratic Triads in the EU Commission

as a bilateral process between the political and the bureaucratic level, but multilaterally, between the commissioner, the heads of cabinet, and the directors-general. Figure 7.1 displays the main triadic configuration at work inside the core executive of the Commission's pyramid, which is the basic unit of analysis.

Has the relationship in these triads moved in the direction of the normal model? This deceptively simple question is not easy to answer. Two points should be made at the outset. First, the interaction between politicians and administrators may be one of the most crucial arenas of institutional politics. But at the same time, there is very little known about how this should be studied. These executive relationships within the upper echelons of public institutions are difficult to measure, hard to access, and difficult to research. There are no standard procedures for how to gauge them. This assessment, therefore, also has a largely exploratory character, with the ultimate purpose of a reappraisal of these relationships.

Second, given the emergence of democratic governance structures around the Commission, we expect a 'normalization' of this political–bureaucratic relationship that should become manifest in a clearer political and hierarchical control and an enhanced administrative responsiveness. Three dimensions will be used to translate these elements of executive relationships into operational terms. The first dimension concerns a detailed breakdown of the political–bureaucratic interaction, which gives a preliminary indication of the organization and character of these political–bureaucratic relationships. The second dimension is used to explore the underlying informal norms and expectations in the political–bureaucratic interaction. The third dimension relates to the perceived influence of the key actors in the relationship.

Table 7.2 displays a simplified representation of the different models of interaction in terms of these three dimensions and their values. On the basis of the exploration of these three dimensions, a cautious conclusion is drawn

Table 7.2 Characteristics of the Ideal-Typical Models of Interactions between Politicians and Administrators

Political-bureaucratic relationship		Normal	Village life	Functional village	Adversarial	Administrative state
	Interaction	Authority imposed by political guidelines, tightly coupled and forced by political cycles, command	Consensual, coupled, aligned and integrative culture, bargaining	Compartmentalized, bargaining	Conflict, opposition, and competition, turf wars, power politics	Expertise, technocratic, distant and loosely coupled, stability
	Norms	Loyalty	Trust, respect, reciprocity	Trust, respect, reciprocity	Distrust, competition	Independence
	Political control and responsiveness	Hierarchy, uni-directional	Reciprocating	Poly-centric,	Poly-centric	Independence

as to whether the relationship between the key actors at the apex has become normalized.

2. The Organization of the Political–Bureaucratic Interface

Interaction, the first dimension, is facilitative behaviour and can lead to different patterns in the political–bureaucratic relationship (see Table 7.2). In the normal model, the overall interaction is determined by political cycles and commissioners can only provide effective political direction if they clearly communicate their policy objectives and their priorities to the officials in the services. Senior officials can only be responsive if they know the political preferences of their commissioners. In the normal, but also in the village, models, politicians and bureaucrats are expected to have regular patterns of interaction and information exchange. In the adversarial model, interaction is expected to be distant and conflict-ridden; in the administrative state model, the communication process is expected to be remote and unaffected by political cycles.

Communication in the triads: the backbone of the relationship

Meetings between the commissioner, the cabinet, and senior officials are institutionalized and take place on a regular basis. Specific principles regarding the arrangement of this communication are set out in a working agreement between the services and the cabinets at the start of the commissioner's term. Most commissioners meet with their senior officials at least once every two weeks in a seminar type of meeting, where senior officials and commissioners discuss various ideas and come to an agreement about the best way forward. Regular interaction, direct and in person, is perceived as essential for a better mutual understanding and flow of information.

While the bi-weekly meetings are used by commissioners and their senior officials to hash out ideas and issues, they do not provide enough time for effective relationship building. Frequent and sustained communication occurs most frequently through phone calls and emails. But relationships are most effectively built during face-to-face interactions, and commissioners and senior staff know that this also requires meetings out of work hours—taking place within the context of more casual get-togethers. These opportunities are critical for executives to cement the working relationship and to bring down hurdles to cooperation; to provide senior officials with the opportunity to get to 'know the mind' of their commissioner, and to work on an understanding of the respective roles themselves, as well as agreement on acceptable and efficient operating modes. A director-general put it as follows:

> The ideal thing is that you have regular contact with the commissioner, and that this regular contact allows you some free space to talk politics. You do need that. Because you need to know what your commissioner wants and to translate that into what is realistic and that takes time. And the commissioner needs to listen to what you feel are viable options. If the commissioner understands what are the real options, and not the ideal options, then we save a lot of time and we can actually be productive.

Organizational routines and the nature of the portfolio of the commissioner affect the intensity and organization of interaction. But interaction and communication patterns between commissioners and their directors-general and heads of cabinets are also highly contingent upon the commissioner's personal work style. Their individual involvement in the policy-making process, their motivation for leading, their strategies for managing information, their willingness to tolerate conflict, and their preferred strategies for resolving conflict determine how the communication and interaction are arranged. A cabinet head described it thus:

> We have a good relationship. The fact that the commissioner comes from a country in which there are good, joined up relationships helps. It is not that we have a commissioner–cabinet world and somewhere far away the DG. She is pretty informal also on talking to the director-general on the telephone. And she is more keen than the former commissioner to know what is going on in the portfolio.

Heads of cabinet and directors-general also need to work in close rapport. The communication between them is one of the building blocks in this political–bureaucratic relationship. They meet each other weekly and instructions from the cabinet to the services are communicated via this channel.[3]

Continuous interaction between the key actors in the triad, between the political and administrative level, forms the backbone of the relationship. It is, however, a set of *additional* factors that determines how this interaction is shaped, as we will see next.

Politicized versus technocratic: issues shape interaction

Highly political salient issues that draw large amounts of (organized) public attention, and whose boundaries of conflict extend to the broader social and political arenas, are more demanding in terms of the political–bureaucratic interaction. When issues are very 'hot', they are more likely to be managed hands-on by the political stratum. Issues differ in terms of their political management, as a director-general pointed out:

> There are sectors that are much easier. Agriculture is much easier than Justice and Home affairs. The latter are very much more complicated, also politically, because the legal basis on which you operate is grey. It is not clear. You don't

have exclusive community competences. You have a mix of national competence and very weak community measures. At the same time the public is increasingly aware that you need European solutions, even if national politicians say no. ... But the ground is full of mines. Justice and Home Affairs, Defence, Foreign Policy are a nightmare.

In some sectors, this demands effective cooperative action between the political and administrative spheres to operate successfully, in others close cooperation is less decisive. Communication patterns vary substantially from area to area, reflecting the specific issue features and the relative influence of politicians and civil servants. On politicized matters, the autonomy of civil servants is generally constrained (cf. Aberbach *et al.* 1981: 250; Peters 1988: 166–7). But on purely technical matters, where the size of the information asymmetry between politicians and civil servants is large, the role of civil servants is larger.

Also within the commissioner's portfolio, political–bureaucratic interaction is organized in various different ways. Commissioners cannot possibly master all policy issues and go head to head with every member of their cabinet or department on the details of each policy proposal. Commissioners must decide what battles to fight. By concentrating on a few prestigious policy areas or pet projects, commissioners create less antagonism in other areas. When issues are both materially and politically inconsequential, there are few incentives—at least for senior officials—to engage in an energy-sapping conflict. These 'zones of indifference'—as Barnard (1938: 169) has called them, are normally areas of smooth cooperation with little discussion.

'Living apart together': diminishing relevance of the spatial dimension

The distance between politics and administration is not only a symbolic one; it is also a physical reality in the Commission. The Berlaymont building in Brussels is the headquarters of the European Commission in the 'European district'. It is the seat of the Commission president, the commissioners, and the cabinets. The DGs and the services of the Commission itself are spread over some sixty odd buildings and scattered across a multitude of different locations across Brussels.

The residential and organizational locus of the top of the Commission, and the physical distance between the political and the administrative spheres, is thought to have an important impact on political–bureaucratic communication (cf. Egeberg 2003).[4] The arrangement facilitates the exchange between the various cabinets in the horizontal coordination of policies and in preparation for the weekly meetings of the College, the cabinet heads, and the deputy heads. The flip side is that the offices of commissioners and director-generals are in separate buildings, that meetings need to be organized in advance, and informal conversations may not be part of the daily work routine as they would have been if they shared the same corridor.

In order to bridge the vertical divide between the political and the administrative levels, Prodi decided in 1999 to house commissioners in the DGs for which they were responsible (Christiansen 2001: 752–3). Commissioners (and their cabinets) had to move out of the Commission headquarters, in the Berlaymont building, and move in with their respective DGs. This was meant to bring about a more intense contact between the commissioner, cabinets, and the services. It soon became clear, however, that whatever was gained in terms of vertical coherence was paid for by a loss of horizontal coordination. Housing the commissioners and their cabinets alongside their departments was found to make communication among commissioners and among cabinets significantly more difficult and time-consuming. This was considered to be one of the factors contributing to a lack of collegiality in the Prodi Commission (Peterson 2004).[5] For this reason, Barroso decided to move his commissioners back to the Berlaymont.

Spatial proximity is thought to be relevant for contacts and political control. But the officials interviewed indicated that being located in different buildings does not automatically mean poorer communication or a diminished responsiveness to the political level. Most offices are located in the European quarter and the Berlaymont building is within walking distance. The Berlaymont, however, is a very large building and it is doubtful whether sharing the same building would have facilitated informal, unplanned meetings among Commission officials.

The interviewees were largely unanimous on this point: distance does not matter. The availability of internet, email, cell phones, and text messages has made communication much easier. In the estimation of the actors in the triad, the geographical diffusion of the Commission's administration over different buildings in Brussels and the physical space between the political and the administrative level has little to no effect on their interaction.[6]

Political cycles: the increasing relevance of the temporal dimension

The timing of the political context is exceedingly important for the interaction at the top of the Commission. Performance management and parliamentary timetables have created a context that imposes temporal demands on public policy-making and political–bureaucratic cooperation. These demands can take the form of externally imposed deadlines for producing deliverables; ongoing rounds of repetitive events and interdependencies, such as the budgeting process, political cycles, and summits.

The time element, inherent in institutionalized representative democracies, has become a far more prominent part of the political–bureaucratic relationship at the top of the EU Commission. Elections produce a kind of shock, although at regular intervals (Heclo and Wildavsky 1974; Kingdon 1995; Jacobsen 2006, 2011). The vote for a new European Parliament, also means a new Commission, new people in political positions, new policies, and a general staff turnover.

New triads of commissioners, cabinet heads, and directors-general enter the organization and have to work through several stages of group development—the social psychological forming, storming, norming, performing, and adjourning (Tuckman 1965) stages that are all necessary and inevitable in order for these triads to grow, to face up to challenges, to tackle problems, to find solutions, to plan work, and to deliver results.

First, when a new commissioner comes in, or a new director-general is appointed, there is usually a period of learning. New commissioners have to find their way in the Commission, and senior officials must figure out how to relate to new commissioners and their cabinets. A director-general noted:

> There is a very difficult period at the beginning of each mandate period, very difficult. In a way, you have national politicians coming in and this place is very different from what they know back home. When some Swiss would come in, they would feel at home, because the Swiss work with federal counsellors in a coalition. You see that commissioners coming in from countries with a long coalition tradition have an easier time, because they know what it is. Politicians coming from majority systems have much bigger difficulties. The clearest example are the Brits, very often they come here and think they can run with it and the whole administration blocks. Then they try to fire people. It doesn't work. It simply doesn't work. Because the system knows that these guys have to compromise. They haven't done their homework in the Parliament, in the Council, in the College. We know as civil service, if we start working in this direction that we will fail. We know it, we have seen it hundreds of times. It simply doesn't work. ... The moment we see that the guy is mastering the game, then we start working.

As the initial contact is built up, the relationship evolves. Then, as time passes, relationships become clearer, according to the interviewees. Knowledge about how the system works grows over time and more stable relationships are established between the political–bureaucratic actors involved. Through regular interaction, commissioners and senior officials get to know each other. This results, most of the time, in a more sophisticated appreciation of the contribution of each of the players and in a mutual respect and trust. In most cases, relationships between commissioners and their senior officials grow and develop over time in a fruitful cooperation. In some cases this evolution may not happen because the relationship is shattered by distrust and suspicion.

Multinationality: a government of strangers?

The Commission has become more multinational as more nationalities have spread out horizontally and vertically across the organization (cf. Suvarierol 2007; Ban 2013). A mix of nationalities in a directorate-general and within individual units has become the norm throughout the Commission.[7] It has made the presence and dominance of specific nationalities and cultures on the work floor less prominent, which provides an international work environment for Commission officials that is experienced as 'fun' and 'vibrant' but also challenging, as a director-general noted:

> You have a group of people who are from the left, from the centre and the right, who are from the north and from the south, who are from different political cultures, and we have to strike a compromise between all that. It is much more complex than in a national administration.

Cultural tensions occur also within this international organization, but these are seen more at the political than at the bureaucratic level. As one director-general put it:

> So, you have very different political cultures. We have them among the civil service also, frankly speaking. But the civil service is much more homogeneous, and when you have worked in the institutions, you get to know how to make compromises, and where to give.

Regular interaction flattens the national differences. Semin Suvarierol (2007: 129–37) shows in her study that working for the Commission entails an organizational socialization process whereby officials learn about other nationalities through working with them. As a result, their perception of national identity changes, and thinking in national categories becomes less overriding. As the multiplicity of nationalities becomes business as usual, the evaluation of other colleagues also falls into a normal work floor pattern. As a commissioner points out:

> When I came to the Commission ... I initially had this reflex of asking 'from where are you coming? From which country are you?' I lost it totally. I don't think of it anymore, which means that this multicultural characteristic of the Commission creates a European culture in the positive sense, which is hopefully better, because it has input from different cultures. In the cabinet I never feel it. Everybody is very different. But, there are some national features, which I cannot explain on the ground of sociology or whatever. But we have this tendency to say 'oh that is a typical German' or 'that was very French'. But you lose it, I think, when you work in this institution.

Working day in, day out, at the Commission means that officials stop thinking of their colleagues as Germans or French and instead regard them as colleagues.

A 'Normalized' EU Commission

A layout of normality

Policy-making in the Commission is not insulated from political cycles and political contestation. It is this context that shapes the interaction among the triads at the top of the Commission. A political licence, stemming from the relation to the EP and the broader political environment, has made commissioners the prime movers within the triads. They are expected to define the programmatic objectives, to create political vision, and mobilize resources. Officials deliver the technically suitable solutions to pursue these goals. It entails a regular contact among commissioners, their heads of cabinet, and senior officials about the commissioner's portfolio. These patterns of communication at the Commission's political–bureaucratic interface are associated with the normal model, or with the village life model, but fit less well with the administrative state model. Still, interaction patterns are only one aspect indicative of the normalization of the relationship. Another indicator is to be found in the norms that underlie these relationships.

3. Norms and Expectations of a Working Relationship

Different types of political–bureaucratic relations come with different norms that are relevant for the day-to-day workings of the Commission. In the normal model, for example, senior officials are expected to comply with the directives of the commissioners (see Table 7.2), and loyalty is an informal norm within this model. In the administrative state model, administrators are expected to be resistant to politicians rather than responsive. In the adversarial model, informal norms are likely to be combative, to display suspicion, and collaboration is likely to be difficult. Village systems, on the other hand, are grounded in trust and an integrated set of norms in the working relationship.

Norms like trust, loyalty, respect, personal chemistry, and reciprocity can have a critical function in a working relationship. These norms are not stipulated in formal contracts or memoranda of understanding. They operate as informal codes of conduct and emerge from the unofficial expectations and discretionary behaviours that result from repeated interaction among the members of the core executive (Romzek and Utter 2012: 443–4). Given the interdependence among the actors, these elements are likely to be at least as important for effective interaction as formal arrangements, and perhaps even more so (cf. Hart and Wille 2006). They are like the 'snakes and ladders' on the popular game board. Self-defeating elements, like distrust or lack of chemistry—snakes— can take the relationship down, whereas the empowering ones—ladders—take it up.

Mutual trust and divided loyalty

Mutual trust is an essential element, according to the interviewees, for a productive relationship. A trusting relationship is absolutely necessary if the parties are to work cooperatively. The interviewees indicated that an underlying certainty about the 'bottom lines' that apply in the interaction must be established. They have to be sure that they can count on one another, even if 'the going gets tough'.

Good professional relationships are more like those among rock climbers than among a bowling group, writes Behn (2001: 161): 'the reciprocal agreements under which professional relationships function are based on some form of trust—not necessarily trust on every level, but certainly a trust that your partnership will continue to function within some widely understood professional norms of reciprocity'. A cabinet head formulated it as follows: 'Trust and loyalty are ultimately more important than friendship. In any working environment you need to have "rapport" with your boss.'

Mutual trust refers to the confidence that commissioners and officials have in each other's competence, confidentiality, openness, and honesty (Hart and Wille 2006). There are a number of underlying norms that facilitate cultivating and maintaining a trusting relationship. Both parties in the relationship should honour any formal and informal commitments made. This means that they do not criticize each other in public; that once they have given their word, they can depend on this being kept; and that they support each other once a decision is taken, even when it is called into question by the outside world. They should not feel as if the rug will be pulled from underneath them. A director-general noted:

> The commissioner has to be certain that I will not do anything behind her back and against her will. They never have to think that I am disloyal. We are all going in the same direction, we have the same goals.

Although loyalty is considered to be an essential element in most theories of political–administrative relationships, the interviewees considered this to be less relevant than trust; even in the commissioners' relationships with their closest advisers, divided loyalties (to career, EU, member states, Commission, and the political boss) are perceived as facts of life. As a one cabinet head commented:

> You cannot function if there is not a situation of mutual trust. Loyalty is less important. Commissioners are obliged to get used to a system where staff are not seeing them as the only or principal object of their loyalty. You have to get used working in that sort of environment.

A director-general described the loyalty to the commissioner as an offshoot of his loyalty to the Commission:

> The greatest loyalty of the official is to the institution. But it is the same: if you are loyal to the institution, then you are also loyal to the commissioner. But if at a certain point a commissioner did something that is not correct, I would not have any hesitation, whatever the consequences are, of denouncing that. The first loyalty is to the institution, and the loyalty to the commissioner comes after that, or is even a by-product of that.

Respect

The relationship is also organized and shaped by another invisible force: the generalized respect that each actor enjoys from the other. Obtaining it and retaining it is a strong motivation or concern of most political–bureaucratic players.

The competition for respect constitutes an invisible world operating in parallel and interaction with the official world of rules and assigned responsibilities. Not only because the need for esteem and reputations are prominently present in these working relationships, but also because the more adept political or bureaucratic officials become in building their circles of respect and in protecting their prerogatives, the more valuable their resources become in the eyes of the others (cf. Heclo 1977: 197). Widespread respect creates leadership, whether or not one enjoys a superior status or hierarchical authority or commanding personality. It subtly builds up (or undermines) reputations; and it creates areas of autonomy, as an official explained: 'They should respect each other such that the commissioner isn't interfering with the director-general's business and the director-general isn't interfering with the commissioner's business.' A director-general claimed: 'In the case of the commissioner, we are so different, there is a certain distance. But maybe, who knows, maintaining a certain distance helps for building a reciprocal respect, which is the essential basis for a good relationship.'

Personal chemistry

Without the right policies, good relations do not get very far. But, at important moments, good relations can turn policies the right way. This is particularly so for those dyads and triads with highly frequent interaction. Personal chemistry lowers the transaction costs in the interaction between politicians and bureaucrats. Commissioners and senior officials do not need to like each other, but it certainly helps. Personal chemistry can therefore be critical. As one cabinet head explained:

> Chemistry is very important. Particularly, in the relationship with the director-general, maybe if the hierarchical element is a bit diluted. There is no

doubt if the commissioner wants to sack me tomorrow, this could happen. If you have a director-general you don't like, fairly soon things get difficult and it wouldn't be the same sort of working relationship. There is no straightforward decision, when you say I cannot work any longer with my director-general. That is not how in this place things are going. That means that the personal chemistry is very important, because if that doesn't work you come out in a very long drawn out [way] that can be very, very damaging ... it could have enormous blocking effect on policy-making and the normal conduct of business. Personal chemistry is more important than teamwork.

Working for a female commissioner can also bring about a special kind of chemistry, given that the top of the civil service in the Commission is a male-dominated arena. One director-general who worked for a woman commissioner felt that the gender difference made the relationship more remote. Another director-general described his relationship with his commissioner as

very trustful and quiet, warm. We have empathy for each other. I like her as a person, and also as a woman. There is that kind of thing. It is not sexual, but there is an attraction. So that makes it easier.

Although there are cases where there is a good fit and strong chemistry between commissioners and bureaucrats, there are also many instances where there is a chronic lack of 'rapport'. A director-general describes how the chemistry evaporated in the relationship with his commissioner:

I can tell you this it was caused by personal behaviour and manners ... With the commissioner the difficulty was that, initially, we were almost friends. He came to my home for dinner with his wife a few times. We went out the four of us. We were in a situation that there was almost personal friendship. In a way I was expecting this to continue, and suddenly I was surprised that somebody who I considered a friend was behaving so differently.

The emergence of conflicts can disrupt a working relationship. There are, broadly speaking, two kinds of conflict in the workplace: when people's ideas, decisions, or actions relating directly to the job are in opposition, or when two people just don't get along. The latter is often called 'a personality clash'. Whereas a conflict of ideas can sometimes be productive—if the actors involved are willing to 'brainstorm' solutions together and compromise—personality clashes very rarely yield productive results of any kind. A clash may start with a dispute on minor issues and escalate from there to mutual loathing. A director-general described a disagreement with his political bosses in unmistakable terms:

I can try to educate the commissioner; or I can try to be naughty, saying, 'I told you so', sending the commissioner straight into a brick wall. And if you have been in a brick wall three times, then maybe you turn around and say 'he was right'. I don't like to do it, but if people are very stupid, than I do it. I have not done it with this commissioner. But I have done it with the former one, because he didn't listen. Then he learns, but it is much more painful; and of course he hates me for it. It is obvious.

A long list can be compiled of directors-general who failed to get along with their commissioners and were therefore required to leave the service, usually for reasons of *incompatibility* (Spence 2006a: 143–4; see also Page 1997; Nugent 2001). For disgruntled officials, the classic bureaucratic option used to be to 'outwait' the commissioner in cases of 'difficulties in communication', although this has become less viable now that a transfer policy for senior civil servants and easy exits have become institutionalized in the Commission.

Reciprocity: a two-way street

Some political–bureaucratic combinations inevitably work better than others. Cabinet heads and senior officials acknowledge that it is their job to prepare themselves—intellectually and psychologically—for the challenge of developing a cooperative relationship with their political supervisor. They must adapt their style of work to suit that of their commissioners, not the other way round; and to reach out and facilitate the start of constructive relations is an administrative responsibility.

Senior officials know they have to learn to work with commissioners who can have different objectives and ways of working. Officials cannot simply pursue their own bureaucratic interests and run the risk of a conflict with their political bosses. It is the *reciprocal* nature of the relationship that is treasured. Commissioners realize that they depend on the resources of the directors-general. These *reciprocating* values explain why officials show restraint when they are engaged in interaction with the other (cf. Mouritzen and Svara 2002: 274); they clarify why senior officials do not openly undercut the political control of their commissioners; and why commissioners do not tend to undermine the independence of their directors-general. Both sides act in terms of norms of 'appropriate behaviour' that make these relationships work.

In short, even if there are triads where organized suspicion has become the norm, the prevailing informal standards in the political–bureaucratic relationship are a mixture of mutual trust, respect, and reciprocity. This tells us that the key actors in the triad appear to build a village life model of interaction.

4. Political Control and Administrative Responsiveness

In the 'normal' understanding of a political–bureaucratic relationship, political authority is characterized by a chain of command, as the classical organization theory posits. One key feature of the model is that there is a 'natural' hierarchy, in which civil servants ultimately defer to political office-holders. But do these strict principal–agent relationships hold in reality? Hierarchy is an important component of the normal model, but can vary in a real working relationship along a continuum from high administrative subordination, where political influence is strongly uni-directional, to high administrative independence. A myriad of factors—such as information asymmetries, expertise, delegated authority—can undermine the hierarchical structure between politicians and bureaucrats (cf. Krause 1999). The interviews were used to gain insight into how the various players of the triad perceive their relationship. How do commissioners and their senior officials view the political–administrative relationship in their day-to-day reality? And do these conceptions of the relationship correspond to the standards of the normal model?

Hierarchy or professional equality?

The simple version of the normal model assumes a degree of hierarchy of authority, of simplicity of decision, and of effective political supremacy that seems unrealistic. This type of division of labour is considered unworkable in today's public organizations, which demand a more nuanced and dynamic view of the political–administrative relationship. In their day-to-day contact, commissioners and directors-general perceive one other as equals. Each set of actors, taken as an aggregate, brings unique assets and shortcomings to the process of government. Only at the end of the day is the relationship between commissioners and their director-generals one of superior to subordinate. As a commissioner commented on the relationship with the director-general:

> Partnership is very important, that we listen to each other, that we share the responsibility, and that we both have a feeling of ownership. Of course there are moments that a decision must be made, when we might differ—although normally I don't have a problem of convincing him, or he to convince me in a discussion. But there are moments in this partnership that I take my responsibility, which is very clear, and the director-general also has to understand this. At the end of the day, it is me who is responsible. I try to get his understanding and sharing whenever I can, but there might be a moment, when I decide against him, when I find it necessary.

Interviewed directors-general largely agreed that, 'in the end', commissioners occupy a superior position. They not only have the final authority over a decision, they also bear the responsibility for it. Senior officials in the Commission see it as their duty to help commissioners articulate and accomplish their goals. At the same time, in cooperating with the commissioner, directors-general seek room to maintain their own professional judgement and they cherish their autonomy. Senior managers are not merely compliant, they are supportive of commissioners (cf. Svara 2006: 7–9).

Is the relationship between commissioners and their directors-general different from that between commissioners and their cabinet heads? A senior official describes the difference as follows:

> The relationship is a bit different, but it is less different than received wisdom in the Commission might make you believe. It is clear that the head of cabinet only exists and draws all his legitimacy from the commissioner, whereas the director-general has an established role to a greater extent. He is having more independent legitimacy. ... It is clearly a hierarchical role. It is good that there is a greater clarity about who is responsible for what. And still the commissioner is ultimately responsible for whatever happens. And that is clearly felt. ... We, I mean the commissioner, relies very heavily on the director-general to step in and to replace the commissioner to do things which are expected from the commissioner. I guess what we have is a less pronounced sort of teamwork.

Independent or interdependency?

In the pre-reform era of the Commission, the bureaucracy was able to behave in a manner that had considerable leeway. In the interviews, this perspective of bureaucratic autonomy was no longer in evidence. Commissioners, heads of cabinets, and senior service emphasized the interdependency of their relationship; they need one another; and neither group can succeed without the other. Commissioners and cabinets cannot achieve their organizational priorities and goals without the expertise and support of the services. Conversely, the senior officials know that they lack the authority and political clout to pass policy proposals without the full support of the political level; without the appropriate political power resources they would be ineffective at performing their core tasks.

The relationships between commissioners, heads of cabinets, and directors-general are interrelated and most likely to fall somewhere between a strict hierarchical relationship and teamwork based on professional equality. A cabinet head described the relationship with his commissioner as one that is multi-faceted:

> It is hierarchical, teamwork, complementary. It is all those things. It is complementary most, in the sense that I am staying here, making sure that the world here keeps on turning while the commissioner is away. ... But now we work together we very much depend on the success of each other.

Furthermore, the relationship is best understood when conceptualized as a dynamic system of interdependency, in which commissioners, cabinet heads, and senior officials respond to one another, and also to events and conditions in the larger policy environment. Commissioners, for instance, often adapt their positions in their interaction with their senior officials and cabinet advisers. A director-general described it as a form of mutual adjustment, from which both benefit:

> Again, it is a question of confidence, but I think that these hearings [from the EP] have improved the relationship between the administrative level and the political level. The commissioners are prepared by the services. Of course they can add their political touch, but the material is prepared by us, following the instructions. For commissioners, it is important to have a good performance in the hearing, because it is their reputation.

Loss of face for the commissioner deals a direct blow to the reputation of the civil service, too, and the director-general is well aware of this fact.

Conflict or consensus?

Commission officials recognize that, in addition to their technical and professional capabilities, their ability to establish, develop, and create effective political–bureaucratic relationships is critical to long-term success. Creating these productive partnerships is perceived as crucial to achieving the Commission's goals and objectives. A director-general noted:

> You have to say to the commissioner, that doesn't work. I have reasonable discussions with my present commissioner, but when I came here, the situation was awful, because there has not been that trust between the commissioner and my predecessor.

There are 'differences of opinion', as senior officials phrased it, as well as a general consensus that a 'healthy dose' of conflict can enhance the quality of policy proposals. The interviewees viewed conflicts as forming a desirable, unstructured system of checks and balances that is more or less part of the organizational design. As long as conflicts address ideas and not power, and as long as conflicting opinions do not escalate into confrontations, they are not perceived as essentially negative. Rather, they are seen as a natural part of productive partnerships. Yet however fruitful differences of opinion may be, the ultimate goal is consensus, says a cabinet head:

> We have different debates during our meetings. Those will come out in front of the commissioner. We have quite open discussions between the director-general and the commissioner. They usually don't end up with a real conflict, because we

manage it more intelligently. It is not good to have the commissioner openly disagree with the director-general in front of all the directors. We would spot them coming early enough to be able to manage expectations on both sides and that could lead naturally to a consensual outcome.

It is important to show political–bureaucratic unity, not only to the external world, but also to the officials working in the DG, As a commissioner indicated: 'It is good that they know we are on the same lines and we are going in the same direction.'

Given their interdependencies, politicians and top officials realize that their relationship must be collaborative, not adversarial. However tenuous they sometimes might be in practice, the language used to describe the (desired) interaction between commissioners and senior officials is characterized by notions such as 'teamwork' and 'partnership'. This political–bureaucratic relationship, since it is so close, is not always completely free of sources of tension, with occasional flare-ups that range from irritation to open conflict. Viewing the relationship as one that is either harmonious or conflict-ridden is too simplistic. Elements of both cooperation and conflict are thus likely to emerge when bureaucrats and politicians work with each other. Obviously, this problem is not unique to the EU Commission.

Partnership in flux

What we observe at the top of the EU Commission is a rather heterogeneous political and bureaucratic sphere. There are considerable variations in the relations between cabinets and services, ranging from harmonious and productive to tense and begrudging. As in any working relationship, some dyads or triads are close and convivial, while others are more distant and formal, if not tense and uneasy. Operations are based on what Heclo (1977) calls 'craft knowledge'—understanding acquired by learning on the job—because 'no systematic body of knowledge or special training exists to instruct political and bureaucratic executives on how to handle their mutual relationships'. Day-to-day practices in the triads vary a great deal and are more aptly expressed in terms of ebb and flow than as a fixed format of less or more cooperation.

'There is not a uniform one-size' noted a director-general about the relationships between commissioners, heads of cabinets, and directors-general. One of the reasons for this variability is that executive roles are carried out in a mixture of formal and informal ways and arrangements. Formal roles have a rather predictable character, but the informal executive arrangements comprise a changing group of people, whose relationships with each other fluctuate. By definition, there is more flexibility in the informal tasks and relationships than in the formal ones. As a result, core executive politics are essentially fluid, and influence is contingent and relational.

5. Political–Bureaucratic Interaction in a Normalized Executive

One of the more persistent images coming out of the interviews with the Commission's core executive officials is the awareness of the necessity for cooperation. Actors in each of the spheres stress that political and bureaucratic roles come together in a mutually supportive way and that their collaboration is geared towards accomplishing purposes which politicians and bureaucrats individually cannot achieve. The conclusion that the interests of commissioners or the political level are systematically at odds with the interests of the administration does not hold. The daily reality is that commissioners, senior officials, and cabinet heads are dependent on each other. They have different resources and they realize that the better they are able to cooperate, the more chances they have of achieving their goals. All can be weak and ineffective, or all can make important contributions to the policy proposals.

A number of conditions support a departure from the administrative state model. To start with, as a consequence of the strengthening of political and administrative oversight structures, accountability no longer plays a *sporadic* role in the EU Commission, but has become a *continuous* endeavour. This has been accompanied by a stronger separation of the political and bureaucratic spheres, as described in Chapter 6, yet at the same time the need for stronger hierarchical control and more cooperation between these two spheres took hold. Being able to undertake comprehensive reviews demands less autonomy at the bureaucratic level, and a better informed political level.

Moreover, a changed playing field for the Commission's political and administrative levels has stimulated a stronger common disposition among executive officials to cooperation. The politicization and professionalization of commissioners and their cabinets, as demonstrated in Chapter 3 and 4, rebuts the idea of innocuous and unfit political amateurs at the political level, incapable of following through on decisions. The Commission's administration, on the other hand, no longer dominates as the main source of expertise in the policy process. Information from sources outside the Commission—from the EP, Council, think-tanks, consultancy firms, NGOs, management consultants, academic centres—has gained a prominent place in the European policy-making space. The increased contestability of policy information and advice has caused the preparation of policy proposals to evolve from the delivering of technical policy expertise to 'recommending between contestable options' (cf. Rhodes *et al.* 2009: 170).

The relationship between politicians and bureaucrats in the Commission has competitive features, although the above discussions have tended to show that there is more of an equilibrium between political and administrative officials. It is a relationship that is not fundamentally one of a zero-sum game, in which any gain for politicians is a loss for bureaucrats and vice versa (cf. Aberbach 1981: 251). Analysis of the interviews confirms patterns already known from the literature. In fact, 'few issues pit politicians against bureaucrats in frontal combat' (Aberbach *et al.* 1981: 252); and that 'virtually every point of potential conflict is also a point of unavoidable mutual dependence' (Heclo and Wildavsky 1974: 373). Furthermore, the stronger centralization within the Commission seems to have succeeded in overcoming some aspects of departmentalism; and this is reinforced by career patterns in which officials do tend to work across a range of sectors. Neither the functional village life, nor the adversarial, nor the administrative state models appear to offer a good approximation of executive relations at the Commission's pyramid.

If there is a dominant pattern of interaction among the triads of commissioners, cabinet heads, and directors-general, then this would formally be the hierarchical *normal* model, in which political leaders prevail over bureaucrats. But at the same time, in the reality of executive decision-making, this pattern of relationship is perceived as being too simplistic by those working at the top. The day-to-day interaction among commissioners, cabinet heads, and directors-general tends to foster the features of a mixed bag: a combination of Guy Peters's (1988) village life and Svara's (2001) state of complementarity. Instead of conflict, mutual dependency and cooperation characterized the interactions within the triads. The most compelling explanation for this observed pattern in the political–bureaucratic relationship is that it is best understood as part of the larger development of the institution—that of the *normalization* of the Commission. Summarizing the features of this process and reflecting on the forces that have driven this process will be the object of the next chapter.

Notes

1. 9 Feb. 2010.
2. CIE 1999*b*: 7.12.2 and 7.12.3.
3. According to the Working Methods of the Commission 2010–14.
4. This was also the situation under the presidency of Santer (as under Delors) when commissioners resided collectively in the Berlaymont, and later the Breydel.
5. The Prodi Commission faced heavy criticism for its lack of coordination and collegiality. The communication among commissioners and their cabinets became significantly more difficult. Under Santer, meetings and informal conversations among members of different cabinets were a common part of the daily work routine, as they could easily be arranged along the same corridor. Under Prodi, where offices might be at the other end of town, meetings needed to be organized in advance, and informal conversations faded away.

Notes

6. A few Directorates are located outside Brussels. Then the distance becomes again a factor of relevance.
7. A director-general should not have the same nationality as the commissioner responsible for their service; directors-general, in turn, should be of different nationalities than their deputy directors-general. The purpose of these policies is to ensure a wide spread of nationalities in senior positions and to avoid national clusters.

8

The Normalization of the EU Commission

> Europe will not be built at once, or as a single whole.
>
> (Monnet 1978: 300)

1. From International Organization to a Normal Executive

Snapshots of change

This book outlines the evolution of executive relationships at the top of the EU Commission. It describes how a change in political and administrative accountability arrangements arising from processes of treaty reforms and administrative reform have 'normalized' the European Commission, transforming it from an international organization into a regular core executive; and how this 'normalization' has become manifest at the level of its executive relationships. The evolution of the institution is placed in the context of the very politics and history that created it.

To illustrate this evolution, let us examine some snapshots of the weekly meeting of the College of Commissioners. The first photograph shown in Figure 8.1 is of a meeting of the first Commission under the presidency of Walter Hallstein.[1] The picture shows a relatively small, informal get-together with nine commissioners hailing from the six founding member states. All are men—the only woman present is taking the meeting's minutes. This first Commission started to work on the European Single Market and a Common Agricultural Policy.

The second snapshot was taken five decades later, at the meetings of the last Commission under the presidency of Barroso. Much has changed since the early days of the first Commission. Attended by twenty-seven commissioners, a third of whom are women, these meetings of the Commission under Barroso bear more resemblance to a summit. The Barroso Commission must deal with policies ranging from the development of an economic growth strategy to policies on financial coordination, illegal immigrants, asylum seekers, climate change, terrorism, consumer protection, and plans to reform

From International Organization to a Normal Executive

Figure 8.1. The Changing Nature of the European Commision: Meetings of Hallstein's Commission and the Barroso II Commission
Source: European Commission

the Common Agricultural Policy (CAP), to name only a few. The EU political order has evolved almost to the point where there is virtually no area of political or social life that is not potentially within its remit.

The snapshots offer an impression of the changing nature of governing Europe. The 1950s and 1960s were a period in which the Commission was still the central seat of political authority. Commissioners and their civil servants were key and influential actors. The term 'Eurocrats' had a positive connotation.[2] The Commission was regarded as a powerful actor and had the exclusive right of initiative of new policies. The role of the European Parliament was still limited. A retired senior official reflecting on his years in Europe summarized it as follows: 'Back in the 1960s and 1970s the Commission had "heroic stature". It had brought peace, it was bringing down borders.'

The snapshots of the Barroso meeting illustrate how policy-making in the 2000s has become a process of interaction between many different actors across a variety of terrains among different levels of government. The policy areas have become much more diversified and crowded. Both the power and the role traditionally enjoyed by the EU Commission in the policy-making arena have become much more constrained and contingent. As the retired senior Commission official described this changed view on the Commission: 'The Commission is now widely seen as bureaucratic and too big. It is perceived as far removed from citizens and it struggles to get credit and recognition from public opinion, or even from its partners in the member states.'

From technocratic body to political executive

Back in the 1950s, the architects of the Commission conceived of the institution as a technocratic body that was to be relatively independent of national and supranational control. It was intended as the Union's civil service with limited and defined powers, representing nothing more than an administrative executive, writes Curtin (2009: 63). This notion matched the early idea of the EU as a technical and regulatory regime, legitimated on output criteria (Majone 1994) or, as Vivien Schmidt (2006) put it, an area of 'policy without politics'. As an international organization, democracy and accountability were assured through the national political process, supplemented by some weaker forms of politicization at the European level (Moravcsik 1998).

Today, the EU has branched out into many policy areas and the Commission has a share in almost every function of EU governance. For the Commission to continue playing a significant role at the European level, it had to remain a credible and capable organization, in terms of its agenda-setting responsibility and policy leadership role. European integration has imposed increasingly political requirements on the organization of the Commission, in terms of its responsiveness, accountability, and effectiveness.

Since the mid-1980s, the accountability structure in which EU Commission officials operate has been shaped by political and administrative reforms. The design and emergence of new accountability forums and arrangements in and around the EU Commission was unavoidable to satisfy new accountability demands. These highlight the Commission's political and administrative adaptive capacity to the increasingly changing and demanding environment in which it is entrenched. These wider imperatives facing the Commission have contributed to the evolution from a technocratic to a more political body.

The Commission has thus gradually acquired the features of a normalized executive. In this concluding chapter, the features of this normalization will be placed in a broader context. The chapter starts with an outline of the key features of this 'normalized' EU executive. Next, a comparison is made between the Commission and other international and national executives; and the trends that explain the Commission's normalization process are summarized. The chapter concludes with a description of the contours of the new accountability regime.

2. Key Features of a Normalized EU Executive

The design of new accountability structures and the revision of rules regulating the *responsibilities* of the Commission's executive officials have been translated into new requirements regarding the qualities and the roles of commissioners, senior officials, and heads of cabinet. These have changed the organization of political and administrative recruitment and redefined the dominant conceptions of accountability, political control, and bureaucratic performance. As a result, the EU Commission has acquired a set of features that enable us to group this under the heading of the *'normal* model'. These key features are summarized in Table 8.1. Let me briefly recapitulate the main findings of this study to show how the Commission fits this model.

Executive accountability modernized

The creation of new forums and instruments, especially at the supranational level, has resulted in an array of political and bureaucratic accountability arrangements in and surrounding the EU Commission (see the overview in Chapter 2). If accountability is defined as the presence of arrangements that oblige executive officials to disclose information, to explain their conduct, and to justify their behaviour (Bovens 2007), then the broadening of the system has expanded the instruments with regard to five elements of the accountability equation:

- the agent (clearly assigned collective but also individual accountability by means of 'responsibilisation' of Commission officials);
- the forums (new powers and institutions: EP, European Audit Office);
- the provision of information (reports, audits);
- the standards for assessing executive action;
- the repertoire of sanctions at the disposal of forums.

A web of accountability arrangements has been woven around the key executive actors in the EU Commission. This layering and thickening of

Table 8.1 Features of the Commission's Normalization

Elements of Executives	Features Normal Model	Emerging Features of the EU Commission
Rules and responsibilities	Distinct responsibilities politicians-bureaucrats	Executive accountability modernized *Strengthened accountability and responsibility*
	Parliamentary control	Strengthened relationship with legislative *Ex post accountability and ex ante directions*
Recruitment	Political selection politicians	The politicization of the Commission *Politicized selection, increased political control and responsiveness to EP*
	Merit selection bureaucrats	The depoliticization of the Commission's bureaucracy *Depoliticized selection, professionalization, performance, and strengthened procedures* Denationalization of the executive *Multinational composition cabinets and political–bureaucratic top*
Role expectations	Distinct roles politicians and bureaucrats	Weberization of executive politics *Demarcation of political–bureaucratic role expectations*
Relationships	Hierarchical relationship	Executive relationships *Formally: hierarchical relationship, informally: complementarity*

the accountability mechanisms has increased the possibilities for holding Commission officials accountable. It was intended to increase the responsiveness and responsibilities of Commission officials; and it has provided an accountability architecture which has established a clearer link between the political and the administrative level. Some even consider the Commission to be the most controlled executive in the world, subject as it is to an extraordinary range of checks and balances (Lord 2004).

Strengthened legislative control over the executive

The development of the EP's legislative powers, and its increased power over the appointment of the Commission, has been significant for the evolution of the Commission. With the notion of the 'democratic deficit' that arose in debates about the legitimacy of the EU at the start of the 1990s (Rittberger 2005, 2012), the awareness grew that, where executive powers in EU governance proliferated, accountability should do likewise (Curtin and Wille 2008). It led to:

- An expansion of the EP's legislative and budgetary powers and the establishment of a stronger interconnection between the legislative and executive branches of EU government.
- A range of ex ante constraints and ex post incentives was established to grant the EP a system for more ex ante control and ex post accountability in and over the Commission (Harlow 2002; Hix 2008; Judge and Earnshaw 2008: 267, 272).
- Parliamentary control of executive politics also manifested itself in the existing trend of making the appointment procedure ever more liable to politicization.[3]
- The EP has become a far more vociferous and demanding interlocutor and has contributed to the design of a more politically accountable Commission.

A politicized Commission: from bottom–up to top–down

Implementation of political and administrative reforms in the EU Commission implied a shift from *bottom–up* politicization towards *top–down* politicization. Not only the huge diversity of national interests—in European circles, the adjective 'political' was long synonymous with 'national'—but also the system of comitology, the politicized issue networks (Beyers and Kerremans 2004), meant that for a long time, *bottom–up* politicization remained an integral part of the work of the EU Commission.

The general tendency of the political and administrative reforms described in this book has been towards 'top–down politicization': an evolution of effective political and bureaucratic accountability arrangements that has made it possible for the political level to exert control over the design and execution of the policy-making process. It has moreover enhanced the increased steering capacity of political officeholders over the bureaucracy and strengthened the political–bureaucratic divide in the executive along the lines of the 'normal' model.

This top–down politicization has manifested itself in the Commission in various ways, as explained in Chapter 3:

- Presidentialization and the shift of power towards the actors at the centre of the EU Commission are two contributing factors to the shift towards top–down politicization. Centralization of resources to the Secretariat General has contributed to a strengthened control from the centre. And the fact that the president is elected by the EP affords the officeholder a stronger position from which to formulate his/her political programme and to defend it against resistance from all quarters. He or she will also find it easier to choose (or to refuse) certain candidates for his team, although his/her choices will still have to be made in agreement with the different capitals.

- The Commission's five-year guidelines define the commissioners' political missions and give a plain indication of the programmatic objectives during the commissioners' term of office.
- As part of evolving political accountability, each commissioner is expected to be responsible and answerable to the EP, i.e. to defend and justify the decisions and actions falling within their portfolio. This reinforced an awareness of individual accountability of commissioners and their directors-general for what is going on in their portfolio.[4]

The Commission is a more partisan and a more politicized body than ever before. It can no longer impose its decisions without a fuller consent by the governed. Policies are not struck in isolation inside the EU Commission. This means that executive officials in the Commission have to spend much more of their time explaining situations, setting out the various options and trade-offs, and persuading those involved to join with them.[5] This can lead to frictions and the contestation of decisions between the Commission and the EP,[6] but it is the way things work in any government.

A depoliticized administration

With the evolution of structures of democratic governance, the need for a productive and efficient bureaucracy that serves the EU (and its political officials) became progressively relevant. The series of internal administrative reforms in the EU Commission were critical components in the creation of an effective policy process and management system. They operated as a *structural means* to 'depoliticize' patterns of member-state influence in the Commission's political and administrative system in order to enhance political control and accountability. As discussed in Chapter 5, changes in the Commission administration have occurred in a number of ways.

- Professionalization of the senior civil services has resulted in changes in the prevailing recruiting and reward procedures, as well as in the profile of these services and their approach to civil service leadership. Nationality, long a decisive factor in the appointment of executive leadership in the more bottom–up 'politicized' Commission, has been replaced by a system based more on professionalism and competence.

The Commission's rigid career structure has become more permeable, with enhanced opportunities for horizontal differentiation and merit-based promotions.
- Among senior civil servants, this professionalization of the senior civil services has led to new role conceptions, such as strategic and managerial capacity, while the abilities to lead and deliver services have become new key competences. New codes of conduct pointed to an increased codification of responsibilities and obligations.
- The modernization of the administrative system—governing by targets and audit, managing and accounting—aimed to produce an administration more responsive to top–down control. Little by little, policy-making has developed into a powerfully managed process. Written political guidelines and the work process, too, have become enmeshed in activity-based management, strategic policy planning, impact assessment requirements, and evidence-based policy-making.

Denationalized executive relationships

The internal administrative reforms lessened the influence of the member states in the organization, and normalization also implied a denationalization of executive relationships in several respects.

- In the main advisory arrangements: the commissioner's cabinets have now become smaller, and more European, in contrast with the past, when cabinets were often national enclaves, and the nationality of the head of cabinet was directly reflected in the nationality of the lead commissioner.
- In terms of structure and selection: the territorial principles of organization (secondment, flagging, parachutage) that had underpinned the Commission for so long lost their significance. Merit principles gained priority over national interests in the selection processes. However, nationality has by no means become irrelevant. It may even be argued that denationalization has caused the principles of national balance to play an even more significant role in the composition of the senior civil service and the cabinets.
- The evolving of the Commission into an executive composed of twenty-seven different nationalities has transformed this institution into a more international environment in which the administrative culture has become progressively 'Europeanized'. The enlargements have led to a considerable increase in administrative heterogeneity in the EU administration.[7] Successive rounds of enlargement have served to enrich the European administrative model with a more open recruitment and

career system and a stronger institutionalized separation between politics and administration. Further eastern enlargement and the growing diversity within the EU administration has changed its administrative culture and may also have reduced the role nationality plays in the attitudes and behaviour of the officials (cf. Suvarierol 2008; Trondal 2010; Egeberg 2012; Ban 2013).

The 'Weber-ization' of executive politics

The selection of commissioners has turned the Commission into a political (rather than a technocratic) body, whereas the selection of the top of the services has become increasingly 'depoliticized'. The changes in organizational design not only gave rise to a change in recruiting patterns, but also reflected altered role expectations. Commissioners are expected to establish a clear policy role; and this has grown steadily more important over the past decade, partly because of the greater scrutiny by the EP and partly because clear political guidelines have been formulated and a policy agenda has been set for the Commission. In their role as professional advisers to the commissioners, heads of cabinet and directors-general assist in this endeavour, both in their own way. New expectations have resulted in a clearer demarcation of the political and the administrative parts. The conception of the Commission as a 'pure hybrid' (Image IV in Aberbach *et al.* 1981), where the roles of commissioners and bureaucrats overlap, has gradually disappeared, as is pointed out in Chapter 6.

Executive relationships: hierarchical but mutually cooperative

Political and administrative changes have not only affected the roles of key executive officials in the Commission but also the dynamics of the relationship between them.

- The role differentiation between commissioners and their senior officials and the recognition of the domination of policy by politicians matches the notion of the normal model. In this conception of executive interactions, administrators accept their formal role as 'subordinate' actors to the decision process that takes place at the level of the political executive.

- Despite a clearer differentiation of the respective roles—linked to the normalization of the EU Commission—commissioners, their heads of cabinet, and their top officials stress the pre-eminence of interdependency, complementarity, and teamwork in their relationship. Their view of the political–bureaucratic relationship is one of a pragmatic professional transaction. Both sides have the space to be strong, provided that there is mutual trust and respect, both of which are crucial in an environment where accountability pressures on both politicians and bureaucrats have increased. The image of the Commission as a 'runaway bureaucracy' has become a poor reflection of this relationship, as is pointed out in Chapter 7.

The Commission: an evolving executive

The founders of the European Commission had a technocratic institution in mind, designed as the engine of European integration. To execute such a task it had to be organized independently. But, as Egeberg (2006a: 31) points out: 'organizing autonomous institutions within a political setting immediately raises questions about accountability and legitimacy'. With the emergence of new accountability forums and arrangements, introduced during the various political and administrative reforms, new norms were brought into the Commission that impose new and specific expectations on the core executive actors working at its political–administrative interface. This study described the differences between the Commission's executive relationships now and at the time of its original design, and it gradually has become clear that this institutional evolution had a clear face, leading to a 'normalization' of this EU executive and of its core executive relationships.

In the normal model executive relationships have been associated with a clear differentiation between politics and administration; and with a clear hierarchical organization, with politicians in charge. *Separation* of political–bureaucratic roles and *subordination* of administrators to politics are the two key dimensions. The separation dimension represents the differentiation between the political–administrative roles, and uses the four different images of Aberbach *et al.* (1981) as a simple and standard way of categorizing the degrees of role separation. The subordination dimension is represented by a continuum of clearly subordinated relationships to politics on the one end, to high administrative independence at the other end; we can use Guy Peters's (1988) five interaction models to categorize the extent of subordination.

Depicting the Commission's shifts on these two dimensions of the political–bureaucratic relationship is critical for a proper understanding of how these executive relationships have evolved. The shift is graphically summarized in Table 8.2 projecting the 'pre-reform' and the 'post-reform' Commission. This table shows, from a longitudinal perspective, a change in the Commission's executive relationships along the *separation* dimension, from role overlap towards a stronger level of role differentiation. Over time, the pure hybrid is replaced by a role model with clearer separation between the spheres of politics and administration. The table also shows how executive relationships

Table 8.2. Shifts in the Core Executive Relationship in the EU Commission

		SEPARATION POLITICAL–BUREAUCRATIC ROLES			
SUBORDINATION POLITICS		high		low	
		Image I	Image II	Image III	Image IV
high	Weberian	Normal model			
	village		POST-REFORM COMMISSION		
	Functional village				
	Adversarial				
low	Administrative state				PRE-REFORM COMMISSION

in the Commission moved along the political *subordination* dimension, from a situation in which the level of autonomy of the bureaucracy was high towards a situation with a stronger political direction and control over the Commission's civil service. The shift on both dimensions contributed to a normalization of the political–bureaucratic relationship.

For a long time, the Commission has been perceived as occupying a hybrid position, somewhere in between an executive authority and a bureaucratic structure (Coombes 1970). Though many still have trouble in determining 'the nature of the beast', the conclusions of this study are that the executive branch in Europe is being transformed profoundly, and that role the Commission plays, as a result of the political and administrative reforms, is progressively becoming that of a normalized executive.[8]

3. Politics and Bureaucracy as Usual?

As the famous 'duck' test tells us: 'If it looks like a duck, swims like a duck, and quacks like a duck, then it probably is a duck.' To what extent are politics and bureaucracy in the EU Commission similar or different from the other ducks, i.e. the core executives in the member states and in international organizations? To interpret the Commission's evolution in the light of political and public administration trends that have taken place at the national and international level, let us move beyond the Commission in order to see, on base of a loose comparison, whether the features of normalization are specific for the EU Commission, or whether they can be observed across executives in the member states and international organizations.

The Commission bureaucracy: not a unique case

The Commission is not a unique case compared to other international bureaucracies. Since the Second World War, the international sphere has increasingly been organized by international organizations (Zweifel 2006). This has led to a growth of international bureaucracies (Bauer and Knill 2007; Trondal 2010) that are linked to these international organizations. Although there are large differences in the fields of policy-making and the range of legal responsibilities delegated to these international bureaucracies, they often act on the basis of fairly similar behavioural logics to the bureaucracies in national states (Trondal 2010). They are organized along a formalized division of labour, mostly vertically specialized with an administrative leader at the top. In their internal structure the work is organized and divided primarily according to non-territorial criteria—portfolios—which are equivalent to ministries in national governments (Hague and Harrop 2010: 338; Nugent 2010: 117).

The sector or functionally based administrative structure of the EU Commission is not an unusual one at the international level. A comparison of the EU Commission with the OECD and the WTO secretariat (Trondal 2010, 2011, 2012) reveals that the Commission shares important organizational characteristics with them both. Admittedly, the administrative capacity at the helm of the Commission is significantly greater than in the other international organizations; the 'logic of hierarchy' predominates in the Commission administration, whereas it exists only marginally in other international bureaucracies, such as the OECD and WTO. The administrative reforms put in place in the Commission also fit well in the worldwide trend towards diffusion of public-sector reforms among national executives and international organizations (Pollitt and Bouckaert 2004; Bauer 2007*a*, 2007*b*; Bauer and Knill 2007; Demmke and Moilanen 2010; Trondal *et al.* 2010; Eymeri-Douzans and Pierre 2011).

The Commission's political executive: a unique case internationally

Most international governmental organizations have a 'political' level next to their administrative level. The Worldbank and the IMF have a Board of Governors. The United Nations has a General Assembly. The WTO has a Ministerial Conference. The OECD has a Ministerial Council. The

Commission has its College of Commissioners. One of the important issues of the growth of these international organizations is that they compare badly with nation-states in their lack of democratic procedures (Zweifel 2006; Zürn *et al.* 2012). International organizations encompass large geographical domains and are accountable to many people and to many different governments. The lack of a 'single people' as a point of reference, and of a general election including all individuals that are potentially governed by the international organization, is perceived by some as an important impediment to their legitimacy (Dahl 1999; Held 2004; Mehde 2007: 173).

The classic international government organization is politically organized primarily according to territory, so that key decision-makers formally represent the constituent government (Egeberg 2006c). The Council of the EU, for instance, shares such basic features of an international organization. International organizations are legitimized indirectly by the consent of the participating governments and above all by their capacity to deliver effective policy (Held and Koenig-Archibugi 2004).

What distinguishes the EU Commission from all other international organizations is its relatively autonomous political *leadership*, organized according to a 'sectoral' logic.[9] The Commission has, and has always had, a clear and definable political executive with its own political leadership (commissioners) that can be distinguished from the bureaucracy, in that it sets priorities, makes decisions, and is able to act relatively independently of national governments and the Council of ministers (Egeberg 2006c). In contrast to many international government organizations, the work at the political level of the Commission is organized and divided primarily according to non-territorial criteria (Egeberg 2006c: 20–5). Likewise, the Commission is the commissioner's primary organizational affiliation (Egeberg 2012: 946): 'the structure within which they are embedded on a daily basis'.

The political accountability architecture of the Commission's political executive—whose appointment and operation is linked to a directly elected forum (the EP)—is even more distinctive. Although several international organizations are related to parliamentary assemblies (with special international parliamentary status), these are usually not strongly representative institutions (Rittberger 2005: 207).[10] The EP is the most influential parliamentary assembly in the universe of international organizations. In terms of accountability arrangements, appointments, the electoral participation of citizens, leadership, representation, and responsibility, the EU is the most democratic of all international organizations (Zweifel 2006).[11] No other international organization comes even close to having comparable arrangements for democratic accountability. Not only are the appointments of prospective commissioners vetted by the EP, the College can also be dismissed from office by a vote of no confidence or censure. The Commission's political programme is 'authorized' by a parliament, which has been directly elected by universal suffrage since 1979.[12] Although its record may still be controversial and discussed by observers and scholars, the mechanisms for democratic accountability are in place (Rittberger 2005; Corbett *et al.* 2007; Hix *et al.* 2007).[13]

Bureaucratic accountability in the shadow of political hierarchy

The Commission's political accountability has not only been translated into a political responsibility of commissioners for their portfolio—scrutinized by a parliament—but the chain of command links the political executive to the senior civil service responsible for the administration.[14] The genius of an effective democratic accountability regime is that it relies on a governance structure of superior–subordinate relationships—with each actor assigned responsibilities linked to a politicized accountability structure, and senior officials providing the crucial bridge between the political and bureaucratic levels.

These vertical accountability relationships, through which administrative answerability in the Commission is organized in the 'shadow of the political hierarchy' (cf. Scharpf 1997; Schillemans 2008; Van Gerven 2009), are relatively unique at the level of international organization. They have resulted in the contours of a new executive accountability relevant to the Commission's operation and in a structure of the EU Commission and an *executive relationship* that has come to resemble the normal model of democratic governance.

4. The Contours of a New Accountability

The evolution of political and administrative accountability

No longer secondary or peripheral to the Commission, political and bureaucratic accountability had now became a critical ingredient for the institution, taking precedence over the technocratic and legal approach to accountability. An elaborate mixture of new accountability mechanisms and practices was created that altered the *locus of control* over the Commission's activities—from the bureaucratic to the political level—as well as the *degree of control* over the Commission's activities.

Politics was a variable that mattered strongly to the evolution of the Commission's new accountability architecture. The literature on EU Commission reforms may have focused nearly exclusively on the impact of the administrative—the so-called Kinnock reforms (Kassim 2004a, 2008; Bauer 2007b, 2008; Schön-Quinlivan 2011), but the Commission's transformation cannot be grasped without an understanding of how these internal reforms were triggered exogenously by a new political context. The increased

The Normalization of the EU Commission

assertiveness of the EP played a significant role in the unfolding of the Commission's normalization process. The rise of and pressures from this up-and-coming accountability forum resulted in a more politicized and powerful EP that was felt at the inter-institutional level (Ringe 2005).[15] It pushed internal administrative reforms onto the Commission's agenda, contributing to a further normalization of this executive institution.

One of the lessons from this study is that political and administrative reforms, which are often treated as completely distinct processes, are closely linked and should be studied together. The key to understanding normalization processes is to think of these as co-evolving with political–administrative systems. Such an approach to executive relationships shows that political and bureaucratic actors and arenas cohere in important ways, characterized as they are by the complementarities in their relationships. As the institutional arrangements that comprise these political–bureaucratic relationships are adapted, these relationships are recreated, too. This evolutionary process is explored in the analysis provided in this book.

Change within continuity: slow-motion transformation

The normalization of the Commission, like many processes of change, unfolded slowly over a relatively long stretch of time (cf. Pierson 2004: 90–102; Thelen 2005; Mahoney and Thelen 2010). The design and evolution of the Commission's new political–bureaucratic accountability architecture was pulled together by four different types of change that developed at different time frames—some slowly, some more rapidly, depending on the context.

Normalization was realized by a replacement of old rules by new ones, and by adding new rules alongside existing ones, the so-called layering or thickening of arrangements. Changes of this kind occurred as the member states accorded new parliamentary powers to the EP and new political accountability arrangements were set in place. Political treaty reforms not only replaced the old rules, but also became a means to add new rules to the old ones.

Likewise, internal administrative reforms were rapidly implemented through the replacement of rules, thus forming an example of what leading institutional theories explaining change refer to as a 'critical juncture'. The shock of the collective resignation of the Santer Commission in March 1999 created the momentum for previously unforeseen agency and innovation, which enabled a rapid upgrading of the system of checks and balances surrounding the emerging EU executive. This crisis served as a 'window of opportunity' for reformers within the Commission, as well as for political forces seeking to strengthen the EP's stature as an oversight body. It brought a serious willingness to review the Commission's political responsibilities and triggered a programme of internal reforms (Harlow 2002: 186: Schön-Quinlivan 2011).

Yet, a closer look at the historical setting of this institutional 'tipping point'—and the reforms and transformation that followed—show that Kinnock's reform plans were built on models and reform ideas in which the 'seeds of change' were already planted. Many of the internal reform measures (announced in the White Paper of the Prodi Commission) had been discussed, suggested, and even recommended in previous years. Reports on the Commission's 'management deficit' and recommending options to improve the internal functioning of the Commission had appeared in the 1970s (see Spence 2000; Cram 2001; Seidel 2010; Schön-Quinlivan 2011: 191–200).[16] The established reform agenda dated back way before Neil Kinnock started his reforms.

Most of these changes that seemingly appeared overnight were long in the making. What is more, normalization, and the evolution of the Commission's new accountability architecture, resulted in large part from small incremental changes via a *conversion* of rules. The EP slowly gained influence by means of inter-institutional bargaining over the allocation of decision-making powers and by altering the formal treaty-based rules (Héritier 2012: 49). When rules are open to contending interpretations and variations in enforcement, they are more likely to be subject to continuous process of changes.[17] Likewise normalization grew out of a neglect of, or a shift in, interpretation or enforcement of old rules that remained intact—a form of change called 'drift'. Commissioners started, for instance, to make their way to parliament to give account, even when there was no formal need to do so.

Changes of this kind have shaped slow-motion normalization. Drift, like layering, does not require making any direct changes to the old institutions and does not rely on altering the rules themselves. These modes of change, which, it should be noted, are more likely in situations or environments with strong veto players, have been much easier to accomplish than changing the rules or the formal treaties (Mahoney and Thelen 2010).

The idea that the Commission's change was due to a rapid replacement of rules in the administration is misleading. One lesson has become clear: the Commission's basic mode of institutional transformation, and its normalization, is to be found in small, more gradual modes of change rather than in response to the big exogenous shock of its collapse in 1999. The Commission, as an institution, represents compromises and contested settlements, and as a result is tension-filled and always vulnerable to shifts. Pressures for change are built into such institutions (Mahoney and Thelen 2010: 4–22), thus inextricably linking continuity and change.

New rules and evolving practices: the significance of active accountability

It is clear that the interaction between treaty and administrative reforms has produced a more refined system of accountability through the introduction of new accountability mechanisms (and hence new accountability *relationships*) and the assignment and redefinition of *roles* and *responsibilities*.

The different forums (parliaments, courts, administrative bodies, general public) demand different kinds of information and apply different criteria as to what constitutes responsible conduct. This has combined to create an 'accountable environment' (Behn 2001) in which '*active* notions of accountability' (Bovens 1998, 2010) are managed, yielding increased clarity and agreement about behavioural expectations and notions of individual responsibility, and reducing uncertainty about the boundaries within which official responsibilities are acted out. The institution of new accountability mechanisms has contributed to the awareness of distinct 'virtues' of public officials—conceptions of what tasks and duties are to be taken seriously, and of the actions (and consequences) for which these officials may be held accountable. The emergence of these new accountability *relationships* has contributed to a shift in the role expectations of politicians and senior officials. It has emphasized the political–bureaucratic distinction and contributed to a further *normalization* of executive relationships.

The findings illustrate the importance of the juxtaposition of a *passive* and *active* conception of accountability (Bovens 1998, 2010) for analysing the normalization process. Accountability not only depends on how public organizations are controlled—and the kind of accountability mechanisms that are available—but also on how executive officials have 'internalized' accountability values. If new accountability arrangements are introduced, these reforms need to be translated into collective practices, which are based on definitions of appropriate behaviour. As Olsen (1997: 175) points out, they 'cannot be imposed on the world full-blown by Napoleonic decrees'.

Hence, the creation of accountability arrangements is, in itself, not a sufficient condition for realizing accountability in an organization. Focusing exclusively on a passive definition of accountability, therefore, will fail to elicit a full picture of the normalization process. Using an active definition of accountability helps to illuminate the issues that arise when realizing accountability in public organizations. Managing expectations and informal norms within the organization have the potential to make a significant impact on how formal accountability requirements are interpreted by officials. The active notion of accountability is critical to understanding why executive officials can behave differently under the same accountability conditions (Hall *et al.* 2007: 412); sometimes they comply with the accountability expectations and sometimes they do not. The way in which public officials render account not only depends on the robustness of the accountability architecture, but is also determined by how public officials take their cues from the formal accountability systems and from the informal norms and expectations with respect to their responsibility.

The Commission's accountability: part of an evolving political order

Comparing the EU with other international organizations, such as the World Bank, the IMF, and the WTO, it is clear that the Commission, more than any other institution, is a 'supranational' institution, with its own currency and flag, its own territory, its own executive, legislature, and court (Zweiffel 2006). The creation of a market system, accompanied by the establishment of legal, political, and bureaucratic institutions at the EU level, implied new governance structures and an emergent polity that was constructed alongside the newly enlarged market (McNamara 2010). Processes of *constitutionalization*, treaty reforms, and enlargement have led to a hardening of the 'core' of the European Union: 'they have contributed to an image of the EU that is more *statist*, in that it has a clearer sense of its underlying norms and values, as well as in having a more clearly defined outer boundary' (Christiansen 2005).

EU governance accountability is, however, not only confined to neat single-level interactions at the supranational level (Bovens *et al.* 2010: 193). The practices of EU governance consist of a plurality of actor–forum interactions at a plurality of levels, that evolve in a dynamic and incremental fashion, with different modes of democratic legitimation which increasingly influence each other. Various, sometimes contending, perspectives on EU integration and accountability, grounded in different understandings of what 'better' accountability regimes consist of, and how they may enhance EU legitimacy (Bovens *et al.* 2010), are woven within the EU system. Its accountability regime has developed not so much by design, but by bricolage (cf. Mattli and Stone Sweet 2012).

A more composite form of democracy, as in Europe, leaves plenty of scope for parallel developments in the different arenas and for enacting alternative modes of legitimation. But it means that the evolution of the EU order is producing outcomes that are difficult to foresee, even if the post-war trend has been towards more steady cooperation and integration (Olsen 2010: 145). This book concludes, therefore with a cautious look at the future of the EU Commission. The normalization of executive relationships, while unavoidable to satisfy the new accountability demands, at the same time poses a set of new complex dilemmas. Has the EU been able to establish itself as a legitimate authority, as a political actor in its own right? And what future is there for the Commission?

The Normalization of the EU Commission

Notes

1 The Commission consisted of nine members—two from France, Italy, and Germany, one from Luxembourg, Belgium, and the Netherlands.
2 In July 1961, *The Economist* introduced the term Eurocrats for the new species of Commission officials (Seidel 2010: 109).
3 The potential for politicization was initially opened up by making the nomination the object of qualified majority voting, rather than 'common accord', in the European Council. The involvement of the European Parliament has further added to the potential for politicizing the appointment.
4 In the founding treaties, the Commission was designed as a uniform political actor, where commissioners had no significant role of their own.
5 This is not necessarily a negative development. Political controversies may help to make the EU more transparent and understandable.
6 Under the Lisbon Treaty, the EP has gradually evolved into 'the institution that aims at protecting' the common interest.
7 New member states joined the EU—such as the UK, Ireland, and the Nordic countries—that belonged to 'administrative families' that differed strongly from the continental model of the founding members of the EU (especially France and Germany) that had strongly influenced the Commission bureaucracy in the early years.
8 Several other studies appear to corroborate this by pointing to separate patterns or single features that are part of the Commission's normalization. These pieces of evidence support the idea of an EU executive that is changing. The expansion of new and strengthened accountability regimes at the level of the EU has been mapped in the literature by Curtin and Wille (2008), Curtin (2009), and Bovens *et al.* (2010). Indications of a political role of commissioners was described by Egeberg (2006*b*), when mapping commissioners' role behaviour, which proved not to be that much different from that of national ministers. Changes in the composition of the political–bureaucratic top, documented by Georgakakis (2010, 2013), show that commissioners increasingly have been drawn from the class of political heavyweights, as is also documented by Wonka (2007) and Döring (2007). Trends that indicate progressive professionalization (and depoliticization) of the Commission's bureaucracy have been documented by Kassim (2004*a*, 2008), Bauer (2007*b*, 2008), Balint *et al.* (2008), Ellinas and Suleiman (2008), Ban (2010), Schön-Quinlivan (2011), Bauer and Ege (2012), and Ongaro (2012). Kassim (2004*b*) has provided further evidence of how the role of the president has become more pivotal through a strengthening of the secretariat-general and how this contributed to an increased presidentialization and centralization within the Commission (Kaczyński *et al.* 2008; Trondal 2010, 2012; Kassim *et al.* 2013. Ban (2013) has documented the impact of reform (in combination with enlargement) on professional values. Michelle Cini (2007) did the same for the ethical infrastructure in the Commission. The denationalization of the cabinets and administration and the limited role of nationality in the Commission have been documented by Egeberg (1996, 2012), Suvarierol (2008), Egeberg and Heskestad (2010), and Ban (2013).

Notes

9. The essentially sectoral and functional accountability organization explains why patterns of cooperation and conflict at the Commission so often followed sectoral lines rather than territorial lines (Egeberg 2006c: 23).
10. The parliamentary organizations are usually stand-alone institutions, which makes it difficult, if not impossible, for them to develop any legislative or oversight functions with regard to governmental institutions at the international level. The power of parliamentary assemblies in international organizations is weak. They merely fulfil a consultative function and lack budgetary, legislative, and supervisory powers.
11. Discussions about the alleged 'democratic deficit' of international organizations have centred very prominently on the EU. Compared to other international organizations, the EU has one of the highest level of discourse about the democratic deficit (Stein 2001: 530; Rittberger 2005: 204–5; Zweifel 2006). And these concerns about the legitimacy deficit in the EU have carried implications that affected the path of democratic institutional reforms (Rittberger 2005). The history of the European Parliament can be summarized as an enduring struggle to become a true parliament with powers and functions similar to national parliaments.
12. The EU is the only transnational organization with a directly elected parliament (Zweifel 2006: 19).
13. Although international organizations lack democratic procedures of this kind, scholars of global governance disagree about to what extent IGOs suffer from a democratic deficit. Moravcsik (2004) and Grant and Keohane (2005) argue that international institutions are legitimized indirectly by the consent of the participating governments, and above all by their capacity to solve the problems that led to their creation (a form of output legitimacy) (Held and Koenig-Archibugi 2004). And like states, these international organizations are subject to a 'new accountability' agenda—mounting for an expansion of accountability along multidimensional lines (Goetz and Jenkins 2005; Grant and Keohane 2005). Horizontal control mechanisms, watchdog groups, and participation of civic groups are all developed to improve systems of checks and balances around these international organizations.
14. Commissioners are not formal heads of their departments (or their DGs)—that is the director-general. Mehde (2009: 75–7) and Verhey (2009: 66) call this a conceptual mismatch. But Mehde makes the mistake of thinking that, if commissioners are not the formal boss of the bureaucracy, a disconnect occurs between the responsibility of the commissioner for the portfolio and the responsibility of the director-general. The code of conduct for commissioners (SEC 2004 1487/2) says the following: 'the chain of responsibility continues down to department level in the person of the director-general, who is answerable to the commissioner and the college for the proper implementation of the guidelines set but the college and the commissioner and in particular for the management of the Directorate-General or service in line with the distribution of powers ... '
15. It resulted in a more powerful EP with an intensification of party competition and politicization, based on a government–opposition dynamic that was observable at the inter-institutional level (Ringe 2005).

16 Seidel (2010: 101) argues that, since the first Hallstein presidency, the Commission has been engaged in reflection on ways of reforming its structures and procedures.
17 These institutional rules are often incomplete contracts with unclear terms and need to adjust to new external conditions (Héritier 2012).

Epilogue: Quo Vadis?[1]

> ... the past is a burden on the present, as well as a source of understanding
>
> (Judt 2011: 84–5)

1. The Tragedy of the Commission: More Normal, Less Powerful

Jean Monnet, the founder of the EU Commission, was firm in his conviction that the European nations had to unite in order to survive. 'Continue, continue, there is no future for the people of Europe other than in union' was his relentless message. In 1950, in the face of rising international tensions, Monnet felt that the time had come to attempt an irreversible step towards uniting the Europeans.

More than sixty years later, political and administrative reforms seem likely to yield a stronger, more dynamic, more modern, high-performance policy-focused Commission that is in a stronger position to do the job it was assigned by its EU founders (Peterson 2008). The irony is that the performance of the successfully reformed Commission appears less and less to determine its own fate and future. More and more, elementary decisions about the European integration process and the role of the Commission therein appear to be being taken in national capitals, leaving the Commission out of the loop. After six decades of steady, if discontinuous, progress towards a normalized executive, the Commission continues to be an evolving institution in an 'unfinished polity'.

Normalized but shrunken

During the Delors years in the late 1980s and early 1990s, the Commission was regarded as a powerful actor. Some argue that there has been a marked decline in the influence of the Commission since the days when it was leading the march to complete the internal market (Nugent 2010: 136). And it is more than just that the policy pioneering days are over. The increasing influence of EP and the Council, plus the growing importance of the 'new modes

Epilogue

of governance' (such as the OMC) have changed the Commission's influence in several policy areas.

Adapting to the emergence of the European Council as the authoritative decision-making body on most vital issues of cooperation, EU states have refashioned domestic procedures and practices to provide chief executives with effective negotiation machineries. The institutionalization of summit decision-making in the EU over the past thirty years has contributed at the level of member states to the empowerment of chief executives in Europe (Johansson and Talberg 2010). It also has led to the paradoxical development of the EU Commission into a stronger supranational institution in an EU that is becoming more and more intergovernmental.

Widespread political opposition to anything approximating a European 'superstate' has blocked the creation of a large, unified executive bureaucracy in Brussels (Kelemen and Tarrant 2011: 922).[2] Thus, while the Commission may be able to retain regulatory powers previously delegated to it, new grants of regulatory authority are increasingly made to bodies outside the Commission. Yet, the extent to which there has been a decline in the position of the Commission should not be exaggerated, as Neil Nugent says: 'it still commands extensive power resources, it still has key duties to undertake, and in some respects its powers have actually increased as it has adapted itself to the ever-changing nature of and demands upon the EU' (Nugent 2010: 137). It has the capacity to impose mandatory regulations on an entire continent (Mény 2012: 157). Moreover, it has changed from performing a strong administrative role to performing a political role (cf. Borrás 2009). Nonetheless, the Commission has an image problem. Even though it has succeeded in pushing through numerous political and administrative reforms, the perception that it is bureaucratic and undemocratic lingers.

Less technocratic more politicized

Throughout its history, the Commission's conception of the EU policy process has been pervaded by a technocratic ethos (Judge and Earnshaw 2008: 294). The emphasis was placed upon 'substantive legitimacy or 'output legitimacy', i.e. the notion that, so long as the common project produced evident benefits in the form of prosperity, economic opportunities, and job creation, voters would accept it, and even come round to welcoming it. This depoliticized idea of the role of the EU Commission was linked to processes of placing EU executive power at some distance from elected bodies, in the non-majoritarian hands of the 'unelected' (Harlow 2002: 58; Curtin 2009: 294). Scepticism about the ability of democratic processes to make sensible policy choices caused a parallel shift in power from elected officials to 'technocrats', who were shielded from political influence (Vibert 2007; Roberts

2010). After all, the European project was mainly about technical matters such as competition, regulation, and rules for the single market, all of which could happily and unproblematically be dealt with out of sight of the voters (as is the case in most countries). So long as the EU did not touch the most important political issues for ordinary voters—such as tax, spending, education, defence, or health care—its apparent lack of democracy and accountability would not matter.

Over the past few decades, doubts have been growing about whether 'output legitimacy' was enough in the context of the EU (2002: 168). With the enormous expansion of EU competences into areas of 'high visibility politics', it was felt that a technocracy would no longer suffice to legitimate the European enterprise (cf. Follesdal and Hix 2005). The period of permissive consensus, in which a political elite determined the modalities of European government without demands for any significant measure of accountability, was assumed to be over.

Democratic politics and the politicization of the institutions are considered to be essential for a genuine democratic identification with the EU and for the evolution to a more responsive political elite (Harlow 2002; Mair 2008; Hix 2008; Curtin 2009). More open contestation and coalition-building would encourage politicization and the development of genuine democratic politics at the EU level. This would mean a more politicized role for the EU Commission that could lead to a clearer accountability connection between policy commitments and outcomes. Based on the democratic accountability substructure that is already in place, the EU Commission, as a normalized executive, would appear to be gearing up to fulfil this role (Hix 2008: 185; Bovens *et al.* 2010).[3]

Democratization without design

An important drive for the Commission's normalization has been the parliamentarization of the EU's political process. Proposals for further empowerment of the EP rest upon the normative assumption that the EU should institutionalize the values of representative democracy (Judge and Earnshaw 2008: 292). A parliamentary Europe will underline the institutional normalization of the EU Commission. Much of the Commission's future depends on what a further continuation of this process means and what form it will take.

Thus far, democracy has more or less been a by-product. The creeping process of EU integration (Majone 2009) and judicialization (Sweet Stone 2010; Kelemen 2012) has been accompanied by a creeping process of democratic adaption at the supranational level. Implied political innovations have developed incrementally, sometimes as lip service realized by political pressures, and sometimes as the product of cautious piecemeal political engineering. But this slow, incremental, political institutional change has acquired the character of democratization by stealth. There is no proactive strategy and no balance of participatory instruments at the different levels of governing. And there is no vision of what the EU should or could be (cf. Mény 2012: 159).

A continuing issue in all this is the balance between an intergovernmental and a federal system. Those leaning towards a bigger role for national parliaments and governments naturally favour the first. The Lisbon Treaty has given national parliaments a bigger role. The role of the EU Commission has been twofold, since the EU sought to develop 'dual legitimacy' in the Lisbon Treaty. But the idea of 'dual legitimacy' is replete with conceptual tension; 'direct' and 'indirect' legitimation claims do not sit easily alongside each other, as both the member states and the European institutions have roles to play in providing authorization, representation, and accountability in the EU (Judge and Earnshaw 2008: 273–4). The increased role of national parliaments in EU policy-making has the potential to encourage national debates about European affairs and could contribute to a parliamentarization of the EU at the national level.[4] At the European level, the stronger role of national parliaments could foster transnational debates and cooperation between national and European political elites. But it could also send ambivalent messages, making the future role of the EU Commission rather imprecise and undecided; particularly when it comes to its weak outward accountability.

2. The EU: Strong 'Inward' Accountability, Weak 'Outward' Accountability

Despite the accountability architecture that is in place at the level of the EU (cf. Hix 2008; Bovens 2010), the Commission is still in a weak position when it comes to the legitimacy issue—its so-called 'outward' accountability. The normalization of EU Commission and European Parliament has not appeared to spill over to the relationship of the EU institutions with the European voter, who still seems lost in the EU's labyrinth of accountability. In order for a sense of 'normal' democratic legitimacy to exist, there must be a basic system of electoral accountability, with a match between the level at which decisions are taken and the level at which, in the final analysis, the electorate can hold the decision-makers to account.

EU elections appear to hold little political relevance compared to national electoral cycles. Voter turnout in the EU elections has been steadily waning, dropping from 62 per cent in 1979 (in an EU of nine) to 43 per cent in 2009 (in an EU of twenty-seven) (Malkopoulou 2009). In the seven direct European

Parliament elections held to date, turnout has fallen by an average of 3 per cent each time, with the largest fall-off occurring in the 1999 elections (7 per cent). These low turnout levels diminish the legitimacy of the electoral process and of the European Union as a whole; in any case, they testify to the limited impact of the post-Santer reforms on the ultimate democratic principal, the European electorate.

The absence of a politicized European debate has reduced the ability to capture public attention and has been clearly detrimental to the EP's capacity to present itself as a relevant political actor (Mair 2008). This is not only evident from voter turnout in the European Parliament election, but also from the esoteric items finding their way onto its agenda (such as regulation of the degree of curvature permitted in bananas or the minimum size of strawberries allowed to be sold) that seem to have little bearing on the issues foremost in the minds of EU citizens. The polarization of EU integration is an issue in national elections, but not one that has dominated the European elections. The EP has increased its power with every EU treaty, but has seen no parallel growth in its legitimacy.

'Governments are "accountable" if voters can discern whether governments are acting in their interest and sanction them appropriately' (Manin et al. 1999: 40). The complicated system of (s)election and accountability governing the European Commission appears not to have given citizens confidence that the 'people who run Europe' are actually accountable to them (Page 1997; Bogdanor 2007; Malkopoulou 2009). The EU lacks a political leader capable of taking the responsibility and the blame for policy choices. The voter has no easy way of sanctioning the headless (or multi-headed) Union (Mény 2012: 162). This poses a considerable problem for the legitimacy of the EU. 'The state is invisible', as Micheal Walzer (1967: 194) notes, 'it must be personified before it can be seen, symbolized before it can be loved, imagined before it can be conceived.' If enhancing EU accountability architecture is accompanied by a continual decrease in voter turnout, the logic of strengthening accountability as a means of democratizing EU governance is undermined.

New political and administrative arrangements have turned accountability practices 'inward': by and large the Commission is now highly accountable towards the other EU institutions, while 'outward' accountability has remained markedly underdeveloped. The legitimacy of the European institutions has failed to gain ground over the past decade. Indeed, the opposite is the case: opinion polls, elections, the rise of anti-European parties, all indicate that it has, in fact, deteriorated (Mény 2012: 154). It is one of the paradoxes of politicization: the thickening of democratic and political structures does not automatically lead to an accountability that is popularly embedded in the EU polity (McNamara 2010).

Epilogue

Supranational democracy and legitimacy

Improving the Commission's outward accountability must necessarily figure in the ambition of the EU to become a democratic polity and in a broader process of citizen control. A central feature of representative democracy is that the voters elect and remove those who govern. In EU elections it should, therefore, become possible to substantially determine and influence the composition and colour, not only of the EP, but also of the Commission. Simplifying the complex EU system of accountability may contribute to a better understanding and knowledge of the role, the working procedures, and the decisions of the Commission and the European Parliament. But this means that EU institutions have to invest in the capacity to present themselves as relevant and independent political actors (McNamara 2010);[5] and that more efforts should be made to politicize the debate in the EU and to structure it around the most politically salient questions (cf. De Clerck-Sachsse and Kaczyński 2009).

It is becoming increasingly clear that, in order to move forward, we must transcend old barriers and, to echo Mény (2002), use the truly novel models of supranational democracy and legitimacy. A core message that emerges from this study is that a basic political and administrative accountability architecture is in place. Whether the possibilities this offers will ultimately be exploited remains to be seen. But, as Fareed Zakaria (2003: 256) put it: 'without [an] inner stuffing, democracy will become an empty shell'.

Notes

1. 'Quo Vadis Europe?' was the question posed by Joschka Fisher at his speech on 12 May 2000 at Humboldt University in Berlin. In this speech he pleaded for a federal Europe.
2. While the European Commission is often depicted as a 'burgeoning bureaucracy', it in fact remains a remarkably small executive with approximately 25,000 employees (Kelemen and Tarrant 2011: 929). Since the beginning of the 1990s, it has become clear that member-state governments are unwilling to countenance any significant expansion of the Commission and instead prefer delegating new regulatory tasks to bodies outside the Commission hierarchy.
3. The EU does not need further treaty reforms to encourage democratic politics.
4. The Lisbon Treaty extends the information rights and powers of national parliaments.
5. Perhaps we can compare the processes involving the European polity with the nation-building process described in Weber's book 'Peasants into Frenchmen' in which the author traced out how an excess of state policies were necessary to glue a fragmented society into the French nation at the end of the 19th century.

APPENDIX
Research Design

Conceptual Development

The research for this book focused, at the outset, on the executive relationships in the EU Commission. Executive relationships remain notoriously difficult to study. The theoretical and methodological challenges are numerous. Theoretically, propositions remain ruthless simplifications of what for the most part are complex, variegated, and ambiguous political and administrative systems and processes. Perhaps the aim to develop causal generalizations—let alone an explanatory theory—about executive relations is not the most helpful stance to take for students of politics and public administration in the first place. It might be more fruitful to take an interpretive perspective: to penetrate the real-world realities of politics and administrative decision-making, coordination, management, and policy preparation in the richest possible ways to help us understand how key actors in these executive relations make sense of what they do, and why they do it, rather than impute fairly simplistic motivations and behavioural propensities about them.

As I worked out the relationships between commissioners, cabinet chefs, and senior officials, I became increasingly intrigued with the related but somewhat different question of how newly emerging accountability arrangements have affected these executive relationships and how this has impacted the institutional character of the EU Commission. As a result, the research shifted to become organized around a somewhat different, but I thought and think, even more compelling theoretical puzzle. As evidence in the research mounted of differences between the Commission's executive relationships now and at the time of its original design, it gradually became clear that the institutional evolution had a clear face, with the emergence of new accountability forums and arrangements, introduced during the various political and administrative reforms, leading to a 'normalization' of this EU executive and of its core executive relationships.

This institutional evolution raised theoretical issues of import well beyond the confines of the EU Commission, touching on fundamental questions about institutional change, the establishment of new accountability arrangements as a result of democratization and administrative reforms. Taken as a whole, the book embodies an argument about institutional evolution and the interaction of political and

Appendix: Research Design

administrative reforms, and its impact on executive relationships, which I believe is also relevant to other executives. But spelling this out is a task that others may pursue in the future.

Methods

Methodologically, both institutional change and politicians and public administrators in executive relations are difficult to study. Institutional change is problematic to research because a fruitful yardstick that assesses qualitative alterations to an institution, and that allows for generalizations over time, is not easy to find. Executive politics is hard to study because of problems of gaining access, confidentiality, partial involvement, and post hoc rationalization which make it particularly difficult to uncover the political process inside the public sector through surveys. In-depth archival analysis and direct real-time observation are far more helpful methods in this regard (Rhodes *et al*. 2007). However, both require deep access that is time-consuming and difficult to obtain (Child *et al*. 2010: 126). An alternative that is opted for in this study is the use of interviews and an analysis of documents. This approach builds directly on past research in the Dutch executive with Paul 't Hart and colleagues from Leiden University (2002; Hart and Wille 2006), in which we studied executive relationships.

Documents

Data have been drawn from primary and secondary sources. Most of the detailed working and official documents are available on-line. I have used the documentation published by the Commission, especially on the administrative reforms. Analysis of the new regulations and codes of conduct were used to gain more insight into the rules governing the selection and appointment procedures. Moreover, the use of biographical data provided information on the careers of key actors. Documents and biographical information were available on the Commission website (<http://ec.europa.eu/index_en.htm>). Further, I used the Commission's White Papers and press releases, speeches of commissioners, reports by the European Parliament and its standing committees, as well as the two reports of the CIE, both published in 1999, in addition to a wide range of general and media sources.

Interviews

The research relies on fifty in-depth, face-to-face interviews conducted with commissioners, directors-general, and heads of cabinet in the Barosso I Commission. The objective of this study was to provide an inside-out account of executive relationships in an era of change.

Effort was made to interview officials and officeholders with experience in working at the top; some officials had been working there for a long time, others were relative newcomers. Interviewees were distributed across a range of sectors and policy portfolios. In addition to their own affiliation, most officials had experience in more than one field. Individuals who were interviewed served in a variety of capacities, but they

Appendix: Research Design

all had professional-level leadership and policy positions. I interviewed more males than females and talked to officials from nearly all twenty-seven nationalities in the Commission. Fifteen additional interviews were conducted with relevant informants: MEPs, to learn about the accountability expectations of the EU Commission, and officials working at the apex, like assistants of the director-general and members of cabinet.

Most of the interviews took place in the interviewees' office in Brussels in the period 2006–9. But other locations included conference rooms, cafeterias, coffee shops, and some off-site restaurants. Interviews typically lasted an hour or so; a few were as short as forty minutes, while others were over two hours in duration. Topics covered included cooperation and the working relationship, perceptions of daily practices, career routes, role expectations, and the contacts with the European Parliament.

The interviews were conducted face to face in a semi-structured (nearly conversational) manner. All conversations were recorded with a voice recorder with the permission of the respondents, and transcribed. In one case only, the respondent/interviewee withheld permission for recording, and the author had to rely on hand-written notes. All respondents were promised complete anonymity and confidentiality regarding their comments. The interviews were conducted on the understanding that the participants would not be named as interviewees. With these ground rules established there was usually no reluctance to talk, no leaving questions unanswered or avoiding topics. The main purpose was to build a sense of openness about what it is like to work in the EU Commission. The atmosphere during the conversations was relaxed, pleasant, and informal. Obviously, however, it was by no means a conversation between equals. During interviews, powerful, influential people—though in the ostensibly dependent role of interviewee—are quite capable of controlling the interview. Politicians and senior officials are skilled 'interviewees' who tell you what they want to tell you and no more. As a result, they are tough objects of study. They understand the decision process in the light of their own selective interpretations. They may rationalize the part they have played in cooperation, and the more politically charged the decision process, the more this is likely to happen (Child et al. 2010: 126). Even if there appeared to be virtually no no-go areas in the conversation, some topics were treated with professional generalizations.

I used the interviews for a number of reasons. First, since I sought information regarding the expectations and perceptions of commissioners, head of cabinets, and senior officials, it made sense to talk to them. The flexibility allowed by an interview instrument was a second reason to opt for this method. The questions were open-ended, and because the interviews were semi-structured, it was possible to add follow-up questions that followed logically from the interviewee statements. The interviews allowed me to cover a large number of topics in depth. I talked with interviewees about the key elements that generate a good relationship. To avoid problems associated with self-reporting, the interviews were not limited to self-reporting. The questions not only concerned the individual's own attitudes and behaviour, but also those of their colleagues. Hence the interviewees were able to act not only as respondents, but also as informants and to talk about their counterparts. This provided the opportunity to reconstruct the parameters of the cooperation within political–bureaucratic dyads

Appendix: Research Design

and triads. The fact that their accounts were consistent with one another increased confidence in the frankness and accuracy of the accounts provided. The interviews and reports were especially useful, because it is nearly impossible to get information on these relationships on any other way.

As result of the precautions and the responses that the interviews elicited, I am confident that the choice of interview subject was appropriate to the task and that the findings reported in this book paint an accurate picture of the political–bureaucratic relationships at the top of the EU Commission during the Barroso years.

Data-Analysis

Interviews were tape-recorded and transcribed. The analysis focused on the communalities and differences between politicians and bureaucrats by focusing on recruitment and role expectations. I also paid particular attention to how people assessed the role of their counterpart in the triad, as well as how they perceived their triadic relationship and what elements were relevant for the relationship. In addition, I considered contextual elements, such as the working of the EP and the portfolio, and whether the interviewees could detect changes in these categories.

In coding the answers and interviews, I relied to some extent on the standardized coding scheme used in a previous study on political–administrative relationships in the Netherlands (Hart and Wille 2006). Armed with these interview data, I tried to answer some key questions about the executive relations at the top of the Commission.

References

Abélès, M., and Bellier, I. (1996) 'La Commission Européenene: Du compromis culturel à la culture politique du compromis', *Revue Française de Science Politique*, 46(3): 431–56.
—— and McDonald, M (1993) 'An Anthropological Approach to the European Commission', Brussels, report for the European Commission (unpublished).
Aberbach, J., and Rockman, B. (2000) *In the Web of Politics: Three Decades of the U.S. Federal Executive* (Washington, DC: Brookings Institution Press).
—— Putnam, R. D., and Rockman, B. A. (1981) *Bureaucrats and Politicians in Western Democracies* (Cambridge, Mass.: Harvard University Press).
Argyris, C., and Schön, D. A. (1978) *Organizational Learning: A Theory of Action Perspective* (Reading, Mass.: Addison-Wesley).
Aucoin, P., and Heintzman, R. (2000) 'The Dialectics of Accountability for Performance in Public Management Reform', *International Review of Administrative Sciences*, 66: 45–55.
—— and Jarvis, M. D. (2005) *Modernizing Government Accountability: A Framework for Reform* (Ottowa: Canada School of Public Service).
Balint, T., Bauer, M. W., and Knill, C. (2008) 'Bureaucratic Change in the European Administrative Space: The Case of the European Commission', *West European Politics*, 31(4): 677–700.
Ban, C. (2009) 'The Challenge of Linking Organizational and Individual Accountability in the European Commission'. Available at: < http://carolynban.net/>
—— (2010) 'Reforming the Staffing Process in the European Institutions: Moving the Sacred Cow out of the Road', *International Review of Administrative Sciences*, 76(1): 5–24.
—— (2013) *Management and Culture in an Enlarged European Commission: From Diversity to Unity?* (Basingstoke: Palgrave Macmillan).
Barberis, P. (1998) 'The New Public Management and a New Accountability', *Public Administration*, 76: 451–70.
Barnard, C. I. (1938) *The Functions of the Executive* (Cambridge, Mass.: Harvard University Press).
Bauer, M. W. (2007a) 'Introduction: Management Reforms in International Organizations', in M. W. Bauer and C. Knill (eds), *Management Reforms in International Organizations* (Baden-Baden: Nomos), 11–23.
—— (2007b) 'The Politics of Reforming the European Commission Administration', in M. W. Bauer and C. Knill (eds), *Management Reforms in International Organizations* (Baden-Baden: Nomos), 54–69.

References

Bauer, M. W. (2008) 'Organisational Change, Management Reform and EU Policy-Making', *Journal of European Public Policy*, 15(5): 627–47.

—— and Ege, J. (2012) 'Politicization within the European Commission's Bureaucracy', *International Review of Administrative Science*, 78(3): 403–24.

Behn, R. D. (2001) *Rethinking Democratic Accountability* (Washington, DC: Brookings Institution Press).

Best, H. (2007) 'New Challenges, New Elites? Changes in the Recruitment and Career Patterns of European Representative Elites', *Comparative Sociology*, 6(1–2): 85–113.

—— and Cotta, M (eds) (2000) *Parliamentary Representatives in Europe, 1848–2000: Legislative Recruitment and Careers in Eleven European Countries* (Oxford: Oxford University).

Beyers, J., and Kerremans, B. (2004) 'Bureaucrats, Politicians, and Societal Interests: How is European Policy Making Politicized?' *Comparative Political Studies*, 37(10): 1119–50.

Bogdanor, V. (2007) *Legitimacy, Accountability and Democracy in the European Union* (London: Federal Trust Report).

Boin, A. (1998) *Contrasts in Leadership: An Institutional Study of Two Prison Systems* (Delft: Eburon).

—— and 't Hart, P. (2000) 'Institutional Crises and Reforms in Policy Sectors', in H. Wagenaar (ed.), *Government Institutions: Development, Design and Change* (Dordrecht: Kluwer), 9–31.

Borchert, Jens, and Stolz, K. (2002) 'Fighting Insecurity: Political Careers in the Federal Republic of Germany', paper presented at the APSA Annual meeting Boston, 29 Aug.–1 Sept.

Borrás, S. (2009) 'The Politics of the Lisbon Strategy: The Changing Role of the Commission', *West European Politics*, 32(1): 97–118.

Boucher, S. (2009) *If Citizens have a Voice, Who's Listening? Lessons from Recent Citizen Consultation Experiments for the European Union* (Brussels: EPIN Working Papers).

Bovens, M. (1998) *The Quest for Responsibility: Accountability and Citizenship in Complex Organisations* (Cambridge: Cambridge University Press).

—— (2006) *Analysing and Assessing Public Accountability: A Conceptual Framework*. European Governance Papers (EUROGOV), C-06-01. Available at: <org/eurogov/pdf/egp-connex-C-06-01.pdf>

—— (2007) 'Analysing and Assessing Accountability: A Conceptual Framework', *European Law Journal*, 13(4): 447–68.

—— (2010) 'Two Concepts of Accountability: Accountability as a Virtue and as a Mechanism', *West European Politics*, 33(5): 946–67.

—— Schillemans, T., and 't Hart P. (2008) 'Does Public Accountability Work? An Assessement Tool', *Public Administration*, 86(1): 225–42.

—— Curtin, D., and 't Hart, P. (eds) (2010) *The Real World of EU Accountability: What Deficit?* (Oxford: Oxford University Press).

Broin, P., and Kaczyński, P. M. (2010) *Treaty of Lisbon: A Second Look at the Institutional Innovations* (Brussels: CEPS Paperbacks).

References

Burke, J. P. (2007) 'From Success to Failure? Iraq and the Organization of George W. Bush's Decision Making', in G. C. Edwards III and D. King (eds), *The Polarized Presidency of George W. Bush* (New York: Oxford University Press).

Campbell, C. (1988) 'The Political Roles of Senior Government Officials in Advanced Democracies', *British Journal of Political Science*, 18(2): 243–72.

Capano, G. (2009) 'Understanding Policy Change as an Epistemological and Theoretical Problem', *Journal of Comparative Policy Analysis: Research and Practice*, 11(1): 7–31.

Caproso, J. A. (1997) 'Does the European Parliament Respresent a No. of 1?', *ECSA Review* 10(3): 1–5. Available at: <http://aei.pitt.edu/54/1/N1debate.htm>.

Child, J., Elbanna, S., and Rodrigues, S. (2010) 'The Political Aspects of Strategic Decision Making', in Paul C. Nutt and D. C. Wilson (eds), *Handbook of Decision Making* (Chichester: Wiley-Blackwell), 105–38.

Christiansen, T. (1997) 'Tensions of European Governance: Politicized Bureaucracy and Multiple Accountability in the European Commission', *Journal of European Public Policy*, 4(1): 73–90.

—— (2001) 'Intra-Institutional Politics and Inter-Institutional Relations in the EU: Towards Coherent Governance?', *Journal of European Public Policy*, 8(5): 747–69.

—— (2005) *Towards Statehood? The EU's Move towards Constitutionalisation and Territorialisation*, ARENA Working Paper, 21/2005 (Oslo: Arena). Available at <http://www.arena.uio.no/publications/working-papers2005/papers/wp05_21.pdf>.

—— and Gray, M. (2004) 'The European Commission in a Period of Change: A New Administration for a New European Union?', *Eipascope*, 3: 20–4.

CIE (Committee of Independent Experts) (1999*a*) 'First Report on Allegations Regarding Fraud, Mismanagement and Nepotism in the European Commission', 15 Mar.

—— (1999*b*) 'Second Report on Reform of the Commission: Analysis of Curent Practice and Proposals for Tackling Mismanagement, Irregularities and Fraud', 10 Sept.

Cini, M. (1996) *The European Commission: Leadership, Organisation and Culture in the EU Administration* (Manchester: Manchester University Press).

—— (2000) *Organizational Culture and Reform: The Case of the European Commission under Jacques Santer* (Fiesole: European University Institute Working Papers, RSC 2000/25).

—— (2004) 'Norms, Culture and the Kinnock White Paper. The Theory and Practice of Cultural Change in the Reform of the European Commission', in D. G. Dimitrakopoulos (ed.), *The Changing European Commission* (Manchester: Manchester University Press), 63–73.

—— (2007) *From Integration to Integrity: Administrative Ethics and Reform in the European Commission* (Manchester: Manchester University Press).

Coleman, J. S. (1990) *The Foundations of Social Theory* (Cambridge, Mass.: Belknap Press of Harvard University Press).

Coombes, D. (1970) *Politics and Bureaucracy of the European Union* (London: George Allen & Unwin).

References

Corbett, R., Jacobs, F., and Shackleton, M. (2007) *The European Parliament* (London: John Harper Publishing).

Cotta, M., and Best, H. (2007) 'Parliamentary Representatives from the Early Democratization of Europe: Political Representations and the Great Change of European Societies', in M. Cotta and H. Best (eds), *Democratic Representation in Europe: Diversity, Change and Convergence* (Oxford: Oxford University Press), 1–26.

Cram, L. (1994) 'The European Commission as a Multi-Organisation: Social Policy and IT Policy in the EU', *Journal of European Public Policy*, 1(2): 195–217.

—— (2001) 'Whither the Commission? Reform, Renewal and the Issue-Attention Cycle', *Journal of European Public Policy*, 8(5): 770–86.

—— (2002) 'Introduction to Special Issue on the Institutional Balance and the Future of EU Governance: The Future of the Union and the Trap of the "Nirvana Fallacy"', *Governance*, 15(3): 309–24.

Curtin, D. (2009) *Executive Power of the European Union: Laws, Practices and the Living Constitution* (Oxford: Oxford University Press).

—— (2011) 'Top Secret Europe', inaugural lecture delivered upon appointment to the chair of Professor of European Law at the University of Amsterdam on 20 Oct., inaugural lecture 415, University of Amsterdam.

—— and Egeberg, M. (2008) 'Tradition and Innovation: Europe's Accumulated Executive Order', *West European Politics*, 31(4): 639–61.

—— and Meijer, A. J. (2006) 'Does Transparency Strengthen Legitimacy?', *Information Polity*, 11(2): 109–22.

—— and Wille, A. (2008) 'Introduction', in D. Curtin and A. Wille (eds), *Meaning and Practice of Accountability in the EU Multi-Level Context* (Mannheim: Connex Report Series, 7), 1–17.

Dahl, R. A. (1989) *Democracy and its Critics* (New Haven: Yale University Press).

—— (1998) *On Democracy* (New Haven: Yale University Press).

—— (1999) 'Can International Organization be Democratic? A Skeptic View', in I. Shapiro and C. Hacker-Cordon (eds), *Democracy Edges* (Cambridge: Cambridge University Press), 19–36.

—— (2006) *On Political Equality* (New Haven: Yale University Press).

Dargie, C., and Locke, R. (1999) 'The British Senior Civil Service', in E. C. Page and V. Wright (eds), *Bureaucratic Elites in West European States* (Oxford: Oxford University Press), 179–204.

De Clerck-Sachsse, J., and Kaczyński, P. M. (2009) *The European Parliament: More Powerful, Less Legitimate? An Outlook for the 7th Term* (Brussels: CEPS Working Document, 314).

De Wilde, P., and Zürn, M. (2012) 'Can the Politicization of European Integration be Reversed?', *Journal of Common Market Studies*, 50(s1): 137–53.

Dehousse, R. (1998) 'European Institutional Architecture After Amsterdam: Parliamentary System or Regulatory Structure?', *Common Market Law Review*, 35: 595–627.

Demmke, C., and Moilanen, T. (2010) *Civil Services in the EU of 27: Reform Outcomes and the Future of the Civil Service* (Frankfurt am Main: PeterLang).

References

Dickinson, M. J. (2003) 'Bargaining Uncertainty, and the Growth of the White House Staff, 1940–2000', in B. Burn (ed.), *Uncertainty in American Politics* (New York: Cambridge University Press).

DiMaggio, P. J., and Powell, W. W. (1983) 'The Iron Cage Revisited: Institutional Isomorphism and Collective Rationality in Organizational Fields', *American Sociological Review*, 48(2): 147–60.

Dimitrakopoulos, D. (ed.) (2004) *The Changing European Commission* (Manchester: Manchester University Press).

—— and Kassim, H. (2005) 'Inside the European Commission: Preference Formation and the Convention of the Future of Europe', *Comparative European Politics*, 3: 180–203.

—— and Page, E. (2003) 'Paradoxes in EU Administration', in J. J. Hesse, C. Hood, and B. G. Peters (eds), *Paradoxes in Public Sector Reform: An International Comparison* (Berlin: Duncker & Humblot), 317–33.

Dogan, M. (1975) *The Mandarins of Western Europe: Political Role of Top Civil Servants* (New York: John Wiley).

—— (1999) 'Les Professions propices à la carrière politique: Osmoses, filières et viviers', in M. OFFERLE (ed.), *La Profession politique: XIXe–XXe siècles* (Paris: Belin).

Dolowitz, D., and Marsh, D. (2000) 'Learning from Abroad: The Role of Policy Transfer in Contemporary Policy Making', *Governance*, 13(1): 5–24.

Donnelly, M., and Richie, E. (1997) 'The College of Commissioners and their Cabinet', in Geoffrey Edwards and David Spence (ed.), *The European Commission*, 2nd edn (London: Cartermill International), 33–62.

Döring, H. (2007) 'The Composition of the College of Commissioners: Patterns of Delegation', *European Union Politics*, 8(2): 207–27.

Druckman, J. N., and Warwick, P. V. (2005) 'The Missing Piece: Measuring Portfolio Salience in Western European Parliamentary Democracies', *European Journal of Political Research*, 44: 17–42.

Duchene, F. (1994) *Jean Monnet: The First Statesman of Interdependence* (New York: W.W. Norton & Co.).

Dunleavy, P., and Rhodes, R. A. W. (1990) 'Core Executives Studies in Britain', *Public Administration*, 68(1): 3–28.

Dunn, D. (1997) *Politics and Administration at the Top: Lessons from Down Under* (Pittsburgh, Pa.: University of Pittsburgh Press).

Durant, R. F., and Diehl, P. F. (1989) 'Agendas, Alternatives, and Public Policy: Lessons from the U.S. Foreign Policy Arena', *Journal of Public Policy*, 9(2): 179–205.

Edelman, M. J. (1964) *The Symbolic Uses of Politics* (Urbana, Ill.: University of Illinois Press).

Egeberg, M. (1996) 'Organization and Nationality in the European Commission Services', *Public Administration*, 74(4): 721–35

—— (2003) 'How Bureaucratic Structure Matters: An Organizational Perspective', in B. G. Peters and J. Pierre (eds), *Handbook of Public Administration* (London: Sage), 116–26.

—— (2006a) 'Balancing Autonomy and Accountability: Enduring Tensions in the European Commission Development', in M. Egeberg (ed.), *Multilevel Union*

221

References

Administration: The Transformation of Executive Politics in Europe (London: Palgrave Macmillan), 31–50.

Egeberg, M. (2006b) 'Executive Politics as Usual: Role Behaviour and Conflict Dimensions in the College of European Commissioners', *Journal of European Public Policy*, 13(1): 1–15.

—— (2006c) 'The Institutional Architecture of the EU and the Transformation of European Politics', in M. Egeberg (ed.), *Multilevel Union Administration: The Transformation of Executive Politics in Europe* (Houndmills Basingstoke: Palgrave Macmillan), 17–30.

—— (2006d) 'Europe's Executive Branch of Government in the Melting Pot: An Overview', in M. Egeberg (ed.), *Multilevel Union Administration: The Transformation of Executive Politics in Europe* (Houndmills Basingstoke: Palgrave Macmillan), 1–16.

—— (2012) 'Experiments in Supranational Institution-Building: The European Commission as a Laboratory', *Journal of European Public Policy*, 19(6): 939–50.

—— and Heskestad, A. (2010) 'The Denationalization of Cabinets in the European Commission', *Journal of Common Market Studies*, 48(4): 775–86.

Ellinas, A., and Suleiman, E. (2008) 'Reforming the Commission: Between Modernization and Bureaucratization', *Journal of European Public Policy*, 15(5): 708–25.

—— and —— (2012) *The European Commission and Bureaucratic Autonomy: Europe's Custodians* (Cambridge: Cambridge University Press).

Eichbaum, C., and Shaw, R. (2007) 'Minding the Minister? Ministerial Advisers in New Zealand Government, Kotuitui', *New Zealand Journal of Social Sciences Online*, 2(2): 95–113.

Elgie, R. (2011) 'Core Executive Studies Two Decades On', *Public Administration*, 89(1): 64–77.

Eymeri-Douzans, J., and Pierre, J. (eds) (2011) *Administrative Reform, Democratic Governance and the Quality of Government* (London: Routledge).

European Commission (2000a) *Reforming the Commission: A White Paper*. Part I, COM/2000/0200 final (Brussels: European Commission).

—— (2000b) *Reforming the Commission: A White Paper, Action Plan*. Part II (Brussels: European Commission).

—— (2001) *White Paper on European Governance 2001*. COM(2001) 428, July (Brussels: European Commission).

—— (2004) *Completing the Reform Mandate: Progress Report and Measures to be Implemented in 2004*, COM (2004) 93 final, 2 Feb.

Finer, H. (1941) 'Administrative Responsibility in Democratic Government', in W. Bruce (ed.) *Classics of Administrative Ethics* (Boulder, Colo.: Westview Press, 2001), 5–26.

Friedrich, C. J. (1940) 'Public Policy and the Nature of Administrative Responsibility', in C. J. Friedrich and E. S. Mason (eds), *Public Policy* (Cambridge, Mass.: Harvard University Press), 333–42.

Frederickson, H. G., and Smith, K. B. (2003) *Public Administration Theory Primer* (Boulder, Colo.: Westview Press).

References

Follesdal, A., and Hix, S. (2006) 'Why there is a Democratic Deficit in the EU: A Response to Majone and Moravcsik', *Journal of Common Market Studies,* 44(3): 533–62.

Fouilleux, E., Maillard, J. de, and Smith, A. (2005) 'Technical or Political? The Working Groups of the Council of Ministers', *Journal of European Public Policy*, 12: 609–23.

Franklin, M., Marsh, M., and McLaren L. (1994) 'Uncorking the Bottle: Popular Opposition to European Unification in the Wake of Maastricht', *Journal of Common Market Studies,* 32(4): 455–72.

Fukuyama, F. (2011) *The Origins of Political Order* (London: Profile Books).

Fung, A., Graham, M., and Weil, D. (2007) *Full Disclosure: The Perils and Promise of Transparency* (Cambridge: Cambridge University Press).

Georgakakis, D. (2009) 'Tensions within Eurocracy', *French Politics*, 8(2): 116–44.

—— and de Lassalle, M. (2006) 'Who are the Directors-General? European Construction and Administrative Careers in the Commission', paper presented at EU–Consent workshop, Paris, June.

—— and Rowell, J. (2013) *The Field of Eurocracy: Political Sociology of the EU Staff and Professionals* (Basingstoke: Palgrave, forthcoming).

Gill, J. I., and Saunders, L. (1992) 'Toward a Definition of Policy Analysis', *New Directions for Institutional Research*, 76(Winter): 5–13.

Goetz, A. M., and Jenkins, R. (2005) *Reinventing Accountability: Making Democracy Work for Human Development* (Basingstoke: Macmillan Palgrave).

Goetz, K. (2011) 'Time and the EU', in E. Jones, A. Menon, and S. Weatherill (eds), *The Oxford Handbook on the EU* (Oxford: Oxford University Press), 703–15.

Grant, R. W., and Keohane, R. O. (2005) 'Accountability and Abuses of Power in World Politics', *American Political Science Review*, 99(1): 29–43.

Grøn, C. H. (2009) 'Same Procedure as Last Year? An Analysis of Constellations of Trust and Control in Management in the European Commission', Department of Political Science University of Copenhagen, Ph.D. thesis.

Haas, E. B. (1958) *The Uniting of Europe* (Stanford, Calif.: Stanford University Press).

Hague, R., and Harrop, M. (2010) *Comparative Government and Politics: An Introduction* (Basingstoke: Palgrave Macmillan).

Hall, A. T., Bowen, M. G., Ferris, G. R., Royle, M. T., and Fitzgibbons, D. E. (2007) 'The Accountability Lens: A New Way to View Management Issues', *Business Horizons*, 5: 405–13.

Hall, P. (1993) 'Policy Paradigms, Social Learning and the State', *Comparative Politics*, 25: 275–96.

—— (2010) 'Historical Institutionalism in Rationalist and Sociological Perspective', in J. Mahoney and K. Thelen (eds), *Explaining Institutional Change: Ambiguity, Agency and Power* (Cambridge: Cambridge University Press), 204–23.

Harlow, C. (2002) *Accountability in the European Union* (Oxford: Oxford University Press).

Hart, 't P., and Uhr, J. (2011) *How Power Changes Hands: Transition and Succession in Government* (Basingstoke: Palgrave).

References

Hart, 't P., and Wille, A. (2006) 'Ministers and Top Officials in the Dutch Executive: Living Together, Growing Apart?', *Public Administration*, 84(1): 121–46.

—— and —— (2012) 'Bureaucratic Politics: Opening the Black Box of Executive Government', in J. Pierre and B. G. Peters (eds), *Handbook of Public Administration* (New York: Sage), 369–79.

—— Wille, A., Boin, R., Dijkstra, G., van der Meer, F., van Noort, W., and Zannoni, M. (2002) *Politiek-ambtelijke verhoudingen in beweging* (Amsterdam: Boom).

Heady, B. (1974) *British Cabinet Ministers: The Role of Politicians in Executive Office* (London: George Allen & Unwin).

Heclo, H. (1974) *Modern Social Politics in Britain and Sweden: From Relief to Income Maintenance* (New Haven: Yale University Press).

—— (1977) *A Government of Strangers: Executive Politics in Washington* (Washington, DC: Brookings Institution Press).

—— and Wildavsky, A. (1974) *The Private Government of Public Money* (London: Macmillan).

Held, D. (2004) 'Democratic Accountability and Political Effectiveness from a Cosmopolitan Perspective', *Government and Opposition*, 39(2): 364–91.

—— and Koenig-Archibugi, M. (2005) *Global Governance and Public Accountability* (Oxford: Blackwell Publishing).

Héritier, A. (2012) 'Institutional Change in Europe: Co-decision and Comitology Transformed', *Journal of Common Market Studies*, 50(s1): 38–54.

Herman, M. G., and Preston, T. (1994) 'Foreign Policy: The Effect of Leadership Style on Executive Arrangements', *Political Psychology*, 15(1): 75–96.

Hix, S. (1999) *The Political System of the European Union* (Houndmills Basingstoke: Palgrave).

—— (2008) *What is Wrong with the European Union and How to Fix it* (Cambridge: Polity).

—— Noury, A., and Roland, G. (2007) *Democratic Politics in the European Parliament* (Cambridge: Cambridge University Press).

Hood, C. (1991) 'A Public Management for All Seasons?', *Public Administration*, 69: 3–19.

—— (2002) 'The Risk Game and the Blame Game', *Government and Opposition*, 37(1): 15–37.

—— (2007) 'What Happens When Transparency Meets Blame-Avoidance?', *Public Management Review*, 9(2): 191–210.

—— and Heald, D. (eds) (2006) *Transparency: The Key to Better Governance* (Oxford: Oxford University Press).

Hooghe, L. (2001) *The European Commission and the Integration of Europe: Images of Governance* (Cambridge: Cambridge University Press).

—— and Marks, G. (2005) 'Calculation, Community, and Cues: Public Opinion on European Integration', *European Union Politics*, 6(4): 421–45.

Huntington, S. P. (1991) *The Third Wave: Democratization in the Late Twentieth Century* (Oklahoma: University of Oklahoma Press).

Ingraham, P. (1995) *The Foundation of Merit* (Baltimore, Md.: Johns Hopkins University Press).

References

Jacobsen, D. I. (2006) 'The Relationship between Politics and Administration: The Importance of Contingency Factors, Formal Structure, Demography, and Time', *Governance*, 19(2): 303–23.

—— (2011) 'Convergence, Divergence or Stability: How do Politicians' and Bureaucrats' Attitudes Change during an Election Period?', *Public Management Review*, 13(5): 621–40.

Joana, J., and Smith, A. (2002) *Les Commissaires Européen: Technocrats, diplomates ou politiques?* (Paris: Presses de Science Po).

Johansson, K. M., and Talberg, J. (2010) 'Explaining Chief Executive Empowerment: EU Summitry and Domestic Institutional Change', *West European Politics*, 33(2): 208–36.

Judge, D., and Earnshaw, D. (2002) 'The European Parliament; Leadership and the Commission Crisis: A New Assertiveness?', *Governance*, 15(3): 345–74.

—— and —— (2008) *The European Parliament* (2nd edn, London: Palgrave Macmillan).

Judt, T. (2011) *A Grand Illusion? An Essay on Europe* (New York: New York University Press).

Kaczyński, P. M., Kurpas, S., and Gron, C. (2008) *The European Commission After Enlargement: Does More Add up to Less?* (Brussels: CEPS Special Reports, Feb.).

Kassim, H. (2004*a*) 'A Historic Accomplishment? The Prodi Commission and Administrative Reform', in D. G. Dimitrakopoulos (ed.), *The Changing European Commission* (Manchester: Manchester University Press), 33–62.

—— (2004*b*) 'The Secretariat General of the European Commission, 1958–2003: A Singular Institution', in A. Smith (ed.), *Politics and the European Commission: Actors, Interdependence, Legitimacy* (London: Routledge), 47–66.

—— (2008) '"Mission Impossible", But Mission Accomplished: The Kinnock Reforms and the European Commission', *Journal of European Public Policy*, 15: 648–68.

—— and Menon, A. (2004) 'EU Member States and the Prodi Commission', in D. G. Dimitrakopoulos (ed.), *The Changing European Commission* (Manchester: Manchester University Press), 89–104.

—— Peterson, J., Bauer, M. W., Connolly, S., Dehousse, R., Hooghe, L., and Thompson, A. (2013) *The European Commission of the Twenty-First Century* (Oxford: Oxford University Press).

Kavenagh, D., and Richards, D. (2003) 'Prime Ministers and Civil Servants in Britain', *Comparative Sociology*, 2(1): 175–95.

—— and Sheldon, A. (2008) *The Powers behind the Prime Minister: The Hidden Influence of Number Ten* (London: Harper Collins Publishers).

Keane, J. (2009) *The Life and Death of Democracy* (London: Simon & Schuster).

Kelemen, D. (2012) 'Eurolegalism and Democracy', *Journal of Common Market Studies*, 50(s1): 55–71.

Kelemen, R. D., and Tarrant, A. D. (2011) 'The Political Foundations of the Eurocracy', *West European Politics*, 34(5): 922–47.

Kingdon, J. W. (1995) *Agendas, Alternatives, and Public Policies* (2nd edn, Boston: LittleBrown).

References

Kinnock, N. (2002) 'Accountability and Reform of Internal Control in the European Commission', *Political Quarterly*, 73(1): 21–8.

Knill, C. (2005) 'Introduction: Cross-National Policy Convergence. Concepts, Approaches and Explanatory Factors', *Journal of European Public Policy*, 12(5): 764–74.

—— and Bauer, M. (2007) 'Theorizing Management Reforms in International Organizations', in M. W. Bauer and C. Knill (eds), *Management Reforms in International Organizations* (Baden-Baden: Nomos), 191–9.

Koenig-Archibugi, M., and Held, D. (2004) 'Introduction', in D. Held and M. Koenig-Archibugi (eds), *Global Governance and Public Accountability* (Chichester: Wiley-Blackwell), 1–7.

Kohler-Koch, B. (2000) 'Framing: The Bottleneck of Constructing Legitimate Institutions', *Journal of European Public Policy*, 7(4): 513–31.

Koppell, J. (2005) 'Pathologies of Accountability: ICANN and the Challenge of "Multiple Accountabilities Disorder"', *Public Administration Review*, 65(1): 94–107.

Kowert, P. A. (2002) *Groupthink or Deadlock: When do Leaders Learn from their Advisers* (Albany, NY: State University Press).

Krause, G. (1999) *A Two-Way Street: The Institutional Dynamics of the Modern Administrative State* (Pittsburgh, Pa.: University of Pittsburgh Press).

Kreppel, A., and Hix, S. (2003) 'From "Grand Coalition" to Left–Right Confrontation: Explaining the Shifting Structure of Party Competition in the European Parliament', *Comparative Political Studies*, 36(1/2): 75–96.

Laffan, B. (1997) 'From Policy Entrepreneur to Policy Manager: The Challenge Facing the European Commission', *Journal of European Public Policy*, 4(3): 422–38.

Lewis, D. E. (2008) *The Politics of Presidential Appointments: Political Control and Bureaucratic Performance* (Princeton: Princeton University Press).

Lijphart, A. (1984) *Democracies: Patterns of Majoritarian and Consensus Government in Twenty-One Countries* (New Haven: Yale University Press).

—— (1999) *Patterns of Democracy: Government Forms and Performance in Thirty-Six Countries* (New Haven: Yale University Press).

Lord, C. (2004) *A Democratic Audit of the European Union* (Basingstoke: Palgrave).

Lowi, T. J. (1964) 'American Business, Public Policy, Case-Studies, and Political Theory', *World Politics*, 16(4): 677–715.

McDonald, M. (2000) 'Identities in the European Commission', in N. Nugent (ed.), *At the Heart of the Union: Studies of the European Commission* (New York: St Martin's Press, 51–72.

MacMullen, M. (2000) European Commissioners: National Routes to a European Elite', in N. Nugent (ed.), *At the Heart of the Union: Studies of the European Commission*. New York: St Martin's Press), 28–50.

McNamara. K. R. (2010) 'Constructing the EU: Insights from Historical Sociology', *Comparative European Politics*, 8: 127–42.

Magnette, P. (2001) 'Appointing and Censuring the European Commission: The Adaptation of Parliamentary Institutions to the Community Context', *European Law Journal*, 7(3): 292–310.

—— (2005) *What is the European Union? Nature and Prospects* (London: Palgrave Macmillan).

References

Mahoney, J., and Thelen, K. (2010) *Explaining Institutional Change: Ambiguity, Agency, and Power* (Cambridge: Cambridge University Press).

Mair, P. (2008) 'Popular Democracy and the European Union Polity', in D. Curtin and A. Wille (eds) *Meaning and Practice of Accountability in the EU Multi-Level Context* (Mannheim: Connex Report Series, 7), 1–17.

Majone, G. (1996) *Regulating Europe* (London: Routledge).

—— (2005) *Dilemmas of European Integration: The Ambiguities and Pitfalls on Integration by Stealth* (Oxford: Oxford University Press).

—— (2009) *Europe as the Would-be World Power* (Cambridge: Cambridge University Press).

Malkopoulou, A. (2009) *Lost Voters: Participation in EU Elections and the Case for Compulsory Voting* (Brussels: CEPS Working Document, 317).

Manin, B., Przeworski, A., and Stokes, S. (1999) 'Introduction', in A. Przeworski, S. Stokes, and B. Manin (eds), *Democracy, Accountability, and Representation* (Cambridge: Cambridge University Press), 1–26.

March, J. G. (1991) 'Exploration and Exploitation in Organizational Learning', *Organization Science*, 2(1): 71–87.

—— (1997) 'Administrative Practice, Organization Theory and Political Philosophy: Ruminations on the Reflections of John Gaus', *PS Political Science*, 30(4): 689–98.

—— and Olsen, J. (1976) *Ambiguity and Choice in Organizations* (Bergen: Universiteitsforlaget).

—— and —— (1984) 'The New Institutionalism: Organizational Factors in Political Life', *American Political Science Review*, 78: 734–49.

—— and —— (1989) *Rediscovering Institutions: The Organizational Basis of Politics* (New York: Free Press).

Marsh, D., Richards, D., and Smith, M. (2000) 'Re-assessing the Role of Departmental Cabinet Ministers', *Public Administration*, 78(2): 305–26.

Mattli, W., and Stone Sweet, A. (2012) 'Regional Integration and the Evolution of the European Polity: On the Fiftieth Anniversary of the Journal of Common Market Studies', *Journal of Common Market Studies*, 50: 1–17.

Mattozzi, A., and Merlo, A. (2008) 'Political Careers or Career Politicians?', *Journal of Public Economics*, 92: 597–608.

Mazey, S. (1996) 'The Development of the European Idea: From Sectoral Integration to Political Union', in J. Richardson (ed.), *European Union: Power and Policy-Making* (London: Routledge), 24–39.

—— and Richardson, J. (1996) 'The European Commission: A Bourse for Ideas and Interests', *Revue Française des Sciences Politiques*, 43(3): 400–30.

Mehde, V. (2007) 'Creating a Missing Link? Administrative Reforms as a Means of Improving the Legitimacy of International', in M. W. Bauer and C. Knill (eds), *Management Reforms in International Organizations* (Baden-Baden: Nomos), 163–74.

—— (2009) 'Political Accountability in Europe', in L. Verhey, P. Kiiver, and S. Loeven (eds), *Political Accountability and European Integration* (Groningen: Europa Law Publishing), 71–8.

References

Meier, K. J., and Bohte, J. (1993) *Politics and the Bureaucracy* (Belmont, Calif.: Thomson-Wadsworth; 5th edn, 2006).

Meijer, A. J. (2012) 'Introduction to the Special Issue on Government Transparency', *International Review of Administrative Sciences*, 78(1): 3–9.

Meltsner, A. (1988) *Rules for Rulers: The Politics of Advice* (Philadelphia: Temple Universithy Press).

Mény, Y. (2003) 'De la démocratie en Europe: Old Concepts and New Challenges', *Journal of Common Market Studies*, 41(1): 1–13.

—— (2012) 'Conclusion: A Voyage to the Unknown', *Journal of Common Market Studies*, 50(s1): 154–64.

Metcalfe, L. (1999) 'Reforming the Commission', *Eipascope*, 3: 3–9.

—— (2000) 'Reforming the Commission: Will Organizational Efficiency Produce Effective Governance?', *Journal of Common Market Studies*, 38(5): 817–41.

—— (2001) 'Reforming European Governance: Old Problems or New Principles?', *International Review of Administrative Sciences*, 67(3): 415–43.

Meyer, C. (1999) 'Political Legitimacy and the Invisibility of Politics: Exploring the European Union's Communication Deficit', *Journal of Common Market Studies*, 37(4): 617–39.

Michelmann, H. (1978) 'Multinational Staffing and Organisational Functioning in the Commission of the EEC', *International Affairs*, 32(2): 477–96.

Monnet, J. (1978) *Memoirs* (London: Collins).

Moore, M. H. (1995) *Creating Public Value: Strategic Management in Government* (Cambridge, Mass.: Harvard University Press).

Moravcsik, A. (ed.) (1998) *The Choice for Europe: Social Purpose and State Power from Messina to Maastricht* (London: Routledge/UCL Press).

—— (2004) 'Is there a "Democratic Deficit" in World Politics? A Framework for Analysis', *Government and Opposition*, 39(2): 336–63.

Mouritzen, P. E., and Svara, J. H. (2002) *Leadership at the Apex: Politicians and Administrators in Western Local Governments* (Pittsburgh, Pa.: University of Pittsburgh Press).

Mulgan, R. (2000) 'Accountability an Ever Expanding Concept?', *Public Administration*, 78: 555–73.

—— (2003) *Holding Power to Account: Accountability in Modern Democracies* (Basingstoke: Palgrave Macmillan).

—— (2007) 'Truth in Government and the Politicization of Public Service Advice', *Public Administration*, 85(3): 569–86.

Murray, A. (2004) *An Unstable House? Reconstructing Commission*, Center for European Reform, working paper. Available at< http://www.cer.org.uk/sites/default/files/publications/attachments/pdf/2011/wp521_unstable_hse_comm-1509.pdf>.

Naurin, D. (2007) *Deliberation Behind Closed Doors: Transparency and Lobbying in the European Union* (Colchester: ECPR Press).

Norris, P. (ed.) (1997) *Passages to Power: Legislative Recruitment in Advanced Democracies* (Cambridge: Cambridge University Press).

—— and J. Lovenduski (1997) 'United Kingdom', in P. Norris (ed.), *Passages to Power: Legislative Recruitment in Advanced Democracies* (Cambridge: Cambridge University Press).

References

Nugent, N. (ed.) (1997) *At the Heart of the Union: Studies of the European Commission* (Basingstoke: Macmillan).
—— (2001) *The European Commission* (Basingstoke: Palgrave).
—— (2010) *The Government and Politics of the European Union* (7th edn, Basingstoke: Palgrave Macmillan).
Olsen, J. P. (1997) 'Institutional Design in Democratic Context', *Journal of Political Philosophy*, 5: 203–29.
—— (2007) *Europe in Search of Political Order* (Oxford: Oxford University Press).
—— (2008) 'Explorations in Institutions and Logics of Appropriateness: An Introductory Essay', in J. G. March, *Explorations in Organizations* (Stanford, Calif.: Stanford Business Books).
—— (2010) *Governing through Institution Building: Institutional Theory and Recent European Experiments in Democratic Organization* (Oxford: Oxford University Press).
—— (2013) 'Accountability and Ambiguity', in M. Bovens, R. Goodin, and T. Schillemans (eds), *The Oxford Handbook of Public Accountability* (Oxford: Oxford University Press, forthcoming).
Ongaro, E. (2012) 'Editorial Instruction: Managerial Reforms and the Transformation of the Administration of the European Commission', *International Review of Administrative Science*, 78(3): 379–82.
Overeem, P. (2012). *The Politics-Administration Dichotomy: Toward a Constitutional Perspective* (2nd edn, Boca Raton, Fla.: CRC Press).
Page, E. (1997) *People Who Run Europe* (Oxford: Clarendon Press).
Page, Edward C., and Wouters, Linda (1994) 'Bureaucratic Politics and Political Leadership in Brussels', *Public Administration*, 72: 445–59.
Panebianco, A. (1988) *Political Parties: Organization and Power* (Cambridge: Cambridge University Press).
Peters, B. G. (1988) *Comparing Public Bureaucracies: Problems of Theory and Method* (Tuscaloosa, Ala.: University of Alabama Press).
—— (2010) *The Politics of Bureaucracy: An Introduction to Comparative Public Administration* (6th edn, London: Routledge).
—— and Pierre, J. (eds) (2001) *Politicians, Bureaucrats and Administrative Reform* (London: Routledge).
—— and —— (eds) (2004) *Politicization of the Civil Service in Comparative Perspective: The Quest for Control* (London: Routledge).
—— Rhodes, R., and Wright, V. (eds) (2000) *Administering the Summit: Administration of the Core Executive in Developed Countries* (Houndmills Basingstoke: Palgrave Macmillan).
Peterson, J. (1999) 'The Santer Era: The European Commission in Normative, Historical and Theoretical Perspective', *Journal of European Public Policy*, 6(1): 46–65.
—— (2004) 'The Prodi Commission: Fresh Start or Free Fall?', in D. G. Dimitrakopoulos (ed.), *The Changing European Commission* (Manchester: Manchester University Press), 15–32.
—— (2008) 'Enlargement, Reform and the European Commission: Weathering a Perfect Storm?', *Journal of European Public Policy*, 15(5): 761–80.
—— and Shackleton, M. (2006) *The Institutions of the European Union* (Oxford: Oxford University Press).

References

Pierson, P. (2004) *Politics in Time: History, Institutions, and Social Analysis* (Princeton: Princeton University Press).

Poguntke, T., and Webb, P. (2005) *The Presidentialization of Politics: A Comparative Study of Modern Democracies* (Oxford: Oxford University Press).

Pollack, M. A. (2003) *The Engines of European Integration: Delegation, Agency and Agenda Setting in the EU* (Oxford: Oxford University Press).

Pollitt, C. (2001) 'Convergence: The Useful Myth?', *Public Administration*, 79(4): 933–47.

—— and Bouckaert, G. (2004) *Public Management Reform: A Comparative Analysis* (2nd edn, Oxford: Oxford University Press).

Powell, W. W., and. Colyvas, J. A. (2008) 'Microfoundations of Institutional Theory', in R. Greenwood, C. Oliver, K. Sahlin-Andersson, and R. Suddaby (eds), *Handbook of Organizational Institutionalism* (Newbury Park, Calif.: Sage), 276–98.

Preston, T., and 't Hart P. (1999) 'Understanding and Evaluating Bureaucratic Politics', *Political Psychology*, 21(1): 49–99.

Prodi, R. (1999) Speech to the European Parliament, Strasbourg, 4 May: <europa.eu/rapid/press-release_BIO-99-191_en.pdf>

Putnam, R. D. (1973) 'The Political Attitudes of Senior Civil Servants in Western Europe: A Preliminary Report', *British Journal of Political Science*, 3: 257–90.

—— (1975) *The Beliefs of Politicians* (New Haven: Yale University Press).

—— (1993) *Making Democracy Work: Civic Traditions in Modern Italy* (Princeton: Princeton University Press).

Ranney, A. (1965) *Pathways to Parliament: Candidate Selection in Britain* (Madison, Wis.: University of Wisconsin).

Raunio, T. (1996) *Party Group Behaviour in the European Parliament* (Tampere: Tampere University Press).

Rhodes, R. (1995) 'Introducing the Core Executive', in R. A. W. Rhodes and P. Dunleavy (eds), *Prime Minister, Cabinet and Core Executive* (London: Macmillan).

—— (2011) *Everyday Life in British Government* (Oxford: Oxford University Press).

—— and Dunleavy, P. (eds) (1995) *Prime Minister, Cabinet and Core Executive* (London: Macmillan).

—— Hart, P. 't, and Noordegraaf, M. (eds) (2007) *Observing Government Elites: Up Close and Personal* (Houndmills, Basingstoke: Palgrave-Macmillan).

—— Wanna, J., and Weller, P. (2009) *Comparing Westminster* (Oxford: Oxford University Press).

Richards, D., and Smith, M. J. (2004) 'Interpreting the World of Political Elites', *Public Administration*, 82(4): 777–800.

Ringe, N. (2005) 'Government–Opposition Dynamics in the European Union: The Santer Commission Resignation Crisis', *European Journal of Political Research*, 44(5): 671–96.

—— (2010) *Who Decides, and How? Preferences, Uncertainty, and Policy Choice in the European Parliament* (New York: Oxford University Press).

Rittberger, B. (2005) *Building Europe's Parliament: Democratic Representation beyond the Nation-State* (Oxford: Oxford University Press).

—— (2012) 'Institutionalizing Representative Democracy in the European Union: The Case of the European Parliament', *Journal of Common Market Studies*, 50: 18–37.

References

—— and Schimmelfennig, F. (2006) 'Explaining the Constitutionalization of the European Union', *Journal of European Public Policy*, 13(8): 1148–67.

Roberts, A. (2004) 'A Partial Revolution: the Diplomatic Ethos and Transparency in Intergovernmental Organizations', *Public Administration Review*, 64(4): 400–24.

—— (2010) *The Logic of Discipline: Global Capitalism and the Architecture of Government* (New York: Oxford University Press).

Romzek, B. S. (2000) 'Dynamics of Public Sector Accountability in an Era of Reform', *International Review of Administrative Sciences*, 66: 21–44.

—— and Dubnick, M. J. (1987) 'Accountability in the Public Sector: Lesson from the Challenger Tragedy', *Public Administration Review*, 47: 227–38.

—— and Utter, J. A. (2012) 'Congressional Legislative Staff: Political Professionals or Clerks?', *American Journal of Political Science*, 41(4): 1251–79.

Rose, R. (2005) *Learning from Comparative Public Policy: A Practical Guide* (Abingdon: Routledge).

Ross, G. (1994) 'Inside the Delors Cabinets', *Journal of Common Market Studies*, 32(4): 499–523.

—— (1995) *Jacques Delors and European Integration* (New York: Oxford University Press).

Rouban, L. (2012) 'The Politicization of the Civil Service', in B. G. Peters and J. Pierre (eds), *The SAGE Handbook of Public Administration* (2nd edn, London: Sage), 380–91.

Rudalevige, A. C. (2005) 'The Structure of Leadership: Presidents, Hierarchies, and Information Flow', *Presidential Studies Quarterly*, 35: 333–60.

Sartori, G. (1969a) 'From the Sociology of Politics to Political Sociology', in S. M. Lipset (ed.), *Politics and the Social Sciences* (New York: Oxford University Press), 65–100.

—— (1969b) 'Politics, Ideology, and Belief Systems', *American Political Science Review*, 63(2): 398–411.

Savoie, D. J. (2008) *Court Government and the Collapse of Accountability in Canada and the United Kingdom* (Toronto: University of Toronto Press).

Scharpf, F. W. (1997) *Games Real Actors Play: Actor-Centered Institutionalism in Policy Research* (Boulder, Colo.: Westview Press).

Schillemans, T. (2008) 'Accountability in the Shadow of Hierarchy: The Horizontal Accountability of Agencies', *Public Organization Review*, 8(2): 175–94.

Schmidt, V. A. (2006) *Democracy in Europe: The EU and National Polities* (Oxford: Oxford University Press).

—— (2010) 'Taking Ideas and Discourse Seriously: Explaining Change through Discursive Institutionalism as the Fourth New Institutionalism', *European Political Science Review*, 2(1): 1–25.

Schmitt, H., and Thomassen, J. (eds) (1999) *Political Representation and Legitimacy in the European Union* (Oxford: Oxford University Press).

Schmitter, P. (1996) 'Examining the Present Euro-Polity with the Help of Past Theories', in G. Marks, F. Scharpf, P. C. Schmitter, and W. Streeck (eds), *Governance in the European Union* (London: Sage Publications), 1–14.

Schön-Quinlivan, E. (2007) 'Administrative Reform in the European Commision: From Rhetoric to Relegitimization', in M. W. Bauer and C. Knill (eds), *Management Reforms in International Organizations* (Baden-Baden: Nomos), 25–36.

References

Schön-Quinlivan, E. (2011) *Reforming the European Commission* (Basingstoke: Palgrave Macmillan).

Schumpeter, J. A. (2010) *Capitalism, Socialism and Democracy* (London: Routledge Classic).

Seidel, K. (2010) *The Process of Politics in Europe: The Rise of European Elites and Supranational Institutions* (London: Tauris Academic Studies).

Selznick, P. (1957) *Leadership in Administration* (New York: Harper & Son).

Settembri, P., and Neuhold, C. (2009) 'Achieving Consensus through Committees: Does the European Parliament Manage?', *Journal of Common Market Studies*, 47(1): 127–51.

Shore, C. (2000) *Building Europe: The Cultural Politics of European Integration* (London: Routledge).

—— (2007) 'European Integration in Anthropological Perspective: Studying the "Culture" of the EU Civil Service', in R. A. W. Rhodes, P. 't Hart, and M. Noordegraaf (eds), *Observing Government Elites: Up Close and Personal* (Houndmills: Palgrave Macmillan).

Smith, A. (ed.) (2005) *Politics and the European Commission* (London: Routledge).

Spence, D. (2000) 'Plus ça change, plus c'est la même chose? Attempting to Reform the European Commission', *Journal of European Public Policy*, 7(1): 1–25.

—— (2006a) 'The Directorates General and the Services: Structures, Functions and Procedures', in David Spence (ed.), *The European Commission* (London: John Harper), 128–55.

—— (ed.) (2006b) *The European Commission* (London: John Harper).

—— (2006c) 'The President, the College and the Cabinets', in D. Spence (ed.), *The European Commission* (London: John Harper), 25–74.

—— and Stevens, A. (2006) 'Staff and Personnel Policy in the Commission', in: D. Spence (ed.), *The European Commission* (London: John Harper), 149–84.

Steets, J. (2005) *Developing a Framework: Concepts and Research Priorities for Partnership Accountability*, GPPi Research Paper, 1. Available at <http://www.gppi.net/publications/research_paper_series>.

Stein, E. (2001) 'International Integration and Democracy: No Love at First Sight', *American Journal of International Law*, 95(3): 489–534.

Stevens, A., and Stevens, H. (2001) *Brussels Bureaucrats? The Administration of the European Union* (Basingstoke Houndmills: Palgrave).

Stevens, H., and Stevens, A. (2006) 'The Internal Reform of the Commission', in D. Spence (ed.), *The European Commission* (London: John Harper), 454–80.

Stinchcombe, A. L. (1965) 'Social Structure and Organizations', in J. G. March (ed.), *Handbook of Organizations* (Chicago: Rand McNally), 153–93.

Stone Sweet, A. (2010) *The European Court of Justice and the Judicialization of EU Governance*, Living Reviews in EU Governance: <http://works.bepress.com/alec_stone_sweet/37>

Streeck, W., and Thelen, K. (eds) (2005) *Beyond Continuity: Institutional Change in Advanced Political Economics* (New York: Oxford University Press).

Strøm, K. (2003) 'Parliamentary Democracy and Delegation', in K. Strøm, W. C. Müller, and T. Bergman (eds), *Delegation and Accountability in Parliamentary Democracies* (Oxford: Oxford University Press), 55–106.

References

—— Müller, W. C., and Smith, D. M. (2010) 'Parliamentary Control of Coalition Governments', *Annual Review Political Science*, 13: 517–35.

Suleiman, E. (2003) *Dismantling Democratic States* (Princeton: Princeton University Press).

Suvarierol, S. (2007) *Beyond the Myth of Nationality: A Study on the Networks of European Commission Officials* (Delft: Eburon).

—— (2008) 'Beyond the Myth of Nationality: Analysing Networks within the European Commission', *West European Politics* 31(4): 701–24.

Svara, J. H. (2001) 'The Myth of Dichotomy: Complementarity of Politics and Administration in the Past and Future of Public Administration', *Public Administration Review*, 61: 176–83.

—— (2006) 'Introduction: Politicians and Administrators in the Political Process—A Review of Themes and Issues in the Literature', *International Journal of Public Administration*, 29: 1–24.

Thelen, K. (2005) *How Institutions Evolve: The Political Economy of Skills in Germany, Britain, the United States and Japan* (Cambridge: Cambridge University Press).

Thomassen, J., and Schmitt, H. (2004) 'Democracy and Legitimacy in the European Union', *Tidsskrift for Samfunnsforskning*, 45(2): 377–410.

Tiernan, A. (2011) 'Advising Australian Federal Governments: Assessing the Evolving Capacity and Role of the Australian Public Service', *Australian Journal of Public Administration*, 70(4): 335–46.

Trondal, J. (2004) 'Re-socialising Civil Servants: The Transformative Powers of EU Institutions', *Acta Politica*, 39(1): 4–30.

Trondal, J. (2008) 'The Anatomy of Autonomy: Re-assessing the Autonomy of the European Commission', *European Journal of Political Research*, 47(4): 467–88.

—— (2010) *An Emergent European Executive Order* (Oxford: Oxford University Press).

—— (2011) 'Bureaucratic Structure and Administrative Behaviour: Lessons from International Bureaucracies', *West European Politics*, 34(4): 795–818.

—— (2012) 'On Bureaucratic Centre Formation in Government Institutions: Less from the European Commission', *International Review of Administrative Science*, 78(3): 425–46.

—— Marcussen, M., Larsson, T., and Veggeland, F. (2010) *Unpacking International Organizations: The Dynamics of Compound Bureaucracies* (Manchester: Manchester University Press).

Tsakatika, M. (2005) 'Claims to Legitimacy: The European Commission between Continuity and Change', *Journal of Common Market Studies*, 43(1): 193–220.

Tuckman, B. W. (1965) 'Development Sequences in Small Groups', *Psychological Bulletin*, 63: 384–99.

Uhr, J. (1993) 'Redesigning Accountability: From Muddles to Maps', *Australian Quarterly*, 65(2): 1–16.

Van Gerven, W. (2007) 'Legal, Ethical, Political and Financial Responsibility of EU Commissioners', paper presented to Committee on Budgetary Control, European Parliament, 4 Oct.

—— (2009) 'Some Remarks Concerning Commissioners: Collective Responsibility in Context, Temporary Committees of Inquiry, Political Independence and

References

Neutrality', in L. Verhey, P. Kiiver, and S. Loeven (eds), *Political Accountability and European Integration* (Groningen: Europa Law Publishing), 115–24.

Vauble, R., Klingen, B., and Müller, D. (2012) 'There is Life After the Commission: An Empirical Analysis of Private Interest Representation by Former EU-Commissioners, 1981–2009', *Review of International Organizations*, 7(1): 59–80.

Verhey, L. (2009) 'Political Accountability: A Useful Concept in EU Inter-Institutional Relations?', in L. Verhey, P. Kiiver, and S. Loeven (eds), *Political Accountability and European Integration* (Groningen: Europa Law Publishing), 55–70.

Vibert, F. (2007) *The Rise of the Unelected. Democracy and the New Separation of Powers* (Cambridge: Cambridge University Press).

Walzer, M. (1967) 'On the Role of Symbolism in Political Thought', *Political Science Quarterly*, 82: 191–204.

Waterman, R. W., and Meier, K. J. (1998) 'Principal-Agent Models: An Expansion?', *Journal of Public Administration Research Theory*, 8(2): 173–202.

Weber, E. (1976) *Peasants into Frenchmen: Modernization of Rural France, 1870–1914* (Stanford, Calif. : Stanford University Press).

Weber, M. (1970) 'Politics as a Vocation', in H. Gerth and C. Wright Mills (eds), *From Max Weber: Essays in Sociology* (London: Routledge and Kegan Paul), 77–128.

—— (1978) *Economy and Society*, ed. G. Roth and C. Wittich (Berkeley, Calif.: University of California Press).

Weingast, B. (2005) 'Caught in the Middle: The President, Congress, and the Political-Bureaucratic System', in J. Aberbach and M. Peterson (eds), *The Executive Branch and American Democracy* (New York: Oxford University Press), 312–43.

Westlake, M. (2006) 'The European Commission and the European Parliament', in D. Spence (ed.), *The European Commission* (London: John Harper), 263–78.

Wildavsky, A. (1987) *Speaking Truth to Power: The Art and Craft of Policy Analysis* (New Brunswick, NJ: Tranaction Publishers).

Wille, A. (2007a) 'Bridging the Gap: Political and Administrative Leadership in a Reinvented European Commission', in M. Egeberg (ed.), *Institutional Dynamics and the Transformation of Executive Politics in Europe* (Mannheim: University of Mannheim, Connex), 7–41.

—— (2007b) 'Senior Officials in a Reforming European Commission: Transforming the Top?', in M. W. Bauer and C. Knill (eds), *Management Reforms in International Organizations* (Baden-Baden: Nomos), 11–243.

—— (2008) 'Van Technocratie naar "Good Governance"', *Beleid en Maatschappij*, 35(1): 40–52.

—— (2009a) 'Political and Administrative Leadership in a Reinvented European Commission', in J. A. Raffel, P. Leising, and A. E. Middlebrooks (eds), *Public Sector Leadership: International Challenges and Perspectives* (Cheltenham: Edward Elgar).

—— (2009b) 'Politicians, Bureaucrats and the Reinvention of the European Commission: From Technical to Good Governance', in L. Verhey, P. Kiiver, and S. Loeven (eds), *Political Accountability and European Integration* (Groningen: European Law Publishing), 91–108.

—— (2010a) 'Modernizing the Executive: The Emergence of Political-Bureaucratic Accountability in the EU Commission', *West European Politics*, 33(5): 1093–116.

—— (2010b) 'The European Commission's Accountability Paradox', in M. Bovens, D. Curtin, and P. 't Hart (eds), *The Real World of EU Accountability: What Deficit?* (Oxford: Oxford University Press), 63–86.

—— (2011a) 'Beyond the Reforms: Changing Civil Service Leadership in the European Commission', in J. Pierre and J. Eymeri-Douzans (eds), *Administrative Reform, Democratic Governance and the Quality of Government* (London: Routledge), 94–105.

—— (2011b) 'Public Sector Leadership in a "Reinvented" European Commission', in J. W. Björkman *et al.* (eds), *Public Leadership and Citizen Value* (The Hague: Eleven International Publishing University), 93–10 .

—— (2012) 'The Politicization of the EU Commission: Democratic Control and the Dynamics of Executive Selection', *International Review of Administrative Sciences*, 78: 383–402.

Woll, C. (2006) 'Lobbying in the European Union: From Sui Generis to a Comparative Perspective', *Journal of European Public Policy*, 13(3): 456–69.

Wonka, A. (2007) 'Technocratic and Independent? The Appointment of European Commissioners and its Policy Implications', *Journal of European Public Policy*, 14(2): 169–89.

Wood, B. D., and Waterman, R. W. (1991) 'The Dynamics of Political Control of the Bureaucracy', *American Political Science Review*, 85(3): 801–28.

Zakaria, F. (2003) *The Future of Freedom: Illiberal Democracy at Home and Abroad* (New York: W. W. Norton & Co.).

Zürn, M., Binder, M., and Ecker-Ehrhardt, M. (2012) 'International Authority and its Politicization', *International Theory, a Journal of International Politics, Law and Philosophy*, 4(1): 69–106.

Zweifel, T. D. (2006) *International Organizations and Democracy* (London: Lynne Rienner).

Index

Aberbach, J. 19, 147, *147*, 158–9
ABM (activity-based management) 138–9
accountability 16–22, 25–6, 188, 199–203
   accountability mechanisms, layering (thickening) of 23, 189–90, 200
   active/passive 202–3
   adjustments to 17–19
   administrative accountability 16–22, *20, 21*, 41, *50*, 51–2, 53, 54, 150–1, *151*, 199–200
   administrative-financial accountability *50, 52*
   and autonomy 40–1
   civil servants and 19, 51–2
   commissioners 79–86, 93–4, 148–52, 192
   depoliticization of 19–20, *20*
   directors-general and 52
   EP and 51, 85–7, 191
   EU Commission and 45–7, 49–54, 198–9
   executive accountability 85–7, 189–90
   heads of cabinet and 113–14, 149–50
   informal accountability 114
   inward/outward 210–12
   legal/quasi-legal accountability 17, *50, 51*, 52, 53
   modernization of 189–91
   political–bureaucratic 16–17, 200–1
   politicization of *20*, 148–52
   presidential accountability 63–4
   Prodi Commission and 34, 138–41
   professional accountability 17, *50*, 52–3
   public accountability 17, *51*, 53
   reforms and 34, 138–41, 213–14
   rules and responsibilities 148–52
   of senior officials 135
active accountability 202–3
activity-based management (ABM) 138–9
administrative accountability 16–22, *20, 21*, 41, *50*, 51–2, 53, 54, 150–1, *151*
   evolution of 199–200
administrative-financial accountability *50, 52*
Amsterdam Treaty (ToA) 26–7, *59*, 61
Annual Activity Reports (AARs) 52, 138
Annual Commission Strategy 138
Article 50-exit (Compulsory Mobility Policy Exit option) 130
audit system 140

Barnard, C. I. 170
Barroso, José Manuel 1, 57, 62, *62*, 63, 65, 71
   'State of the Union' speech 64
Barroso I Commission 57
   activity after leaving 77
   early leaves *75, 76*
   gender balance 72
   and political/administrative division 160
   political alignment 71, 72
   senior managers' educational qualifications *131*
   senior officials' experience of EU Commission *132, 134*
Barroso II Commission 57–8, 70, 186–7, *187*, 188
   background of commissioners 73
   commissioners groups 82
   early leaves *75, 76*
   gender balance 72
   heads of cabinet 117 n. 2
   political alignment 72
Behn, R. D. 175
Benelux countries 36
Berlaymont building 170–1
Borchert, Jens 74
bureaucratic accountability, *see* administrative accountability
Buttiglione, Rocco 57

CA (Common Assembly) 36–7
cabinet system 39, 48–9, 81, 98–101
   civil servants and 100
   code of conduct 101–2, *116*
   composition of 103–6, *104, 105*
   denationalization of 103–6, 116, *116*, 193
   gender balance 104
   modernization of 115–17
   and political–bureaucratic relationships 164–5
   professional qualities 106–7
   reform of 101–2
   selection procedure 65, 97–8, 117 n. 1, *153*, 192
   as training grounds 107
   see also heads of cabinet

237

Index

CCA (Consultative Committees of Appointments) 127
chefs de cabinet, see heads of cabinet
Christiansen, T. 203
CIE, *see* Commission of Independent Experts
Cini, M. 78
civil servants 39, 129, *163*
  and accountability 19, 51–2
  autonomy of 170
  in cabinets 100
  and codes of conduct 193
  communication with 112
  professionalization of 192–3
  and promotion 124, 130, 192–3
  and recruitment 12, 106, 192–3
  responsibilities 12
  role expectations 13, 14
  selection procedures 21
  see also directors-general
codes of conduct
  civil servants and 193
  cabinet system 101–2, *116*
College of Commissioners 33, 34, 197–8
  gender balance 72
  legitimacy 80
  politicization of 57–61
  selection procedure 67
Commission of Independent Experts (CIE) 33–4, 46
  1999 report 164
  Second Report on Reform of the Commission 47
commissioners 4
  accountability of 79–86, 93–4, 148–52, 192
  collegiality 79–83
  competence of 69–70, *70*
  deselection process 69
  and directors-general 168–9, 179–80, 181–2
  and EU citizens 90–1
  executive leadership 78–91
  executive relationships 158–60, *159*
  functions of 158
  gender balance 72
  and heads of cabinet 5–6, 108–10, 168–9, 180–1
  hearings 68, 85
  and legitimacy 80
  and media 89–90
  MEPs and election of 68–9, 93
  pathways of power 73–5
  and political–bureaucratic relationships 164–5
  and politicization of Commission 66–77, *92*
  profile of 73
  recruitment of 5, *67*, 153
  representation of interests 70–2
  role expectations 5, 79–91, 155–8, 194
  rules and responsibilities 5, 78–91

  selection of cabinet 97–8, *153*
  selection procedure 5, 66–77, 153
  and senior officials 168–9
Common Assembly (CA) 36–7
Compulsory Mobility Policy Exit option (Article 50-exit) 130
Consultative Committees of Appointments (CCA) 127
conversion 23
core executives 4, 25
  definition of 11–12
Council of the EU 198
Curtin, D. 188

Dalli, John 95 n. 14
Day, Catherine 1
de-flagging 127
Delors, Jacques 61, *62*, 92
Delors Commission 46
Delors I Commission
  activity after leaving 77
  early leaves 75
  senior managers' educational qualifications *131*
  senior officials' experience of EU Commission *132, 134*
Delors II Commission
  activity after leaving 77
  early leaves 75
  gender balance 72
  senior managers' educational qualifications *131*
  senior officials' experience of EU Commission *132, 134*
Delors III Commission
  activity after leaving 77
  early leaves 75, 76
  senior managers' educational qualifications *131*
  senior officials' experience of EU Commission *132, 134*
democracies
  accountability 16–22, 45–7
  organization of 15
denationalization
  cabinets and 103–6, 116, *116*, 193
  of executive relationships 193–4
depoliticization 19–20, *20*, 21, 143–4, 192–3
Diamantopoulou, Anna 96 n. 20
DiMaggio, P. J. 24
directors-general 4
  accountability of 52
  and commissioners 168–9, 179–80, 181–2
  communication with heads of cabinets 169
  executive relationships 158–60, *159*
  experience of EU Commission 131–3, *132, 134*

238

Index

function of 158–9
job rotation 129–30
and responsibility 151–2
role expectations 135–7, 140, 142, 156–8, 194
selection procedure 126, 137–8
displacement 23
Dunn, D. 18

ECJ (European Court of Justice) 36–7
ECSC (European Coal and Steel Community) 26, 35–7, 38, 41
EEC (European Economic Community) 37
Egeberg, M. 195, 198
elections 210–11
EP, *see* European Parliament
ETI (European Transparency Initiative) 53
EURATOM (European Atomic Energy Community) 37
Eurocrats 187
European Anti-Fraud Office (OLAF, Office Européen de Lutte Anti-Fraude) 52, 95 n. 14
European Coal and Steel Community (ECSC) 26, 35–7, 38, 41
European Commission
  accountability of 45–7, 49–54, 198–9
  colleges *43*
  comparison with other international bureaucracies 196–7
  core executive 4, 11–12, 25
  current role 207–10
  development of 42–7, *44*
  directors-general and 131–3, *132*, *134*
  early leaves 75–7, *75*, *76*
  and EP 47, 58–61, *92*, 199–200
  evolution of 26–7, 195–6, *196*
  expansion of 121–2, 186–9
  fragmentation of administration 120–1
  gender balance 72
  institutional features *42*
  key features of normalized executive 189–96, *190*
  Kinnock reforms 119–20, 122–3, *123*, 124–5, 130, 135
  late-1990s innovations 164–5
  legitimacy of 45–6, 48
  MEPs and 57, 58, 60, *60*, 64, 68–9, 93
  (mis)management of EU funds 121
  nationality problem 120
  organizational DNA 35–7
  and political/administrative division 146–8, *147*
  political executive, uniqueness of 197–9
  political–bureaucratic relationships 162–8, *163*, *166*, *167*
  politicization of 49, 61–6, *92*, *92*
  President, role of 61–6
  reforms of 27, 47–9, 192
  remit 3–4
  and selection procedure 66
  senior appointments 123–35
  tensions in 37–42
  treaty reforms and 3
European Court of Auditors 52
European Court of Justice (ECJ) 36–7
European Economic Community (EEC) 37
European Parliament (EP) 26–7, 45–6, 55 n. 12
  and accountability 51, 85–7, 191
  Barroso and 63
  and Commission president 63
  and deselection procedure 69
  and executive 85–7, 93, 191
  and EU Commission 47, 58–61, *92*, 199–200
  and Lisbon Treaty *59*, 87
  and Maastricht Treaty 59, *59*
  and Nice Treaty *59*
  and selection procedure 66, 67, 68, 69
  and treaty reforms 58–9, *59*
European Transparency Initiative (ETI) 53
executive accountability 85–7, 189–90
executive relationships 5–6, 25
  change in dynamics 194–5
  denationalization of 193–4
  directors-general and 158–60, *159*
  heads of cabinet 158–60, *159*
  models 195–6, 199
  reforms and 213–14
  top-down politicization of 21

FFPE (Commission staff union) 1

G8 summits 64
gender balance 72, 104, 126
Georgakakis, Didier 130–1
geographical balance 125–6, 154–5
Gill, J. I. 99
Grant, R. W. 205 n. 13

HA (ECSC High Authority) 26, 35, 36–7
  independence of members 38
  Monnet's vision of 41
Hallstein, Walter 37, 41, 61, *62*
Hallstein I Commission 186, *187*
  early leaves *75*, *76*
  senior managers' educational qualifications *131*
  senior officials' experience of EU Commission *132*, *134*
Hallstein II Commission
  early leaves *75*, *76*
  senior managers' educational qualifications *131*

239

Index

Hallstein II Commission (*Cont.*)
  senior officials' experience of EU Commission 132, 134
heads of cabinet 4, 81, 97–117
  and accountability 113–14, 149–50
  Barroso II Commission 117 n. 2
  and cabinet members 109–11
  and commissioners 5–6, 108–10, 168–9, 180–1
  and directors-general 169
  evolution of role 115–17, *116*
  executive relationships 158–60, *159*
  functions of 158
  informal processes 112–13
  policy role 111–12
  professional qualities 106
  recruitment 5
  role expectations 5, 156–8, 194
  rules and responsibilities 5
  selection procedure 5, 102–3, *103*
  as shadow managers 108–14
Heclo, H. 162, 182
High Authority, *see* HA (ECSC High Authority)
Hooghe, L. 124

IMF (International Monetary Fund) 197
informal accountability 114
institutional entrepreneurship 24
Internal Audit Service (IAS) 52
inward accountability 210–12
isomorphism 24

Jeleva, Rumania 95 n. 13
Jenkins, Roy *62*
Jenkins Commission
  early leaves *75*
  senior managers' educational qualifications *131*
  senior officials' experience of EU Commission *132, 134*
job rotation 119–20, 127–30
judicial-legal accountability *51*
Judt, T. 207

Keohane, R. O. 205 n. 13
Kinnock, Neil 48–9, 55 n. 2, 119
  Reform Strategy White Paper 48
  reforms 119–20, 122–3, *123*, 124–5, 130, 135
Kroes, Neelie 96 n. 20

legal/quasi-legal accountability 17, *50, 51*, 52, 53
Lisbon Treaty 26–7, 72, 95 n. 12, 204 n. 6, 210
  and Commission president 63
  and EP *59*, 87

Maastricht Treaty 26–7, 43
  and Commission president 61
  and EP 59, *59*
Magnette, P. 45
Malfatti, Franco Maria *62*
Malfatti Commission
  early leaves *75, 76*
  senior managers' educational qualifications *131*
  senior officials' experience of EU Commission *132, 134*
Manin, B. 211
media: relationship with commissioners 89–90
Mehde, V. 205 n. 14
MEPs (Members of the European Parliament)
  and election of Commission 68–9, 93
  and election of president 63–4
  and politicization of College 57, 58
  questions to Commission 60, *60*, 64
Merger Treaty 37
merit selection 12–13, 21, 124–30
  and gender balance 126
  and geographical balance 125–6, 154–5
  selection procedures 126–30
Michel, Louis 96 n. 20
Monnet, Jean 26, 33, 35, 36, 38, 186, 207
  and Europeanization of Commission 39
  vision of ECSC 37, 41
  vision of High Authority 41
Moravcsik, A. 205 n. 13

nationality 120
  and balance of merit selection 125–6, 154–5
  and Europeanization 39–40
  see also denationalization
New Public Management (NPM) 11, 19
Nice Treaty 26–7
  effect on EP *59*
  QMV 71
normalization *190*
  accountability and 16–22, 24
  as adapting and learning 23
  and change, concept of 22–6
  definition of 10
  drivers of 23–4
  as gradual transformation 22–3
  mechanisms of 24
  modes of 23
  normal model 11–15
  normalization concept 24
  normalization perspective 24–5
  study design 28–31, *29*
NPM (New Public Management) 11, 19
Nugent, Neil 81, 208

Index

OECD (Organisation for Economic Co-operation and Development) 197
OLAF (Office Européen de Lutte Anti-Fraude, European Anti-Fraud Office) 52, 95 n. 14
Olsen, J. P 10, 25, 202
Ortoli, Francis Xavier *62*
Ortoli Commission
 early leaves *75, 76*
 senior managers' educational qualifications *131*
 senior officials' experience of EU Commission *132, 134*
outward accountability 210–12

parachutage 40, 100, 102, 106, 124
parliamentary assemblies 198
passive accountability 202–3
Peters, Guy 20, 163, *163*
Pierre, J. 20
political accountability 16–17, 41, *50*, 51, 53, 54, 150–1, *151*
 evolution of 199–200
political–administrative division 147, *147*, 160, 171
 in Commission 146–8, *147*
political–bureaucratic accountability 16–17, 200–1
political–bureaucratic relationships
 communication issues 168–71
 conflict/consensus 181–2
 independence/interdependency 180–1, 194
 late-1990s innovations 164–5
 loyalty 175–6
 models 162–8, *163, 166, 167*, 174, 179, 184, 194, 195
 multinationality and 173
 mutual trust 175, 195
 norms and expectations 174–8
 organization of 168–74
 personal chemistry 176–8
 political authority 178–80
 reciprocity 178
 respect 176, 195
 time issues 171–2
politicization 19–21, *20*
 bottom–up/top–down processes 20–1, *21*, 49, 91–3, *92*, 191–2
 of College of Commissioners 57–61
 definition of 20
 and professionalism 37–9
Powell, W. W. 24
President of the Commission 191–2
 MEPs and 63–4
 and politicization of Commission *92*
 role of 61–6

selection of cabinet 65, 117 n. 1, 192
see also individual Commissions; individual Presidents
presidential accountability 63–4
Prodi, Romano 47–8, 62, *62*, 96 n. 20
 and political–administrative division 146, 160, 171
 reform of cabinet system 101–2
 on reform of selection procedures 128
Prodi Commission 71
 and accountability reforms 34
 activity after leaving *77*
 code of conduct for cabinets 101–2
 and communication 171
 early leaves 75–6, *75, 76*
 and political–administrative division 160
 reforms 34, 47–9, 54 n. 1, 122–3, 138–41
 senior managers' educational qualifications *131*
 senior officials' experience of EU Commission *132, 134*
 White Paper on European Governance 48
professional accountability 17, *50*, 52–3
professionalism and politicization 37–9
professionalization of civil servants 192–3
promotion: of civil servants 124, 130, 192–3
public accountability 17, *51*, 53
public management reforms 19
Putnam, R. D. 30, 142

qualified-majority voting (QMV) 71, 72
quasi-legal accountability *50*
Question Hour 64

recruitment procedures 5, 12–13, 152–5, *153*
 civil servants and 12, 106, 192–3
 heads of cabinet and 5
 and normalization *190*
 parachutage 40, 100, 102, 106, 124, 152
 senior officials and 5, 123–8, *125, 128*, 153–4
 see also selection procedures
Reform Strategy White Paper (Kinnock) 48
reforms 31 n. 6
 and accountability 34, 138–41, 213–14
 administrative 142–4, *143*
 and denationalization 193–4
 financial 139–40
 interaction of 25
 pre-Kinnock agenda 201
 reaction to 138–9, 141
 result-based reporting 149
 slow transformation 200–1
research design 213–16
 conceptual development 213–14
 data-analysis 216
 documents 214

241

Index

research design (*Cont.*)
  interviews 214–16
  methods 214
responsibilities, *see* rules and responsibilities
responsibilization 140
responsiveness 64
retirement: Article 50-exit 130
Rey, Jean 62
Rey Commission
  early leaves 75
  senior managers' educational qualifications *131*
  senior officials' experience of EU Commission *132, 134*
role expectations 194
  civil servants and 13, 14
  commissioners and 79–91, 155–8, 194
  directors-general and 135–7, 140, 142, 156–8, 194
  heads of cabinet and 156–8, 194
  and normalization *190*
  senior officials and 5, 135–42, 144, 155–8
rules and responsibilities 5, 12
  and accountability 148–52
  civil servants and 12
  College of Commissioners and 34
  commissioners and 5, 79–87
  directors-general and 151–2
  heads of cabinet and 5
  and normalization *190*
  senior officials and 5, 148–52, *151*

Santer, Jacques 62
Santer Commission 33, 71
  activity after leaving 77
  and communication 184 n. 5
  early leaves 75
  reform initiatives 46
  senior managers' educational qualifications *131*
  senior officials' experience of EU Commission *132, 134*
Saunders, L. 99
Savoie, Donald 22
Schmidt, Vivien 188
Schumann, Robert 35
Schumann plan 36
Second Report on Reform of the Commission (CIE) 47
Seidel, K. 206 n. 16
selection procedures 5, 12–13
  cabinet members 103–7
  civil servants and 21
  College of Commissioners and 66, 67
  directors-general and 126, 137–8
  educational qualifications and 130–1, *131*
  EP and 66, 67, 68, 69
  external candidates 133
  heads of cabinet 102–3, *103*
  internal candidates 130–3
  member states and 66–8
  political qualifications and 21
  senior officials 5, 123–35, *128*, 153–4
  standardization of 126–7
  see also merit selection
senior officials 123–35
  accountability of 135
  and commissioners 5–6
  communication between 168–9, 170–1
  educational qualifications 130–1, *131*
  executive relationships 158–60, *159*
  experience of EU Commission 131–3, *132, 134*
  job rotation 127–30
  location of 170–1
  merit selection 124–30
  parachutage 40, 100, 102, 106, 124
  and political–bureaucratic relationships 164–5
  recruitment procedures 5, 123–8, *125, 128*, 153–4
  role expectations 5, 135–42, 144, 155–8
  rules and responsibilities 5, 148–52, *151*
  selection procedures 5, 123–35, *128*, 153–4
  see also directors-general
Single European Market 43–4
Special Council of Ministers 36–7
Spence, D. 101, 115
Spierenburg Report 55 n. 11
Stolz, K. 74
Strategic Planning and Programming (SPP) cycle 138–9
Suvarierol, Semin 173
Svara, Jim 163–4

Thorn, Gaston 62
Thorn Commission
  activity after leaving 77
  early leaves 75, 76, 77
  senior managers' educational qualifications *131*
  senior officials' experience of EU Commission *132, 134*
Treaty of Amsterdam (ToA), *see* Amsterdam Treaty
Treaty on European Union (TEU), *see* Maastricht Treaty
triads 165–6, *166*
  communication in 168–71
  see also commissioners; directors-general; heads of cabinet; political–bureaucratic relationships

Index

United Nations (UN) 197

Van Gerven, W. 55 n. 2, 161 n. 3
Verheugen, Günter 1–2, 162
Verhey, L. 205 n. 14

Wallstrom, Margot 96 n. 20
Walzer, Michael 211
Weber, Max 11, 18–19, 212 n. 5
   model of bureaucracy 37–8

White Paper on European Governance (Prodi Commission) 48
Wildavsky, A. 97
Wilson, Woodrow 11
Wonka, A. 70
Worldbank 197
WTO (World Trade Organization) 197

Zakaria, Fareed 212